Tennessee Women in the Progressive Era

Tennessee Women in the Progressive Era

Toward the Public Sphere in the New South

Edited by Mary A. Evins

The University of Tennessee Press • Knoxville

First Edition.

The paper in this book meets the requirements of American National Standards Institute / National Information Standards Organization specification Z39.48–1992 (Permanence of Paper). It contains 30 percent post-consumer waste and is certified by the Forest Stewardship Council.

Library of Congress Cataloging-in-Publication Data

Tennessee women in the progressive era: toward the public sphere in the new south / edited by Mary A. Evins. — First edition.
pages cm
Includes bibliographical references and index.
ISBN-13: 978-1-57233-913-2 (hardcover: alk. paper)
ISBN-10: 1-57233-913-6 (hardccover: alk. paper)
1. Women—Tennessee—History—20th century.
2. Women—Political activity—Tennessee—History—20th century.
3. Feminism—Tennessee—History—20th century.
I. Evins, Mary A.

HQ1438.T2T43 2013
305.420976809'04—dc23
2012046738

Dedicated to our progressive Tennessee foremothers

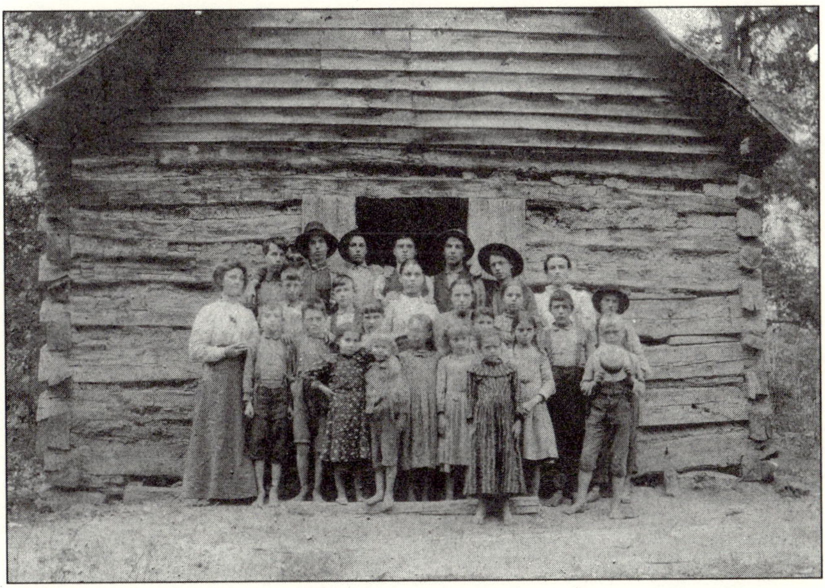

Susan Annie Fancher (Smartt), far left, of Fancher's Mill, White County, Tennessee. She was a teacher in a one-room log-cabin, rural-Tennessee public school, shown here with her students, c. 1904, probably the Isoline community of Cumberland County. Courtesy of the Evins-Smartt family collection.

Contents

Illustrations

Foreword

Beyond the Domestic Sphere and Beyond the Nineteenth Amendment: The Efforts of Tennessee Women Progressives Outside of the Home, 1870s to 1930s

Mary A. Evins

This collection owes its existence to our shared interest in Progressive Era Tennessee women and our realization that previous anthologies that have expressly studied Tennessee women progressives have centered only on the Nineteenth Amendment. No prior compilation on Tennessee women progressives has focused on the work and lives of Tennessee women of the Progressive Era beyond the vote. The achievement of Tennessee suffragists is a feather in Tennessee's historic cap. As a progressive battleground state and with the general assembly's ratification of the woman suffrage amendment, Tennessee demonstrated nationally in 1920 that it had retained its status as a moderate southern state, a border state, holding to its earlier image as having been "last in, first out" of the Confederacy, separating itself from the Deep South and also from a handful of rock-ribbed conservative holdout states in the Northeast that by August 1920 had continued to block the constitutional amendment for woman suffrage. Tennesseans are justly proud of having been "the perfect 36th" state to bring in the Nineteenth Amendment and secure the vote for women.

But progressive women in Tennessee of the later nineteenth and early twentieth centuries were busy outside of their homes and families and involved in a wide range of other activities. In their everyday lives they were vigorous participants in their cities and hometowns and were changing women's place in cultural consciousness. Many women expressly worked toward progressive societal reforms and pushed, even if inadvertently, beyond the domestic sphere to shift the perception and status of females in society. Centering on Tennessee's women progressives—but, yes, beyond the topic of suffrage—our essays provide a window into the worlds of women in the early twentieth century and broaden understanding of what Tennessee's New Women were involved in, what they cared about, how they spent their energies, and how they acted in public roles. We know they were multifaceted, keenly aware of their impacts on society, and intentionally committed to improving the communities in which they lived. Some women were visionaries and apostles for a changed world. We present a selection of their stories.

In writing on the Progressive Era and on progressivism, we suggest two perspectives: time period and social activism. We hew to a classic, textbook, turn-of-the-last-century definition of the era, but we also explicitly utilize progressivism's "long chronology," by which southern progressivism is best understood, from the late 1800s into the decades of the early to mid-twentieth century. We examine women's work from the 1870s to the 1930s but are not even limited by those decades because many progressive processes reach well into and beyond the 1930s. We extend progressivism accordingly. The progressivism with which we interact is the period in American history when society was moving beyond the restrictive behaviors, attitudes, and historic moments of the nineteenth century (including the Civil War) into the new twentieth century of possibility. Women, nationally and in the South, had long been busy with many activities, roles, and employments away from hearth and home and had never honestly been strictly defined or confined by the domestic sphere. Yet at the turn into the twentieth century, women more forthrightly challenged patriarchy, power, and prejudice, both quietly through the daily processes of their lives and overtly through public actions.

The historiography of women's progressivism is extensive; much is cited in the chapters that follow. Striking, however, is that other than the matter of the Nineteenth Amendment and references to women with Tennessee backgrounds such as Ida Wells-Barnett and Mary Church Terrell, Tennessee is woefully absent from national scholarship on women progressives. Nor are Tennessee women progressives especially visible in regional analyses, in which women of other southern states tend to dominate. A wealth of information on Tennessee women progressives exists, however, and is available in three types of sources: theses, dissertations, and the published volumes that derived from those bodies of research; individual journal articles, encyclopedia entries, and biographies in larger women's history collections; and books devoted to histories of specific women's groups, organizations, and issues such as suffrage or temperance. In juxtaposition to those, our volume is focused simply on the era and on the socially conscious work of Tennessee women who lived then. Our collection expands understanding of the breadth of activities in which forward-thinking women progressives were engaged in the years of the later nineteenth and early twentieth centuries.

On this subject we developed a symposium in 2007 titled "Intersecting Missions: The Work of Women in Progressive Women's Organizations in Tennessee, 1870–1930," held in Nashville at the Scarritt-Bennett Center, a former Methodist women's college, in conjunction with a history conference on women's mission work. What emerged from the symposium were several valuable observations about Tennessee progressivism. First, the long chronology absolutely applies. Women's incremental movements into increased public involvement grew organically in different communities, depending on local issues and needs that had to be met. Maturation for women began earlier in certain quarters and continued later in others. Second, Tennessee women progressives and "New Women" are inextricably embedded. They represent the same set of phenomena, despite varying contexts in which one term may be used over the other. The actions of women progressives make them New Women even if they themselves might have rejected the term. Many of the women in our volume, however, explicitly self-identified as either progressives or New Women, and we do not think the others in our volume, who may not have employed the phraseology, would have refused either designation. Southern women typically held to a traditionalism and female propriety that many of their northern sisters would eschew during the same time period; southern women traditionalists may not have been feminists, but many were very active agents of change nevertheless.

Third, Gilded Age women whose wealth, connections, and rank in society were bound up in maintaining the socioeconomic order that ensured their status, were, by virtue of their education, exposure, leisure time, and influence, often on the cutting edge of social change, sometimes purposefully and at other times unintentionally. Position was a determinant of agency. Yet, fourth, the work of Tennessee women progressives ultimately defied class, race, and region. Whether educated or not, whether rural or urban, whether black or white, whether of humble means or well-to-do, whether teacher or farm girl, whether married or single, whether from the mountains or the cotton fields, Tennessee women wanted improved lives for themselves and others, and they went after what they believed should be theirs and society's. Their work may have been humble and not of national importance—starting schools, protecting their families, providing services for the needy, establishing tomato clubs, playing sports—but taken together, such women were developing public expectations, uplifting the state, and bettering the South. In their public service they took on liquor, lynching, racism, legal hamstrings, school boards, dress codes, and the church. Ultimately they challenged attitudes, propriety, fundamentalism, and the social order. Proactively they worked toward formulating new laws, new policies, new functioning structures, and new organizations. Was Tennessee markedly altered through their efforts? Perhaps in some cases not. But their work was foundational for each decade of the twentieth century that followed.

This collection is not comprehensive, it is a beginning. It does not represent every region or section of the state. It focuses heavily on the work of educated women and women who for differing reasons of position and influence were women of privilege. There are more narratives on the work of white women than African American women. Tennessee women were women of faith, and their faith inspired their actions, but the public engagement of Protestant women is especially recovered here. Our essays deal primarily with Methodist, Lutheran, Presbyterian, Church of Christ, and Baptist women—yet we are fully aware that women of other Protestant faiths and Catholic and Jewish women were also quite active in progressive programs in Tennessee during the same period. There was no attempt whatsoever to emphasize one religion or denomination over another, nor are we prepared at this point to draw cultural implications from the overrepresentation of, particularly, Methodist women in progressive work. (There is no doubt that Methodist women were social reform powerhouses, but so were women of other faiths in our volume. Comparison of religious tenets as prime movers is a topic for another analysis.) Our authors' individual subjects of research generated the content of our collection, but our gaps do pinpoint important areas for future investigation. Our volume's value is that it introduces a slice of Tennessee history through the work of some of Tennessee's purposeful progressive women actors.

Another clear intent of our collection is to present women's *work* rather than just biography (although there is some of that). Examination of work, whether paid employment or volunteer efforts, illustrates ways in which women were engaged in their communities, from the halls of government to the high hollows of the Appalachian Mountains, toward changes to improve society. We explore what motivated the women. Our women's efforts may not place them in textbooks, but in the "all politics is local" definition of daily life as political, they were making social and political history. Their locales and areas of attainment may not fit the prescriptive model of the efficient, urban, northeastern progressive, but by making constructive contributions in their Tennessee counties, whether in town or out in the country, they too were progressive reformers. By pushing the envelopes of accepted gender roles and feminine behaviors, they too were New Women.

In the chapters that follow, the progressive women studied investigate through the dedicated efforts of their own labors in Tennessee whether women of faith can act across racial boundaries in the era of legal segregation to challenge their own prejudices and stand morally for what is right, and whether they can they affect average people to join them in shifting attitudes and behaviors. In examining urban settlements and Tennessee antilynching activists, Janice M. Leone and Paula K. Hinton struggle with these processes. Through the histories of a mountain school and county tomato clubs, Jean S. Hamm and Minoa D. Uffelman respond affirmatively to the question, does working with girls alter systemic rural poverty and bring improbable improvements into the hardscrabble lives of mountain and farming families? Less hopeful perhaps, at least within one Tennessee-based church, is Carole Stanford Bucy's evaluation of whether it is humanly possible for women to soften the rigid structures of religious power and patriarchy to open cultures of belief to the simple principle that if women are equal in the eyes of God, they should be equal in the church. Sonya Ramsey's study of African American teachers questions to what extent, and whether, African Americans' adherence to white, middle-class notions of propriety and decorum must be thoroughgoing for black professional women to achieve respect in a racist society. Not dissimilarly, the can-you-sweat-and-still-be-a-lady contribution by Mary Ellen Pethel on women athletes invites a discussion: Does a woman's body strength diminish her femininity and does physical prowess negate southern womanhood? My own essay leaves me with the second-wave feminism realization that if breaking through glass ceilings in the professional arena of childhood education—women's "natural" professional realm—is difficult, how much more challenging it is, and will be in the later decades of the twentieth century and on into the twenty-first century, for women when they confront the many other barriers by which sexist institutions and society block women's human striving for full equality in all aspects of life. These are some of the questions posed through the essays we collectively present in *Tennessee Women in the Progressive Era.*

Each of the studies in this anthology confirms what women's historians and social historians know full well, that the moral and daily actions of women are central to both *real* history and political history. In placing all of our women's contributions in the appropriate Tennessee and national historic contexts, Elisabeth Israels Perry introduces this volume with interpretations of her own and with questions that pique the reading of the chapters to follow.

Personally, to the very fine scholars who have joined together in this shared endeavor, I thank you. I am sincerely appreciative of your sustained progressive efforts toward the historic research into and recovery of the women's work we collectively present here. We all are extremely grateful to the University of Tennessee Press for partnering with us to realize a publication that will further authenticate and solidify the place of Tennessee progressive women in written history.

Introduction

"Preserving the Sanctity of the Home, Ensuring the Freedom of the State": Tennessee Women Progressives in Historical Perspective

Elisabeth Israels Perry

> *Woman's Work*
> *Whatever may be necessary to preserve the sanctity of the home and ensure the freedom of the state*
>
> —Kate Kirkman 1897, Woman's Department, Tennessee Centennial Exposition

The title of this introduction comes from the inscription on a monument in Centennial Park in Nashville, Tennessee. The monument marks the location of the Woman's Building of the Tennessee Centennial Exposition, which was held in the park in 1897. Installed in June 1904 by the exposition's "Woman's Department," the monument honored not just the building they had put up for the fair but also everything the women had done to make the fair a success. In addition, at a time when most middle-class Americans still believed that women's "proper place" was in the home, the monument justified women's active involvement in the public sphere. For this reason, it serves as a launching point for this anthology's subject, the work of Tennessee's "New Women" during the Progressive Era.

Everything about the Woman's Building monument had a special meaning to the women who designed and installed it in Centennial Park. It consists of a rectangular marble shaft about twelve feet tall, which is set onto a double pedestal and crowned by a large granite sphere. A bronze plaque on the shaft bears the following inscription: "THIS MONUMENT

APTLY MARKS THE SITE OF THE WOMAN'S BUILDING AT THE TENNESSEE CENTENNIAL EXPOSITION HELD IN THIS PARK IN THE YEAR 1897." An enigmatic aphorism follows: "THAT THAT IS ROUND CAN BE NO ROUNDER." Derived from a rule of grammar,[1] the phrase refers literally to the monument's crowning sphere and figuratively to the "perfection" of the women's achievement. Following the aphorism is a list of the members of the Woman's Department, and under that two words: "WOMAN'S WORK," which is defined as "WHATEVER MAY BE NECESSARY TO PRESERVE THE SANCTITY OF THE HOME AND ENSURE THE FREEDOM OF THE STATE." These words come from a speech delivered on the day the Woman's Building was opened by the president of the Woman's Department, Kate (Van Leer) Kirkman.

As I've written extensively about the monument in another publication,[2] here I will confine myself to linking its purpose and content to the theme of this anthology. Both the very presence of the monument in the park as well as its definition of "woman's work" speak to this theme. First, its presence: Although the leaders of the Woman's Department never directly said so, I believe they erected the monument because of the insufficient credit they had received for their work. Two weeks before the installation of the women's memorial, the male leaders of the exposition had installed a memorial of their own. This memorial consisted of a large slab of granite which was embedded on the shore of the artificial lake constructed in the park for the fair. Its bronze tablet, which honors the major individuals and groups who had helped organize the event, features the names of the male directors of the fair. The women directors' names are there, too, but confined to a small, lower right-hand corner of the tablet. Since at the time of the fair as well as at the fair's conclusion many observers (including the male directors of the event) had singled out the Woman's Building and the women's work as a prime reason behind the exposition's success, to the women directors the positioning of their names seemed an insufficient tribute. And thus they raised the funds for, designed, and installed a monument of their own.[3]

Second, the monument's content: Its definition of woman's work expressed the women's conviction that a woman's place was in the world, doing what was necessary to "preserve the sanctity of the home and ensure the freedom of the state." What precisely they meant by these words is

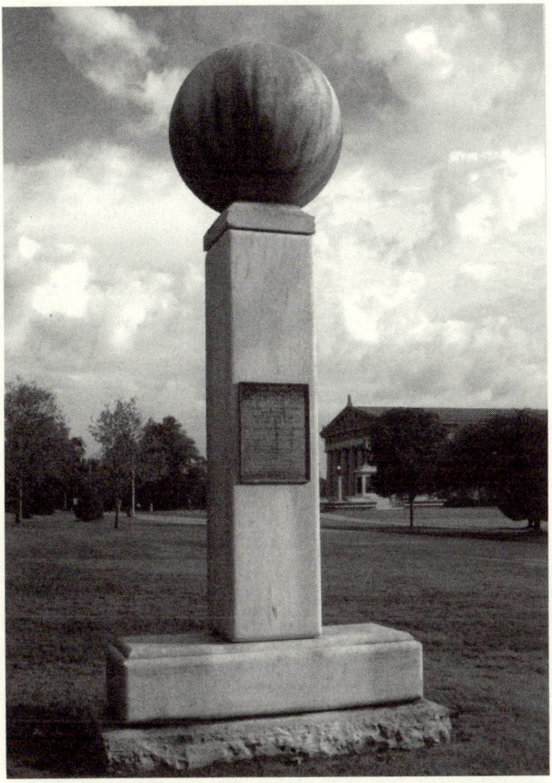

The monument to the Woman's Building of the Tennessee Centennial Exposition of 1897, at its current location in Centennial Park, Nashville, Tennessee, southwest of the Parthenon. Photograph by the editor.

open to interpretation, but the general message is unmistakable: As Kate Kirkman said, when she reviewed the history of Tennessee in a speech she delivered at the opening of the Woman's Building, one should not assume that throughout Tennessee's "century of struggle and triumph woman has been an idle spectator." Indeed, woman "has been a potent if not an equal factor in the march of human progress."[4] By putting her definition of woman's work on their monument, the women directors of the exposition lay claim to a public space from which they would continue to be a

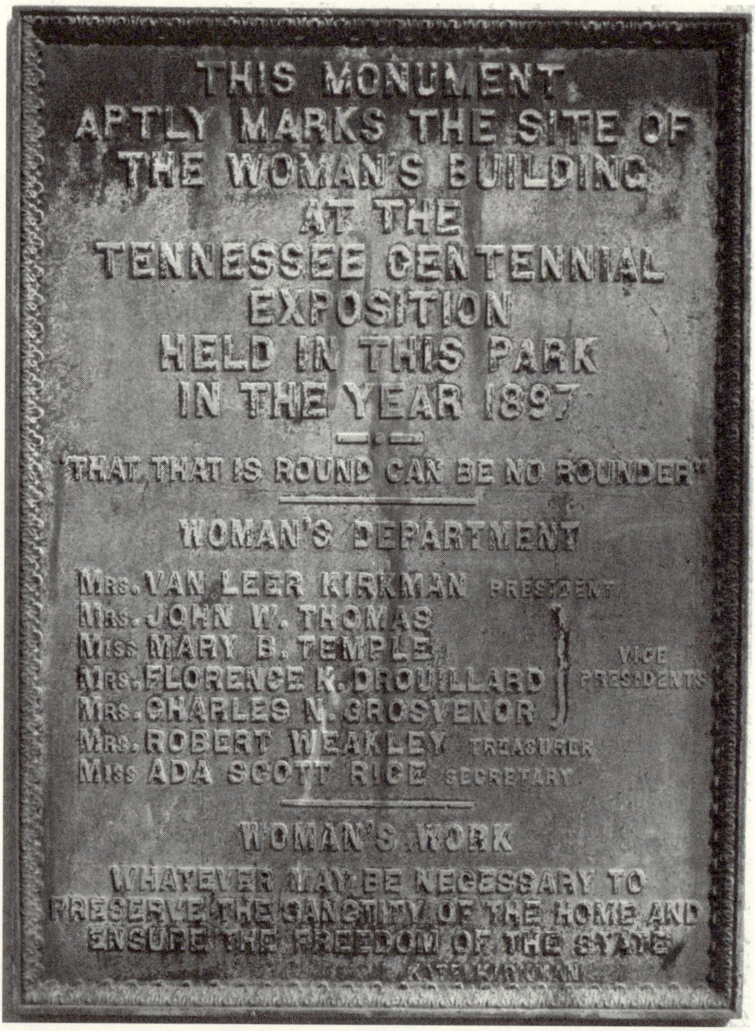

The dedicatory plaque on the Woman's Building monument. Photograph by the editor.

"potent" factor in the life of their state. In short, they insisted upon the appropriateness of women's public activism and wanted recognition for it.

The monument in itself is still not enough, however. In Centennial Park, the replica of the Parthenon of Athens, Greece, built for the fair in 1897 and rebuilt in the 1920s of more sturdy materials, dwarfs the woman's monument and renders it almost invisible.[5] Because park visitors are usually focused on the Parthenon, few (if any) even notice the women's monument, and even if they do notice it, they probably have no idea what it means. I myself lived in Nashville for over ten years before I had ever noticed it. On the day I walked over to see what it honored, I suspected it held significance for the history of women in turn-of-the-twentieth-century Tennessee but had no idea why it had been installed, who the women were who had installed it, or what its enigmatic inscription had meant to them.

Like the Woman's Building monument, this anthology represents an effort to recognize Tennessee women's contributions to the state's welfare during the Progressive Era. But it is more than compensatory history; it also seeks to change the larger story of the Progressive Era in U.S. history. This story has generally been so focused on traditional electoral and legislative politics, all necessarily dominated by stories about men, that many historians of women find it almost unrecognizable from the perspective of insights and conclusions from women's history.

This is a problem I addressed a few years ago in an essay titled "Men Are from the Gilded Age, Women Are from the Progressive Era."[6] This essay suggested that, despite the growing amount of scholarly literature in Progressive Era women's history, historians of progressivism were still not taking account of the "New Women's history" in their general depictions of the reform period. The essay made four points about this state of affairs. First, historians were at last telling the story of the woman suffrage movement as a "part" of progressive reform, but beyond commenting on how "few" women voted after suffrage, or the extent to which women squandered their political effectiveness by disagreeing over key issues of public policy (as if men never disagree!), they rarely made woman suffrage central to progressive reform. Nor did they probe the consequences of the woman's vote for local politics, the arena in which postsuffrage era women were most politically active.

Second, historians were ignoring the importance to progressivism of moral reform movements in which women were often the most active participants. Such movements included antiprostitution, temperance, and dance hall and motion picture regulation. Historians who paid attention to such movements often marginalized them as the expression of "fanatical" bluestockings who didn't want anyone (especially working-class immigrants) to have any fun in life. I argued that, since women were not only prominent in moral reform movements but also had launched many of them, unless historians stopped judging moral reform from their more modern (and usually morally liberal) perspectives, they would never incorporate women into the mainstream of Progressive Era history. I argued further that, even if historians disapproved of moral reform, these movements deserved just as much analysis and interpretation as any other contemporary reform movement, and that such an analysis should be made from the perspectives of the women reformers as well as from the contexts in which these women operated.

My third point was that historians would continue to fail to integrate women into Progressive Era history unless they adopted a more capacious definition of the term "politics." While politics has always entailed much more than elections and voting, traditional political histories usually concentrate only on electoral areas of political activity. I asked historians to recognize that politics includes the entire spectrum of citizen interaction with governmental bodies at all levels of the polity, and argued that once they accepted that idea they would see the extent to which women's activism was essential to the story of progressivism. Fourth and finally, I suggested that historians ought to consider adopting a broader and more flexible periodization for progressivism, one that revolves not around electoral victories, which necessarily involved more men in this period than women, but around the development and fate of reform legislation and public policies. Such a periodization would necessarily start the Progressive Era much earlier than traditional histories date it and would end it much later. More important, it would put women's interests and concerns more toward the center of progressivism.

The essays in this anthology reaffirm that these four historiographical points—the centrality of suffrage to reform movements of the period, the importance of moral reform to women progressives, the need for a broader definition of the term "politics," and the desirability of expanding the era's chronological boundaries—continue to be among the salient lessons coming out of Progressive Era women's history. The very title of the conference from which the essays derive—"Intersecting Missions: The Work of Women in Progressive Women's Organizations in Tennessee, 1870–1930"—acknowledges a "long Progressive Era" for women, one defined more by women's agendas than by men's. Had the conference adopted the standard periodization paradigm—that the Progressive Era began with Theodore Roosevelt's ascension to the presidency in 1901, peaked with the formation of the Bull Moose party in 1912, and ended with that party's defeat or in Woodrow Wilson's departure from office in 1920—participants in the conference would have had much less to talk about than they did.

Indeed, when one looks at the development of the reform impulse in U.S. history in the late nineteenth century from the perspective of women, the line that some historians still draw between the so-called Gilded Age and the Progressive Era becomes quite blurry. Anyone who has studied the explosion of women's involvement in reform movements in the immediate post–Civil War period knows just how fuzzy that line can be. During the Gilded Age, women—mostly from the middle and upper middle classes, both black and white, but also some working women—founded clubs and organizations that initiated social, political, and moral reform movements. In the process of doing so, these women spoke out on what would become the major issues of the Progressive Era long before most politicians acknowledged that government's relationship to issues of human welfare, labor policy, the economy, and the environment needed to change.[7] Moreover, women's agitation for reform helped build the consensus among voters that supported the progressive changes eventually incorporated into law and public policy.

The fairs and expositions of the post–Civil War period provide vivid examples of women's involvement in movements for progressive change long before ideas for reform had reached high levels of government. This was especially true of the fairs held in the 1890s. The Chicago World's

Columbian Exposition of 1893 brought together women from across the country and the world to participate in congresses and parliaments. These meetings, which were well-publicized and popular events, led to the formation of long-lasting networks for woman suffrage and other reform movements. Two years later, the Woman's Building at the Cotton States and International Exposition in Atlanta held a similar series of congresses, covering topics such as suffrage, emancipation, professionalization, legal reform, and education. Belva Lockwood, one of the nation's first woman lawyers and a presidential candidate in the 1880s, spoke, calling for women to pursue a higher mission than "pickles and preserves."[8] Even though the exhibits in the woman's buildings of these two fairs emphasized women's traditional domestic arts, many of the meetings set out progressive agendas.

This was true as well of Tennessee's Centennial Exposition of 1897. Throughout the months of May and October, the women who organized the Woman's Building hosted a series of "convocations" on intellectual, economic, and political topics. Many speakers, including Sophonisba Breckinridge, Kentucky's first woman lawyer, addressed issues of women's work, higher education, and opportunities for professionalization. The topic of woman suffrage held prominent place in the convocations, with widely known southern suffragists such as Lide Meriwether, Laura Clay, Virginia Clay Clopton, and Frances E. Griffin giving inspirational speeches. Nationally prominent women, such as settlement workers Florence Kelley and Jane Addams, gave addresses. National women's organizations, such as the Daughters of the American Revolution, General Federation of Women's Clubs, National Council of Women, and National Council of Jewish Women, made presentations of their work. No African American women appeared on the Woman's Building programs, however, even though the National Association of Colored Women met in Nashville the same year as the centennial. Their absence underscores the limits of southern women's engagement with reform in the 1890s, although some of the essays in this anthology show that by the 1910s those limits were beginning to weaken.[9] Moreover, in the decades following the centennial, as is clear from other essays, the Tennessee women who formed networks and cemented contacts in Gilded Age expositions kept reconnecting with one another in the reform campaigns of the Progressive Era.[10]

Several of the essays in this anthology provide further evidence of the need for an earlier start date for progressivism. Janice M. Leone's essay on Belle Bennett and the Woman's Missionary Council of the Methodist Episcopal Church, South, shows how this organization began its work in the 1890s (and continued long past the 1920s). Carole Stanford Bucy's piece on Silena Holman's debates with Disciples of Christ leader David Lipscomb over women's roles provides vivid details on the late-nineteenth-century temperance and suffrage activism in Tennessee that provided a foundation for modern feminist ideas. Other essays demonstrate that women continued to pursue child health and public health measures long after winning the right to vote, and that they saw these and other reforms as continuing their pursuit of the progressive causes of an earlier era. Jean S. Hamm's essay on the Konnarock Training School in Appalachia links the school's work to Progressive Era roots and shows how it lasted until 1958, while Paula K. Hinton situates Tennessee women's involvement in efforts to stop lynching in the 1910s and shows how those efforts were carried on way beyond the 1920s.[11]

More research will probably continue to push progressivism's chronology beyond traditional limits. Historians have long debated the precise relationship between progressivism and the New Deal, with some arguing for similarities, others for important differences. To help clarify this relationship, more research needs to be done on how women progressives at local levels responded to the challenges of the Great Depression and on the ideological links between their responses and Progressive Era antecedents. For some Progressive Era women's organizations, such as the Women's Trade Union League, the Progressive Era continued not only through the 1930s but lasted until the Cold War and McCarthyism dealt the final blows. Tennessee provides a local example in its campaign to allow women on juries, which succeeded only in the 1950s, thanks to the remnants and heirs of Progressive Era women's networks who made that legislative change possible.[12]

In demonstrating Tennessee women's engagement with politics long before they had the vote, ran for office, or even served on juries, this anthology's essays also support the argument that a broader definition of "politics" permits a fuller incorporation of women's public activities into U.S. political history. The essays by Leone, Bucy, and Sonya Ramsey not only clarify the importance of religious instruction and temperance campaigns to the women they write about but also show how the women envisioned and worked for political outcomes from these activities. Of course, for these reformers, the winning of woman suffrage was central to all of their causes, as legislators often used women's lack of the franchise as a rationale for disregarding political issues of importance to women. Hence, as several of the essays show, the careers of women reformers often began with temperance, only to move rather quickly to women's rights and suffrage, and then on to advocacy work for other causes, such as feminism, labor-industrial reform, and improved race relations.

Most of the Tennessee women who worked for better race relations did not seek that goal because they favored or even envisioned racial integration as an eventual development. During the Progressive Era, this goal was far beyond most people's imagination. But they did want to stop lynching, which they saw as a horrendous moral wrong. Recognizing that local governments were powerless (or unwilling) to stop lynching, they fought (in vain, as it turned out) to make lynching a federal crime and worked tirelessly to expose the false reasoning that lynch mobs used to justify their violence. As the essays by Leone and Hinton show, women church leaders challenged the nation's racial hierarchies by establishing cooperative networks of African Americans and whites who then worked together to stop lynching. These networks, which led to key antilynching organizations, such as the Southern Sociological Congress, founded in 1912, and the later Commission on Interracial Cooperation, were integral to the growing strength of the antilynching movement across the South. This movement is a perfect example of how Progressive Era women turned their engagement with "moral" reform toward political action.

Other manifestations of the political nature of women's Progressive Era reform in Tennessee include, somewhat surprisingly, the canning and tomato clubs that Minoa D. Uffelman writes about in her essay. She shows how, inspired by agricultural reformer Seaman Knapp, Virginia P. Moore transmitted scientific methods to farmers so that they could properly preserve their crops. Moore also encouraged farm women to improve their earnings through canning so that their families could do better in hard times. In 1914 Moore joined other farm demonstration agents in advocating passage of the Smith-Lever Act to support the extension work of land-grant universities, work that substantially improved rural life in Tennessee and elsewhere. Similarly, the elementary school educators of whom Mary A. Evins writes in her essay did "political work." Lucy Gage convinced legislators to fund kindergartens and train their teachers; Julia Green, despite hostility from male school officials, accomplished so much for primary education in Nashville, from transforming the primary school curriculum to bringing national parent-teacher and professional educator associations to Nashville, that to many she became "an almost legendary figure."[13]

Perhaps historians undervalue women's roles in such areas as agricultural demonstration and elementary school education because of the way we "name" some women's activities. If we talk about how they set up canning clubs, founded and worked in social settlements, or organized Girl Scout troops, we call that "social work." If we talk about their development of primary schools, we call that "women's work." If we redefine all of that activity as "community work," work to improve and benefit the larger community, then we cannot fail to recognize its "political" content and impact. Moreover, much of women's community work led them to advocate legislation, campaign for particular laws and public policies, and serve as public watchdogs over government spending and enforcement. This was political work, too, even if Progressive Era Tennessee women activists did not have the vote, used the language of motherhood to justify their actions, and denied they were being "political" in the traditional sense of the word. Whether or not they were mothers, they were still "doing politics," broadly conceived. Identifying their work as such allows us to include it as part of the mainstream political history of the nation.

How does this idea apply to the history of Tennessee women's activism during the long Progressive Era? Even the act of forming a woman's organization, especially at a time when doing so flouted tradition or threatened scandal, could be considered a political act. Can we look more closely (assuming records can be found) at such events as the Centennial Exposition, the establishment of the Woman's Department, and the controversies over who would run the department as sources of insight into the history of Tennessee's New Women? And what of the convocations that were held during the exposition? Contemporary newspapers reported selectively on what was said, but knowing more about the speeches given at those events would uncover clues to women's interests, concerns, and feelings about the topics of their day.

Much work remains to be done on women's roles in political structures traditionally defined. A Tennessee branch of the Progressive party in 1912 existed, but we lack information on how women related to it. Since the national Progressive party was the first to endorse woman suffrage, it was "the" party for women. Did Tennessee women join it? Were they made welcome? Did they serve as canvassers? In other states, women were candidates for office on the Progressive party ticket. What about in Tennessee? How did Tennessee women's views compare with the views of other women progressives from different regions of the country?

For historians, the era of women's political agitation that followed the ratification of the Nineteenth Amendment holds promise for exploring further questions about the impact of women on the nation's political history. As mentioned above, most historians who write about the postsuffrage era emphasize the deep divisions over race, the Equal Rights Amendment, prohibition, and other controversial issues that preoccupied women's organizations after they won the vote. Pointing to how few women actually exercised the elective franchise and how few women won public office after getting the vote, they often conclude that winning the vote for women held little significance. Admittedly, it's difficult not to notice how few women voted in those early postsuffrage years, or to write about how bitterly divided women became over key issues of interest to them. But by focusing on the divisions, low female voter turnout, and failed electoral campaigns, historians have assumed that women were unable to bring any influence to bear on political events.

Tennessee historians might seek to identify such influence by using the "women's pages" of local newspapers to find out what defined "women's" issues in different parts of Tennessee. These pages could tell them about the local political organizations women founded and the local issues these organizations advocated. They might ask what kinds of strategies civic-minded women used to get men to listen to their ideas for changes in public policies, or on what issues women united, despite their differences. What, for example, did they have to go through to get the Sheppard-

Towner Maternity and Infancy Protection Act of 1921 accepted in Tennessee? Convincing legislatures to accept and then match federal money to improve the health of mothers and infants was not easy in other states: Opposition was strong from legislators who charged the advocates of this piece of "progressive" legislation with trying to bring "socialism" into American medical care. Did this happen in Tennessee? Once Sheppard-Towner was accepted and put in place in Tennessee, what effect did it have on the state's infant and maternal mortality? What was the reaction in Tennessee when funding for that act came to an end? These and other avenues of inquiry would help fill out the picture of the actual impact of suffrage on women and on Tennessee politics in the balance of the twentieth century.

Finally, what about the centrality of moral reform to progressivism? We do not have to assume that everything that "progressive" women did was necessarily something we approve of now, but we do have to try to understand moral reform and all attempts at social engineering from within their own contexts, not through the lens of modern hindsight. We need to look at them from the point of view of the women (and men) who fought for and against such controls over human behavior. Who were they? What constituencies did they represent? What were the experiences that drew them to advocate moral reforms? What happened to the people affected by moral reform? If moral reform movements were all about middle- and upper-class control over the masses, how do we explain the participation and approval of working-class individuals and groups in these movements? And how do we explain the differences over reform strategies demonstrated by the different groups who pursued moral reform?

Beyond asking these questions, we can, as Bucy does in her essay on Silena Holman, use women's moral reform activism to show how it enabled its leaders to challenge separate spheres or carve out new leadership roles for women. We might ask, also, what other moral reforms interested Tennessee women that were perhaps of lesser consequence than prohibition but nevertheless illuminate women's lives and interests in this period. How did Tennessee women respond to the larger reform agendas of the Woman's Christian Temperance Union? Did some groups pursue them wholeheartedly, or did divisions play themselves out in local political arenas, and if so, what do these divisions tell us about the larger reform agendas these women (and their male allies) pursued? Finally, Mary Ellen Pethel's essay on the remarkable development of women's sports in Progressive Era Tennessee suggests that, even though women athletes "did not carry banners, hold rallies, or intentionally advance a political movement," "their competitive athleticism publicly contested the Old South order of class and gender." This suggestion should inspire us to investigate the extent to which the public sphere of competitive athletics provided women with a stepping stone to public activism.

These are just a few of the questions that arose in my mind as I considered the essays in this anthology. Readers will surely think of more and, I hope, be stimulated by the essays to pursue more primary research and writing on Tennessee women's history. In the meantime, I end where I began, with the women of the 1897 Tennessee Centennial Exposition and the closing words of Kate Kirkman's final report of the exposition's Woman's Department. "Nothing perishes that is worth preserving," she said. "So woman's part in the Centennial will live on, shining through another century, stimulating women to a higher endeavor; but worth more than woman's work was the example set of the character of the women of Tennessee. And what is owing to the Woman's Department for this? A debt which the unceasing praise of a cycle of years can not repay."[14]

Tennessee women are still waiting for the "unceasing praise" that, in 1897, they not only thought was their due but were sure would come their way soon. Like so many middle- and upper-class organized women in the decades surrounding the turn of the twentieth century, they were unfailingly optimistic about women's future possibilities. When they dedicated their monument, they believed they were living at the dawn of a "Woman's Age" or "Woman's Era." Black and white clubwomen of this time period used these labels to announce their conviction that women were at last coming into their own, would finally be allowed to play significant roles in public arenas, and would, through these roles, redeem the full democratic promise of America. We know now that this conviction would not be fulfilled in their lifetimes. We also know that they never got the "unceasing praise of a cycle of years" for which they so ardently wished.

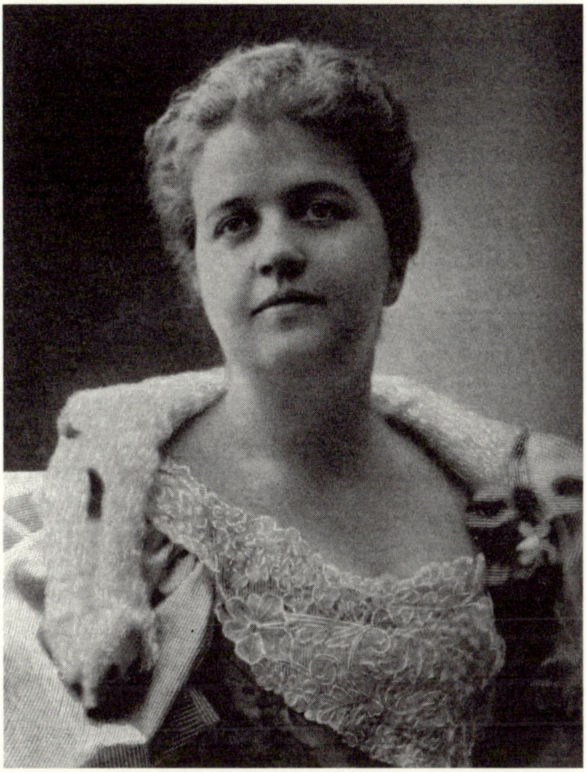

Kate Kirkman, President of the Woman's Department for the Tennessee Centennial Exposition. From Herman Justi, *Official History of the Tennessee Centennial Exposition, Opened May 1, and Closed October 30, 1897*, 1898.

Although we may neither praise nor agree with all that they did, at the very least we must and can preserve a useful memory of *what* they did. Thanks to the scholars represented in this anthology, we have precise and detailed evidence about the meaning of progressivism to some of Tennessee's female activists. Because of their original research, these scholars help us connect Tennessee women to the movements for reform that dominated the early-twentieth-century American experience. The task remains to find out even more, and then to integrate the insights and conclusions that emerge from such findings into the larger pictures of both Tennessee and U.S. history. In the meantime, at least the Woman's Building monument still stands in Nashville's Centennial Park. It should keep calling out to us as we rewrite the history of the New South with the work of women at its center.

NOTES

The opening epigraph refers to Kate Kirkman, in Herman Justi, *Official History of the Tennessee Centennial Exposition, Opened May 1, and Closed October 30, 1897* (Nashville: Committee on Publication, Tennessee Centennial and International Exposition, 1898), 146.

1. "When a thing is round or square it cannot be rounder or squarer. These adjectives do not admit of comparative and superlative forms." See John Bechtel, Slips of Speech (Philadelphia: Penn Publishing, 1895), 63, http://www.gutenberg.org/etext/4983/.

2. See my "Memorializing the 1897 Tennessee Centennial Woman's Building," in *Gendering the Fair: Histories of Women and Gender at World's Fairs,* ed. T. J. Boisseau and Abigail Markwyn (Urbana: Univ. of Illinois Press, 2010), 149–65. The members of the Woman's Department honored on the monument are Mrs. Van Leer Kirkman, president; Mrs. John W. Thomas, Miss Mary B. Temple, Mrs. Florence K. Drouillard, Mrs. Charles N. Grosvenor, who were all vice presidents; Mrs. Robert Weakley, treasurer; and Miss Ada Scott Rice, secretary.

3. They also designed an elaborate ceremony for the unveiling, which I describe at some length in "Memorializing the 1987 Tennessee Centennial Woman's Building." Local newspapers described the installation of both the "men's" memorial as well as the women's; see the *Nashville American,* May 22, 1904, 21, and June 5, 1904, 14. As only two weeks passed between the installation of the men's slab and that of their own monument, I believe the women had been forewarned about the meager recognition they were going to receive on the slab. I speculate that their source of information about the men's memorial was Evalina Thomas, a member of the Woman's Department and wife of John W. Thomas, president of the 1897 Centennial.

4. Kirkman's speech appears in full in Justi, *Offical History,* 146, and in local newspapers (*Nashville Banner,* May 3, 1897, 1; *Nashville American,* May 4, 1897, 5).

5. The Parthenon was the only building not torn down when the fair was over. Since it was made of temporary materials, however, over time it deteriorated, and so the city rebuilt it in concrete in the 1920s. See *The Tennessee Encyclopedia of History and Culture,* http://tennesseeencyclopedia.net/, q.v. "The Parthenon" and "Tennessee Centennial Exposition."

6. The speech was later published in the inaugural issue of the *Journal of the Gilded Age and Progressive Era* 1, no. 1 (Jan. 2002): 25–48.

7. To cite just one issue, organized women campaigned for pure food and drug laws decades before either federal officials or muckraking journalist Upton Sinclair set their eyes on the issue, and Sinclair, author of the famous novel *The Jungle,* came to see it only because the female social settlement workers at Chicago's Hull House suggested he write about labor issues in the stockyards. See Lorraine Swainston Goodwin, *The Pure Food, Drink and Drug Crusaders, 1879–1914* (Jefferson, N.C.: McFarland, 1999).

8. Cited in Bruce Harvey, "World's Fairs in a Southern Accent: Atlanta, Nashville, Charleston, 1895–1902" (PhD diss., Vanderbilt Univ., 1998), 261. Harvey covers the Nashville Woman's Department on 265–74. On women's participation in the 1893 World's Columbian Exposition, see Jeanne Madeline Weimann, *The Fair Women* (Chicago: Academy Press, 1981).

9. On the convocations, see "The Woman's Department," in Justi, *Official History,* 143–58. Throughout the summer of 1897, Nashville's daily newspapers reported extensively on the convocations, sometimes providing verbatim records of the speeches.

10. In 1916, six thousand women in 150 clubs belonged to the Tennessee Federation of Women's Clubs. See Carole Bucy, "Quiet Revolutionaries: The Grundy Women and the Beginnings of Women Volunteer Associations in Tennessee," 8, ms. in author's possession.

11. In an earlier publication, the late Anita Shafer Goodstein recognized Tennessee women's continuing loyalty after suffrage to Progressive Era feminist goals, such as controls on political machines; the passage of more social welfare legislation (especially for mothers and children); public funding for recreational resources; and moral campaigns for prohibition, an end to red-light districts, and stricter supervision of movie theaters and dance halls. In fact, she argued, white women reformers were so intent on achieving these goals that in 1919 they reached across racial barriers to enlist the support of the "best" black women in their causes. See her "A Rare Alliance: African American and White Women in the Tennessee Elections of 1919 and 1920," *Journal of Southern History* 64, no. 2 (May 1998): 219–46, esp. 231–35. Goodstein quotes Nashville suffragist Catherine Kenny referring to "the universal tie of motherhood and sisterhood" as uniting the "best" black and white women as voters.

12. See Ruth Anne Thompson, "Full Citizenship and Jury Service for Women: The Passage of Tennessee's Women Jurors Law, 1951" (master's thesis, Vanderbilt Univ., 1991).

13. Alberta L. Meyer, "Julia Green Dies," *Childhood Education* 38, no. 5 (Jan. 1962): 242.

14. Justi, *Official History,* 154.

Chapter 1

"Practical Religion": The Settlement Work of the Woman's Missionary Council of the Methodist Episcopal Church, South, 1890–1930

Janice M. Leone

> *The field in which you are called to labor is as broad as our country; the necessity for the redemptive work of Christ as great as when he came to earth, and the opportunities for woman's work . . . absolutely incalculable.*
>
> —Belle Harris Bennett, 1903

The settlement house movement in the United States is a standard topic in most studies of Progressive social reform in the late nineteenth and early twentieth centuries.[1] Patterned after European institutions, settlement houses and the work done in them have been credited both with delivering social services and with being committed to "sweeping social change."[2] The first recognized American settlement, the Henry Street Settlement in New York City, and likely the best-known settlement, Hull House in Chicago, often overshadow institutions described as second-tier settlements as well as the southern, church-affiliated settlements whose workers successfully carried on reform work in various southern cities.[3] Typically characterized as settings primarily for religious evangelizing and conversion, these latter settlement houses are easily relegated to a separate category for historical inquiry and excluded from studies of reform in the years from 1890 to 1930.

Yet one southern women's religious organization, the Woman's Missionary Council of the Methodist Episcopal Church, South, led by longtime president Belle Bennett, counters the standard description of settlement activities. The reform work of these women not only lends credence to their presence during the Progressive Era but also places them squarely within the larger Social Gospel movement of the time and suggests an early challenge to the racial hierarchy of the Jim Crow South. As such, uncovering the work of these women contributes to a more complete picture of the Social Gospel movement while at the same time according Belle Bennett and the Woman's Missionary Council (WMC) members their rightful place in the more general history of social reform.[4]

These Methodist women were not alone in their work to improve southern society. They were surrounded, for example, by clubwomen, who tackled a myriad of community projects, including creating kindergartens and building juvenile reformatories, libraries, and schools while generally working to improve conditions for workers, cleaning up cities, supporting YWCAs, and promoting public health. Other clubwomen focused their efforts on industrial workers and immigrants. And many of these women moved into the suffrage battle and politics.[5] For the most part, however, clubwomen, as well as those in religious groups, worked in racially segregated organizations, not unusual for the time period. Even Elizabeth Turner's careful study of Progressive women reformers, including Methodist women, in Galveston, Texas, reveals parallel organizations made up of black and white women who usually began their reform efforts in church groups and then moved on to participate in secular activities. Although these women may have shared community improvement goals, when it came to race issues, they often worked at cross purposes.[6] In her study of North Carolina women, Glenda Gilmore describes white women who worked to maintain Jim Crow at the same time that black women wanted to end it, making it difficult to achieve interracial cooperation.[7] Even Southern Baptists, one of the other prominent denominations in the South during the Progressive years, berated themselves for lagging behind Methodists and Presbyterians in their work "among the black people for the purpose of teaching and helping them."[8] So while the women of Belle Bennett's Woman's Missionary Council joined thousands of other southern women reformers, their early efforts at cross-race cooperation and the extent of their reform activities were rare in these years.

The Woman's Missionary Council began in 1890 as the Woman's Parsonage and Home Mission Society with the charge to collect money for the support of ministers and their families in the American West—especially to provide parsonages—and to carry on mission work in the cities. In 1896 the General Conference of the Methodist Episcopal Church, South, shortened the organization's name to the Woman's Home Mission Society and granted the women members authority to govern their own activities. Belle Harris Bennett, a Kentucky native, served as president of the organization from 1896 until 1910, when the Woman's Foreign Missionary Society of the church merged with the Woman's Home Mission Society to become the Woman's Missionary Council.[9] Bennett continued on then as president of the newly created organization until 1920. By the end of her long tenure as president—twenty-four years, from 1896 to 1920—the Woman's Missionary Council was heavily involved in reform work in a variety of areas. Bennett, with her leadership skills and her belief in what she referred to as "practical religion"[10] and the imperative to change the environment of people in need, deserves much of the credit for moving this woman's religious organization toward increasing educational reforms, interracial work, and social activism during the Progressive Era.

Bennett has been the subject of several articles, brief biographies, and reminiscences.[11] These works tend to be laudatory, uncritical descriptions of her early life of privilege in Kentucky, her baptism in 1884 at the age of thirty-two, and her move into missionary work in 1887. But most accounts agree that Bennett, for the remainder of her life, successfully combined a deep spirituality with social activism as she led the WMC in its various reform efforts. As such, Bennett also symbolized the "new woman," an image of activist women that emerged during the years of the Progressive Era.[12] Although a southerner, Bennett was not inclined to uphold the tradition of the Lost Cause with its promotion of a conscribed antebellum southern ladyhood.[13] Instead, as she traveled worldwide and interacted with church leaders as well as secular reformers to effect social change, Bennett seemed to embrace her role as a new woman. And counter to some claims that religious women stayed within the bounds of traditional womanhood, the public reform work of Bennett and the women of the WMC at the turn of the last century clearly accords them prominence as new women.[14] In accounting for Bennett's success in moving the WMC in the direction of social activism, especially in the area of improving race relations, her methods and motivations as well as her position within the Social Gospel movement must be credited. According to Tochie MacDonell, who served with Bennett as general secretary of the Board of Missions, Bennett easily mixed religious tenets and practices with Social Gospel philosophy. Bennett's practical religion resulted in schools and settlements across the South that were clearly founded on religious principles. In particularly encouraging the building of schools, Bennett pushed for the implementation of "a systematic Bible study . . . that the individual life might be purified and the missionary spirit cultivated and developed."[15] For Bennett the mission of these schools was "to hold up Christ as a personal Savior, to teach the Bible as the revealed work and will of God, and to develop men and women of strong Christian character who will glorify God serving and saving others in the mission of those who teach and control in these schools."[16] As MacDonell noted, "The motive of her . . . missionary zeal was the building of God's victorious kingdom on earth. She sought to show the way of regeneration through Christ to the individual and fought to conquer the evil that clogs the salvation of society. 'Eternal life for the individual, the kingdom of God for humanity,' was the slogan of her life."[17] As head of a women's religious organization, naturally Bennett relied on her faith to support her call to social reform and interracial work at a time when few white Americans were concerned about the status of race relations in the country.[18]

On an even more personal level, Bennett, soon after her baptism, adopted the habit of faithfully observing the Sabbath through Bible study, prayer, hymn singing, and participation in communal worship. This commitment to the Sabbath meant that she avoided all travel and work on Sunday—no small feat for a woman who traveled as much as she did in her duties as WMC president. On the other six days of the week, she made it a habit to set aside some time each day for Bible study, a way to "nourish her soul with the Word of God" rather than spend too much time with her practical religion of reform and service.[19]

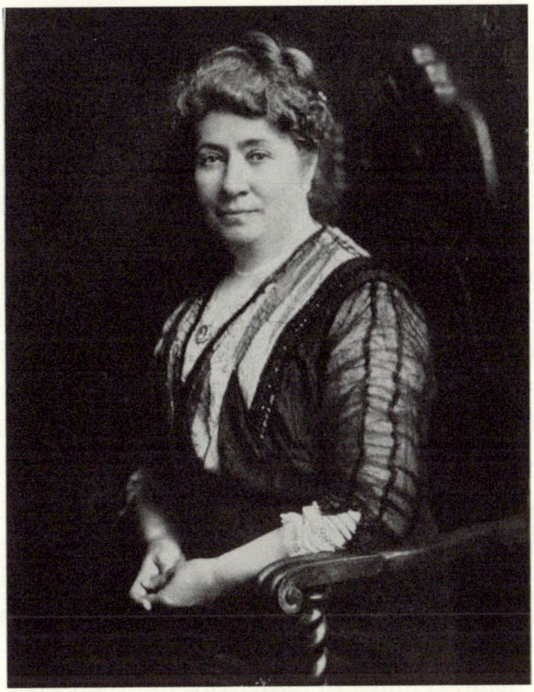

Belle Harris Bennett. From Mrs. R. W. MacDonell, *Belle Harris Bennett: Her Life Work*, 1928.

While it might be tempting to dismiss Bennett as belonging only to the realm of women's Christian missionary work, she also functioned very successfully in the more secular world of reform. And it is this combination of her religious grounding along with secular reform that places her practical religion in the middle of the Social Gospel movement. Defined in its most simplistic terms as the effort to build the kingdom of God on Earth, Social Gospel ideology relied on the resources of mainly Protestant churches to save not only individuals but also society. Two of the most prominent Social Gospel activists, Josiah Strong and Walter Rauschenbusch, articulated the larger societal goals of the movement in their numerous books and publications.[20] And although Bennett's religious beliefs certainly influenced her leadership style, her acceptance of the Progressive-thinking, Social Gospel tenets of the day were obvious as she led her organization by her own example. For instance, Bennett's early call for missionary work among blacks should have come as no surprise to the people who knew her, since "progress was the law of life to her, and she believed in the progress of the whole Negro race."[21] To this end, Bennett spoke in black churches and to black charity associations, taught Bible classes in black churches, and befriended individual African Americans. In the first decades of the twentieth century, she continued this work. In her home state of Kentucky, she taught a Bible study class at St. Paul's African Methodist Episcopal Church from 1900 to 1904 to audiences of up to five hundred people. In addition, Bennett and her brother apparently helped out black churches financially on more than one occasion. From 1915 to 1918, she even served as president of the Madison County [Kentucky] Colored Chautauqua and presided at the annual meetings.[22] Seeing their president actively involved in work with African Americans because she believed in the ability of people to change and improve their lives likely dispelled any reservations that WMC members may have had about doing similar work.

Yet Bennett was not content to let only her example determine the success of WMC reform efforts. In the days before cell phones and e-mails, Bennett and other council officers relied on publications of the WMC, especially the monthly newsletter, *Our Homes,* first published in 1892 and then renamed the *Missionary Voice* in 1910, as well as the published accounts of the annual meetings to promote their reform agenda, especially with regard to black settlement work and race issues in general. By 1908, the WMC had approximately forty thousand members, all of whom were expected to pay at least the annual fee of fifty cents to receive the organization's newsletter.[23] And although Bennett did not edit the publication, she often wrote for the paper, urging readers to participate in the growing home mission work.

It was in *Our Homes* in 1897 that Bennett's first call to work for and with African Americans appeared. After 1912, monthly articles on the progress of black settlement work appeared in the newsletter along with reports of all other activities. Bennett wrote regularly about the growth of home mission work for blacks at the council's annual meeting, and these records were reprinted in the newsletter for all members to read. Her reports ranged from encouraging council members to provide more domestic science and manual training courses at their schools and settlement houses to supporting an antilynching law. By 1920, Bennett could write to her readers about the "racial goodwill" she saw and that "in many of the cities, towns, and counties of these States godly men and women of both races are working out plans and policies for race relationships that will bring forth a spirit of Christian brotherhood such as the world as yet has never known."[24] Bennett obviously believed that progress in race relations had been made, at least during the years of her tenure as WMC president.

In addition to using the newsletter and annual reports to accomplish reform goals, Bennett communicated with WMC members on a more personal level. She spent much of her time on the road, traveling not only throughout the South but also abroad. The newsletter is filled with updates of Bennett's travels and indicates that she kept up a hectic pace for most of her long tenure as president. From 1898 to 1900, for example, the newsletter followed her work from Dallas, Texas, to Missouri to South Carolina to Key West, Florida, and on to the Home Mission Society of the North Mississippi Conference. In each setting she organized new mission societies, encouraged existing ones, raised money for the council's schools, gained subscribers for *Our Homes,* and gave speeches, sometimes as many as three or four over the course of two days. In these efforts, the *St. Louis Christian Advocate* affirmed "Miss Bennett stirs the heart."[25] In 1906, Bennett reported that she had been in the field for seven months during the previous year, a clear indication that her work as ambassador for home mission work continued.[26] And of course, as president, she attended every annual conference of the WMC, often held in Nashville, Tennessee, but just as likely to be in another southern city.

Bennett also used her travels to educate herself about mission work and social reform and then to pass on her ideas for practical religion to WMC members. For example, in 1901 Bennett traveled to England to attend an international conference of Methodists, where she presented a report on the home and foreign mission work of the WMC. While there she also visited numerous settlement houses, especially in London, many run by the Wesleyan Church and the Salvation Army. She noted in several instances that children at these centers received a combination of schoolwork, religious instruction, and training for a trade.[27] Bennett also learned from reformers closer to home. In 1901 she was on the program of the General Missionary Conference in New Orleans. Also giving speeches at the conference were Florence Kelley, Jane Addams, and Booker T. Washington, who gave an address on "The Negro and Industrial Education."[28] A few years later, Bennett spent several weeks in Chicago, studying the city mission work there, and then went on to New York City to investigate its missions.[29]

On a regular basis, she also studied labor, commerce, and immigration issues along with solutions presented by religious and secular organizations in the United States and abroad. Her studies reflected her belief in the importance of knowing the facts to find a viable solution. To this end, in 1901 she hired a woman to teach Christian Sociology at the Methodist Training School in Nashville, where young women trained to be missionaries and deaconesses. Using their training, the young missionaries followed Bennett's method of first gathering information and then passing on that material to fellow Methodist women in church publications, conferences, and educational institutes. As Tochie MacDonell pointed out, in this way home mission women became familiar with expressions such as "sociological investigation" and "social service" long before the Methodist Church itself did. Bennett firmly believed that if reform were to work, her efforts to promote it should begin with the women of the church, that "their influence [would] work like leaven in the Church."[30] Clearly Bennett employed many of the same methods as some of the most prominent Progressive Era reformers, but in her case, she focused especially on the important role for women in reform.

Belle Bennett's reliance on a combination of religious teachings and tenets drawn from social reformers of the day, her strong leadership, practical religion, and use of a wide variety of tactics resulted in an organization that offered expanded educational opportunities for residents in surrounding communities as well as increased interracial cooperation. As such, she deserves credit for helping to lay the groundwork for an increasing emphasis on social reform, especially in the area of education, in New South cities, improving race relations in the Jim Crow era, and for defining women's role in these reform efforts. The activities of the WMC women whom she led for almost thirty years are testament to her success.

Soon after its formation in the 1890s, the WMC began expanding its activities into social reform, beyond just furnishing homes for pastors and their families, to which some church women limited themselves. Belief in the power of education to improve lives led WMC women to establish mission schools in Florida for the children of Cuban immigrants; a mountain school in London, Kentucky, for poor children in the area; an industrial school in Greeneville, Tennessee, for orphans; and night schools for Japanese and Chinese workers on the West Coast. Council women also tackled the problems of immigrants and the poor in urban areas, mainly through their practice of friendly visiting in cities that included St. Louis, Atlanta, Houston, New Orleans, and Los Angeles. Nashville, Tennessee, by the turn of the century home to the country's largest population of Southern Methodists, who also outnumbered the membership of other Protestant denominations, became a center of WMC mission work. Members opened the Door of Hope Home Mission for immigrants in the city in 1893, a need arising in part from increasing industrial growth, especially in textile manufacturing, which attracted large numbers of young women operatives.[31] The first programs of the Door of Hope included a kindergarten and a rescue mission for girls. In 1901, WMC women changed their reform methods from visiting the poor to establishing a residential center among Nashville's needy populations, where deaconesses and kindergarten teachers lived as residents of what became their first settlement house. In 1903, the women officially renamed their mission in Nashville the Wesley House, the first of many such houses intended for white workers and immigrants. Tennessee eventually had Wesley Houses in Memphis, Knoxville, Chattanooga, Jackson, and Murfreesboro. Despite some reservations in these early years about being identified with northern, secular settlement work, WMC women patterned their programs at the Wesley Houses after Jane Addams's Hull House. Kindergartens, sewing and cooking classes, and programs on techniques of childcare, diet, and disease prevention became common offerings at these white settlement houses.

Over the course of the next twenty years, the WMC women expanded their city mission work throughout other southern states. By 1920 they were supporting twelve Wesley Houses staffed by 69 paid professionals and 227 volunteer workers. Wesley staff ministered "to fifty-two thousand five hundred people in twelve communities. There were eighty-nine organized clubs with two thousand four hundred and eleven members, twelve clinics in which were treated seven thousand eight hundred and sixty-seven patients, five day nurseries caring for two hundred children, thirteen kindergartens with eight hundred and eighty-six pupils, five night schools with sixty pupils, four Daily Vacation Bible Schools with seven hundred and sixty pupils and one hundred and forty-five teachers."[32] Also in 1920, the WMC at its annual meeting adopted a committee report calling for an enlarged city mission program. Not only were new settlements established, but existing ones increased cooperation with other public and private social service agencies, such as the Red Cross, YMCA, Camp Fire Girls, and the public schools. Clearly, the WMC intended for its Wesley Houses to be permanent fixtures on the urban social reform scene, and many of them functioned well into the twentieth century.

As noted, Wesley Houses served primarily white women and young children. But following Belle Bennett's lead, WMC women also attempted to serve the African American population in the South. In 1897, Bennett issued the first call to Methodist women for organized missionary work among blacks. In her presidential address that year she noted that

> there are two large classes of society touching our lives every day, whether we be in the country, in the towns, or in the large cities, to which our Society has as yet given no helping hand. We have done nothing for the negroes. Our great Church, as a Church, has done but little. Individual members may, doubtless, have done much; but as an organization the path of duty is plain before us, and as the Woman's Parsonage and Home Mission Society of the Methodist Episcopal Church, South, we must enterprise some special work for this great race of people. As a Convention, I beg your earnest consideration for this cause.[33]

WMC members responded to Belle Bennett's call to action, and once again Nashville, Tennessee, was one of the cities in the forefront.[34] In Nashville the Bethlehem House, the name Methodist women gave to their black settlements, opened its doors in 1913 through the efforts of Sallie Hill Sawyer, a Fisk College graduate and member of Capers Chapel Colored Methodist Episcopal Church who had first approached the Methodist women in 1907 about opening a settlement house for the city's approximately thirty-six thousand African American residents, almost a third of Nashville's total population at the time.[35] Although the WMC was unable to respond positively to Sawyer for almost six years, likely due to the lack of funds for "colored work" rather than an absence of motivation, supporters recommended to the WMC at its annual meeting in 1912 that Negro work be officially established in the city.[36] The WMC women agreed and adopted a constitution and bylaws to govern the Nashville Bethlehem House. The constitution created the interracial Cooperative League for Work Among Negroes in the City of Nashville, Tennessee.[37] In addition to overseeing the operation of the settlement, the objectives of the league included the following:

> To do all in its power to establish a larger sympathy and a better spirit of cooperation between the negro and white people.
> To promote and carry on work for the improvement of the economic, social, and spiritual condition of negroes in Nashville.
> To bring about the union and cooperation of existing agencies and organizations where desirable and to cooperate in every way with the National League on Urban Conditions among Negroes in carrying out the objects of this organization.
> To make such studies in Nashville as may be required to accomplish the above objects.
> To secure and train negro students for social service work.[38]

These objectives of the league as well as religious principles guided the early development of Nashville's Bethlehem House. Although the WMC ran a school for African American girls in Georgia, additional Bethlehem Houses were only established in Augusta, Georgia, Birmingham, Alabama, and Chattanooga, Tennessee.[39]

The specific educational activities offered at the WMC Wesley Houses and Bethlehem Houses reflected Belle Bennett's practical religion. Although the houses served different clientele, the educational activities offered at both institutions were similar. And settlement workers clearly identified what they did as educational work—both traditionally and nontraditionally defined. As one contributor to the WMC newsletter noted in 1911, "We usually think of education in the narrow sense of classroom work, which is in fact but a fragment of the education of any person. Yet it is an indispensable fragment; and as such it has a considerable place in our Wesley Houses and institutional work. A large number of these institutions have kindergartens; many have night schools for foreigners and other day workers; one—the Wesley House at Bristol, Va.—has a primary school for the children in its neighborhood, who have no public school." She went on to note the presence of Sunday schools, industrial training classes, cooking and sewing classes, and carpentry and house-making courses in all the Wesley Houses. According to the same writer, these classes opened "both the minds and souls" and were carried on "in thirty-two centers, under a teaching force of one hundred and sixty-eight salaried and four hundred and thirteen volunteer workers, reaching nearly three thousand five hundred pupils, the educative power of our home mission forces in classroom work alone is not to be despised."[40]

From the founding of the first Wesley House in Nashville, the kindergarten held a prominent place in daily educational activities. In addition to the deaconess or head resident who ran the house, the position of kindergarten teacher was often the only other permanent salaried position.[41] In a time when kindergartens were rare in southern public schools, settlement house kindergartens filled a pressing need in local communities. Taking a modern-day, almost Head Start, approach to their work, kindergarten teachers defined their mission and activities broadly. Obviously a religious motive drove their work with young children as evidenced by the pleasure that the kindergarten teacher at the Georgia Bethlehem House experienced from being able to convey to "the little tots" the true meaning of Christmas at the annual holiday party and to explain why Santa Claus really appeared.[42] Another teacher at the Memphis Wesley House described her students, who often repeated the Bible verses they had been taught, as having been given "a chance not only for higher ideals, but a chance to know Him who said: 'Suffer the children to come onto me.'"[43]

Yet there was more to these kindergarten activities than merely a chance to bring children into the church. Indications are that the kindergarten classes served to prepare children to enter public schools where they were available. The various clubs, projects, programs, and story hours held under the auspices of the kindergarten taught children skills needed to succeed in public schools. As one settlement teacher noted, "Our graded school teachers say they know one of our children as soon as they enter school; they are morally and educationally trained, until they are superior to the other children."[44] Another recounted the story of the mother who sent her wayward child to the Wesley House kindergarten in Nashville with the caution that teachers would not be able to manage him. Yet the teacher was able to report that "after three months of training this same child is often held up to other children as an example of obedience."[45] These behavior lessons were a big part of preparing children to move into the public schools with some hope of success. Once students learned the lessons of kindergarten—whether they included memorizing and reciting Bible verses, working together on group projects, creating gifts to bring home to parents, presenting holiday programs to the public, or meeting behavioral expectations and cleanliness standards—they were presented with diplomas and fully expected to become successful public school students who would improve not only themselves but also their families, homes, and communities.[46] Miss B. Veazey wrote of the six Nashville Bethlehem House kindergarten graduates in 1915, they "will be ready to cope with any first-grade child in free-hand cutting, drawing, molding, sewing, painting, and number work."[47]

For children beyond kindergarten age and teenagers, the settlement houses also offered a wide variety of educational opportunities. Belle Bennett mapped out the need for vocational education in the very first years of the settlements. She noted in 1911 with her usual mixing of the religious and secular that training for paid occupations was almost unknown in the city slums, mill villages, or mining camps. Possessing a remunerative skill would allow young people "to bear witness fearlessly in the midst of adverse and unchristian surroundings."[48] While much vocational education was concentrated in the academic schools the WMC supported across the South, WMC city mission work, especially settlement houses, also sought to provide vocational education. Most of the Wesley Houses and two of the Bethlehem Houses ran night schools that offered everything from English language classes in immigrant communities to basic reading and numbers courses as well as vocational classes. Attendees studied carpentry, stenography, typewriting, sewing, and domestic science. As the head resident at the Nashville Wesley House wrote, "Several of our young women were prepared by our stenography and typewriting classes for positions which they now fill with credit to themselves and satisfaction to us."[49]

Other settlements actually provided more traditional schools for children who did not attend school or who lived in areas where no schools existed, a clear example of how these institutions filled in gaps in the public school system. Knoxville settlement workers noted that many children in their area failed to attend school either because they were "not well enough clad to go the long distance" or their parents were simply indifferent to their children's school attendance, in response to which the Knoxville Wesley House opened a school for these children and endeavored to give them adequate training in their textbooks as well as "real lessons of life and to instill in them the ideals all too sadly lacking in many homes."[50] Several years later, one of the Knoxville deaconesses served as truant officer for the nearby public school and, likely due in part to her position, managed to get three hundred children into the school who would not otherwise have attended. The Wesley House supplied many of these new students with clothing and books. So even if they did not actually provide the school course or classroom, settlement workers nonetheless continued to support educational efforts of their communities.[51]

While they never lost sight of the religious basis for their settlements and city mission work, WMC members' educational work certainly evidenced their support of Bennett's practical religion approach. And WMC women moved very easily in the more secular world of Progressive reform. Their annual reports and newsletters are peppered with references to and writings by reformers of the day including Josiah Strong, Walter Rauschenbusch, Jane Addams, and Florence Kelley.[52] By 1916, they had adopted what they titled the "Constructive Social Program," which included among many issues the call for abolition of child labor, enactment and enforcement of compulsory education laws, establishment and maintenance of juvenile courts and reformatories, constructive censorship of moving picture films, strict enforcement of the law regulating the sale of habit-forming drugs, enactment and enforcement of laws prohibiting the liquor traffic and the sale of cigarettes, prison reform and abolition of convict lease system, and the cultivation of sympathy among all races.[53] These activities were driven by the guiding philosophy of the WMC women. As they noted in their annual report for 1917, "Let no one feel that the Wesley House movement is a small task set by the women of the Church for themselves. It is a movement which believes in the value of human life and has faith in the man at the bottom. It believes not only in the redemption of the sinner, but also in the redemption of the society in which he must have part. It uses the power of neighborhood organization as a means to bring about this rational and social order."[54]

The call for social order reflected the Progressive influence and may account for, at least in part, WMC women's work in improving race relations. With encouragement and leadership from Bennett, the WMC women's commitment to interracial cooperation and their networking among white and black community activists, challenged standard notions of Jim Crow segregation in the New South. The development and funding of the Nashville Bethlehem House serves as a case in point. Following an initial contribution of one thousand dollars from the Tennessee Conference of the WMC, which allowed for the rental of a deteriorating antebellum home to serve as the first Bethlehem House, the WMC pledged to contribute half of the yearly budget with the remainder to be raised locally.[55] Records indicate that workers at the settlement and residents of the surrounding black neighborhood labored to provide the other half of the budget. As early as 1913, Estelle Haskin reported that the Mothers' Community Club at the settlement had contributed over forty dollars to the support of the Bethlehem House kindergarten since "these women do not intend that the 'white folks' shall do all the good."[56] The club continued to contribute a monthly stipend to the kindergarten teacher for the purchase of supplies.[57] Following the death in 1917 of housemother Sallie Sawyer, Bethlehem House workers and residents created the Sallie Hill Sawyer Memorial Fund Committee. In one year alone, 1919, the committee, through various activities, raised one thousand dollars. In the following year, the committee financed the two kindergartens connected with the house at that time.[58]

Not only did WMC women and house staff and residents work together to fund the settlement, but they also worked with community organizations to keep the settlement afloat financially. For example, the Big Brothers, an organization not officially connected to the Bethlehem House, routinely turned over to the settlement its proceeds from the sale of Sunday newspapers at Christmas time. In 1925 alone, $250 from the Big Brothers allowed Bethlehem House workers to deliver "260 well-filled baskets into worthy, needy homes." Big Brothers also made dinner for "57 children from the alleys." During that same Christmas season, children from the Sunday school of the West End Methodist Episcopal Church, a white Nashville church, brought baskets of gifts for the kindergarten children at Bethlehem House. What appeared to be an ongoing gift for the kindergarten children was milk they regularly received from some of the women's clubs in the city.[59] While not direct monetary contributions, these gifts nonetheless aided in the continued operation of the settlement and allowed Nashville residents, both black and white, to become a part of this intracommunity network of support for the house's activities and objectives.

Throughout her remaining tenure as WMC president, Bennett continued to guide the development of interracial activities among the organization's members and in the process encouraged the growth of a network of women involved in interracial settlement work. And not surprisingly, in the first years of the Nashville Bethlehem House, workers created programs that eventually became standard fare at the other settlement houses. By 1915 the yearly report on activities listed a Mothers' Club, a kindergarten, a kindergarten training class, a story hour, sewing school, Camp Fire Girls, Junior Boys' Club, Kitchen Garden Club, Young Men's Cooperative Club, Children's Industrial Work, and Sunday afternoon Bible Hour among the settlement programs. Settlement workers also did house-to-house visiting, contacting an average of 350 people that year. By 1925, in addition to these programs, Brownie and Girl Scout troops had been added to the list of programs offered.[60] These regular activities at the settlement resulted from and reinforced the WMC women's belief in the importance of strong homes as the basis for a good society. Thus the many programs offered for children and mothers were not out of place at the Bethlehem House and were similar to clubs and activities at other settlements, both black and white.

Although the WMC settlement work with blacks was generally guided by the principle of cooperation and practical religion, the early interracial and community networks that resulted from this approach did not suggest racial equality. In fact, in the years immediately following Belle Bennett's call to Negro work, few WMC women moved far away from the notion that blacks were not yet ready to lead themselves without the help of whites. Generally, in these early years of their home missionary work, southern Methodist women regarded African Americans as belonging to a "child race" not yet evolved as far as whites in the "life of humanity."[61] According to Mary Helm, an active member of the WMC who wrote several textbooks for missionary study, whites owed blacks "the debt of love, the debt of the strong to the weak."[62] In these early years, WMC women also held tightly to their belief in the social separation of the races. Lily Hammond, wife of the president of Paine College[63] and an active WMC member, wrote in 1914 on the need to provide just treatment for blacks, but also noted, "What we white people need to lay aside is not our care for racial separateness, but our prejudice."[64] Yet both Lily Hammond and Mary Helm strongly supported the WMC work with blacks, even if it was based on a racist belief in white superiority. According to Hammond, "The finest and strongest Negroes, I believe without a single exception, have come to their high development largely through contact with broad-minded, large-hearted white men and women. For years to come few of them are destined to reach that plane by any other process. I think on this point the real leaders in the South, white and black, are agreed."[65] Given these generally held beliefs of WMC women—the inferior position of blacks in civilization, the necessity of maintaining racial separateness, and the need for superior whites to aid blacks—it is not surprising that early programs at the Nashville Bethlehem House reflected these attitudes.[66]

Yet even though this early network of black and white women did not imply equality, interacting on a daily basis with black workers and residents and the continued encouragement through the actions and words of Bennett led the WMC women to broaden gradually the scope and meaning of cooperation and eventually moved them into work for racial reform. Even the integrated staff, although structured in a racial hierarchy with a white director and a black housemother, served to increase understanding between blacks and whites at the house. Housemother Sallie Sawyer was described as a link between white workers and people in the community "because of her sympathetic and motherly understanding of her own people."[67] Black and white students from area colleges also strengthened interracial networks as they worked with each other and the community on various Bethlehem House programs. Fisk University, the Methodist Training Center, and later Scarritt and Peabody Colleges, all located in Nashville, sent students to work at the house to gain valuable social service training. As Estelle Haskin noted in her yearly report to the WMC, at the Bethlehem House these students received "very definite training and inspiration . . . in larger and better race sympathies."[68]

The increasing scope of cooperation and the expansion of interracial networks were reflected in other activities at the settlement. Estelle Haskin taught classes at Fisk University as part of the school's social service program, which sent numerous students to Nashville's Bethlehem House to gain practical social work experience. The Public Welfare League, an organization of both whites and blacks founded in 1916 to improve the lives of blacks in Nashville, maintained an employment bureau at the Bethlehem House. In 1917 the Public Welfare League and the Bethlehem House Board amended their constitutions to allow "for the joint prosecution of local work." Together these organizations worked on community programs such as Negro health and clean-up week.[69]

The settlement opened its doors to other community organizations as well. It served as the headquarters for the black Red Cross during World War I. The city of Nashville used the Bethlehem House yard as a playground for black children who had few if any other designated places for play. The Negro Public Library and the settlement cooperated to provide weekly story hours for children at various locations, while house workers joined with the extension worker from the YWCA to bring a Friday noonday service to forty black women employed at a hosiery mill near the settlement. In the 1920s, Bethlehem House board members and workers continued to reach out to community agencies. The director of boys' activities at the house worked with the juvenile courts in Nashville to reduce delinquency. House workers contacted the Nashville Censor Board, asking that they also monitor the "colored movie." Unaware that black movies had been overlooked, the board "promised better things."[70] Clearly, these activities not only served to bring blacks together but also increased white Nashvillians' knowledge about conditions in the black community and encouraged the interracial cooperation that WMC women had advocated since the founding of Bethlehem House.

While the number of white women who worked daily at the house was limited, WMC members nevertheless were kept informed of its activities. For a time the secretary of the Woman's Missionary Council chaired the Bethlehem House Board and acted as a link between both groups. Bennett herself visited the Nashville Bethlehem House and encouraged its settlement work.[71] The annual reports of settlement house directors and workers were included in the published proceedings of the WMC national meetings that went out to all members. This information about Bethlehem House activities was readily available to council members.

The daily interactions of people at the Bethlehem House influenced the interracial activities and cooperative efforts of the WMC women. As the work of these women matured over time, WMC leaders began to advise members "to open your hearts anew to the American negro. Go to them in love; do not go in a condescending attitude."[72] Annual reports discussed the need to change attitudes toward blacks since the WMC had moved beyond aid and uplift of blacks. One report noted among WMC women the "slowly rising appreciation of the Negro as a *person* with feelings, with laudable ambitions for education, for a chance to make a good living, and a chance to live in health and self-respect."[73] References to blacks as a child race no longer appeared in the WMC literature by the 1920s. The interracial work at the settlements had made these white women more sensitive to the need for racial reform and led WMC women into involvement in organizations and activities specifically designed to address racial questions.

By 1920, for example, the WMC was working with the Commission on Interracial Cooperation (CIC), an organization formed in 1919 in Atlanta to improve race relations. It was not unusual that these organizations joined in this common objective, since the CIC director, Will Alexander, had served on the Bethlehem House Board in its first years, when he was a divinity student at Vanderbilt University.[74] In attempting to bring women into the CIC, Alexander turned to Bennett for support, and she invited him to address the WMC at its annual meeting, where he suggested that the WMC appoint a committee to study changing race relations. What resulted was the creation of the WMC Commission on Race Relationship to study "the whole question of race relationship, the needs of negro women and children, methods of cooperation by which better conditions may be brought about." The committee sought to bring to WMC women "a better understanding of the task before them and to cooperate with other agencies dealing with the race problem."[75] Alexander credited Bennett with playing an important role in moving southern women into the work of the CIC. Bennett's biographer quotes Alexander as stating, "I have a feeling that Miss Bennett, more than anybody else, had through the years laid the foundation for the new attitude which Southern women are taking. . . . I cannot state this too strongly."[76]

In an effort to carry out the duties of the new committee on race relations, two delegates from the Commission on Race Relationship, Carrie Parks Johnson and Estelle Haskin, attended the biennial session of the National Association of Colored Women's Clubs (NACWC), which met at Tuskegee, Alabama, in 1920. Johnson and Haskin were so impressed with what they learned in a day-long discussion with black representatives at this meeting that they asked these women to put in writing the points discussed that could be "possible hindrances to the happiness and good will of us all." The black women's message was then passed on to a conference of white women held in Memphis in October 1920. Four of the speakers at this conference were black women who "bared their souls and made appeals for better understanding and cooperation, for protection and respect for their womanhood, for opportunities for their race." The WMC members at the conference joined with other attendees to create the Continuation Committee of the Memphis Conference to ensure that the black women's message would be passed on through their missionary newsletter, the WMC annual reports, monthly bulletins of local auxiliaries, and visits to numerous woman's missionary conferences.[77]

While some historians see these early conferences as a starting point for southern Methodist women's work for race reform, the meetings are better described as the culmination of more than two decades of interracial activity and reform on their part, beginning with Bennett's call to action at the turn of the century.[78] By the time Bennett's presidency ended, the WMC was allocating an average of twenty thousand dollars each year for this work.[79] Bennett was also responsible for the appointment of a "Director of Negro Work" within the organization, a move designed to ensure that WMC members would carry on race work even without Bennett.[80] And in fact, in the 1930s, Jessie Daniel Ames, head of the Association of Southern Women for the Prevention of Lynching, tapped into this network of well-organized Methodist women for support in her work to eradicate lynching.[81]

Clearly, the activities of the WMC women at these religiously based, second-tier settlement houses demonstrate that they played a significant role in the development and improvement of their individual communities as they participated in the larger efforts to find solutions to problems brought on by rapid industrialization and urbanization in New South cities. Guided by the capable and influential leadership of long-term WMC president Belle Bennett, with her practical application of religious values, these women not only relied on the teachings of their church and the tenets of the larger Social Gospel movement to guide their work but also adopted many of the reform methods of secular Progressive reformers as they moved into their communities to effect change. In particular, their work with African Americans challenges traditional notions about race relations in the Jim Crow South at the turn of the last century. Although a belief in racial equality did not likely motivate their work with African Americans, the women of the WMC did reach across racial lines to improve race relations, and the settlement house provided them the institution and setting in which to do this. As agents of reform and practitioners of practical religion, the women of the Woman's Missionary Council of the Methodist Episcopal Church, South, deserve to be moved from the margins to the center in any study of the Social Gospel movement during the Progressive Era. Their work should serve to expand the understanding and interpretation of this significant reform movement.

Janice M. Leone

NOTES

The opening epigraph refers to Belle Bennett, "The Message of the President," Proceedings of the Fifth Annual Meeting, Atlanta, Apr. 17–22, 1903, reprinted in *Our Homes* 12, no. 5 (May 1903): 2.

1. The works on progressivism are voluminous. See the following sampling of sources: Mina Carson, *Settlement Folk: Social Thought and the American Settlement Movement, 1885–1930* (Chicago: Univ. of Chicago Press, 1990); Allen Davis, *Spearheads for Reform: The Social Settlements and the Progressive Movement, 1890–1914* (New York: Oxford Univ. Press, 1967); Maureen A. Flanagan, *America Reformed: Progressives and Progressivisms, 1890s-1920s* (New York: Oxford Univ. Press, 2007); Mary E. Frederickson, "'Each One Is Dependent on the Other': Southern Churchwomen and the Process of Transformation, 1880–1940," in *Visible Women: New Essays on American Activism,* ed. Nancy Hewitt and Suzanne Lebsock (Urbana: Univ. of Illinois Press, 1993); Dewey Grantham, *Southern Progressivism: The Reconciliation of Progress and Tradition* (Knoxville: Univ. of Tennessee Press, 1983); Howard Jacob Karger, "Phyllis Wheatley House: A History of the Minneapolis Black Settlement House, 1924–1940," *Phylon* 47, no. 1 (Mar. 1986): 79–90; William A. Link, *The Paradox of Southern Progressivism, 1880–1930* (Chapel Hill: Univ. of North Carolina Press, 1992); Ralph Luker, *The Social Gospel in Black and White: American Racial Reform, 1885–1912* (Chapel Hill: Univ. of North Carolina Press, 1991); Cynthia Neverdon-Morton, *Afro-American Women of the South and the Advancement of the Race, 1895–1925* (Knoxville: Univ. of Tennessee Press, 1989); Milton Speizman, "The Movement of the Settlement Idea into the South," *Southwestern Social Science Quarterly* 44, no. 3 (Dec. 1963): 237–46; Judith Trolander, *Professionalism and Social Change: From Settlement House Movement to Neighborhood Centers, 1886 to the Present* (New York: Columbia Univ. Press, 1987).

2. Elisabeth Lasch-Quinn, *Black Neighbors: Race and the Limits of Reform in the American Settlement House Movement, 1890–1945* (Chapel Hill: Univ. of North Carolina Press, 1993), 2.

3. Ruth Hutchinson Crocker describes second-tier settlements as "those institutions that played an important role in their communities . . . but were not headed by nationally prominent reformers." See Ruth Hutchinson Crocker, *Social Work and Social Order: The Settlement Movement in Two Industrial Cities, 1889–1930* (Urbana: Univ. of Illinois Press, 1992), 6.

4. See Wendy J. Deichmann Edwards and Carolyn De Swarte Gifford, *Gender and the Social Gospel* (Chicago: Univ. of Illinois Press, 2003) in which the authors argue persuasively that a gendered analysis of the Social Gospel movement provides new definitions and interpretations of this reform movement in which women as well as men played a significant role. Edwards and Gifford also call for more primary research into the participation of women in this reform movement.

5. See Joan Marie Johnson, *Southern Ladies, New Women: Rage, Region and Clubwomen in South Carolina, 1890–1930* (Gainesville: Univ. Press of Florida, 2004); Nancy Hewitt, *Southern Discomfort: Women's Activism in Tampa, Florida, 1880s–1920s* (Urbana: Univ. of Illinois Press, 2001); Judith N. McArthur, *Creating the New Woman: The Rise of Southern Women's Progressive Culture in Texas, 1893–1918* (Urbana: Univ. of Illinois Press, 1998); Glenda Elizabeth Gilmore, *Gender and Jim Crow* (Chapel Hill: Univ. of North Carolina Press, 1996); Noralee Frankel and Nancy S. Dye, eds., *Gender, Class, Race, and Reform in the Progressive Era* (Lexington: Univ. Press of Kentucky, 1991).

6. Elizabeth Hayes Turner, *Women, Culture, and Community: Religion and Reform in Galveston, 1880–1920* (New York: Oxford Univ. Press, 1997).

7. Gilmore, *Gender and Jim Crow,* 178.

8. Victor Irvine Masters, *The Call of the South: A Presentation of the Home Principle in Missions, Especially as It Applies to the South* (Atlanta: Home Mission Board of Southern Baptist Convention, 1918), 69.

9. John McDowell, *The Social Gospel in the South: The Woman's Home Mission Movement in the Methodist Episcopal Church, South, 1886–1939* (Baton Rouge: Louisiana State Univ. Press, 1982), 10–15, 126–29.

10. In an early address to members of the Woman's Home Parsonage and Home Mission Society and printed in the society's newsletter, Bennett referred to city mission work as practical religion when she argued for the expansion of their mission work to include greater emphasis on helping African Americans and building more educational institutions. *Our Homes* (Jan. 1897): 3, microfilm, Divinity Library, Jean and Alexander Heard Library, Vanderbilt University, Nashville.

11. Emily Olmstead, *Intimate Glimpses of Miss Belle H. Bennett* (Nashville: Belle H. Bennett Memorial Committee, 1923); Mrs. Robert W. [Tochie] MacDonell, *Belle Harris Bennett: Her Life Work* (Nashville: Board of Missions, Methodist Episcopal Church, South, 1928); McDowell, *Social Gospel in the South;* Carolyn Stapleton, "Belle Harris Bennett: Model of Holistic Christianity," *Methodist History* 21 (Apr. 1983): 131–42.

12. Nancy Cott, *The Grounding of Modern Feminism* (New Haven: Yale Univ. Press, 1987); Johnson, *Southern Ladies*; Elisabeth Israels Perry, *Belle Moskowitz: Feminine Politics and the Exercise of Power in the Age of Alfred E. Smith* (Boston: Northeastern Univ. Press, 1992); Kathryn Kish Sklar, "Two Political Cultures in the Progressive Era: The National Consumers' League and the American Association for Labor Legislation," in *U.S. History as Women's History: New Feminist Essays,* by Linda Kerber, Alice Kessler-Harris, and Kathryn Kish Sklar (Chapel Hill: Univ. of North Carolina Press, 1995); Marjorie Spruill Wheeler, *New Women of the New South: The Leaders of the Woman Suffrage Movement in the Southern States* (New York: Oxford Univ. Press, 1993).

13. For a thorough treatment of women and the Lost Cause, see Karen L. Cox, *Dixie's Daughters: The United Daughters of the Confederacy and the Preservation of Confederate Culture* (Gainesville: Univ. Press of Florida, 2003).

14. Judith McArthur argues that it was secular voluntary associations rather than religious activism that moved women into progressive reform. See McArthur, *Creating the New Woman.*

15. *Our Homes* 10, no. 5 (May 1901): 1.

16. Ibid.

17. MacDonell, *Belle Harris Bennett,* 90.

18. Ibid., 70.

19. Stapleton, "Belle Harris Bennett," 132–33.

20. Josiah Strong, *Our Country: Its Possible Future and Its Present Crisis* (New York: Baker and Taylor, 1885); Josiah Strong, *Religious Movements for Social Betterment* (New York: Baker and Taylor, 1900); Josiah Strong, *Our World: The New World Religion* (Garden City, N.Y.: Doubleday, 1915); Wendy J. Deichmann Edwards, "Women and Social Betterment in the Social Gospel Work of Josiah Strong," in Edwards and Gifford, *Gender and the Social Gospel,* 36–52; Walter Rauschenbusch, *Christianity and the Social Crisis* (New York: Macmillan, 1907); Max L. Stackhouse, ed., *The Righteousness of the Kingdom* (Nashville: Abingdon Press, 1968); Paul M. Minus, *Walter Rauschenbusch: American Reformer* (New York: Macmillan, 1968).

21. MacDonell, *Belle Harris Bennett,* 124.

22. Ibid., 121, 132, 134.

23. *Our Homes* 8, no. 11 (Nov. 1899): 4; 17, no. 1 (Jan. 1908): 5.

24. Woman's Missionary Council (WMC), *Annual Report,* 1919–20, 57, Virginia Davis Laskey Research Library, Scarritt-Bennett Center, Nashville (hereafter cited as Scarritt-Bennett Center).

25. *Our Homes* 7, no. 12 (Dec. 1898): 10.

26. *Our Homes* 15, no. 6 (June 1906): 4.

27. *Our Homes* 10, no. 11 (Nov. 1901): 2.

28. *Our Homes* 10, no. 4 (Apr. 1901): 1.

29. *Our Homes* 14, no. 11 (Nov. 1905): 8.

30. MacDonell, *Belle Harris Bennett,* 88–89. Charles Israel's work on the short-lived Missionary Training School for Christian Workers (MTS), located in Nashville from 1905 to 1915 and under the supervision of the MEC South's General Board of Missions, suggests that Scarritt College's curriculum and methods were followed in the Nashville school also. As Israel notes, students at MTS were trained "for active service in a developing southern urban missionary movement" (2). Charles Israel, "The Missionary Training School: Women, Missions, and the Social Gospel in the Protestant Vatican" (paper presented at a conference on southern women and progressive reform, "Intersecting Missions: The Work of Women in Progressive Women's Organizations in Tennessee, 1870–1930," Scarritt-Bennett Center, Nashville, Mar. 10, 2007).

31. Don H. Doyle, *Nashville in the New South, 1880–1930* (Knoxville: Univ. of Tennessee Press, 1985), 42–50, 122.

32. WMC, *Annual Report,* 1919–20, 91.

33. Belle H. Bennett, "Address of Miss Belle H. Bennett," *Our Homes* 6, no. 1 (Jan. 1897): 5.

34. The earliest WMC settlement work with African Americans actually began in 1912 in Augusta, Georgia. Mary Noreen Dunn, *Women and Home Missions* (Nashville: Cokesbury Press, 1936), 62–63; WMC, *Annual Report,* 1914–15, 318, Scarritt-Bennett Center; "History of Wesley House, 1894–1969," History File, Bethlehem Centers of Nashville, Nashville.

35. Doyle, *Nashville in the New South,* 235. See Sonya Ramsey's chapter, this volume.

36. Shortly before the opening of the Bethlehem House, Estelle Haskin, director of social services at the Methodist Training School, reported on "the heavy handicap of lack of funds, room, and equipment to perpetuate the colored work of the department." By this time, the WMC was already supporting a growing number of city mission projects throughout the South at an approximate cost of seventy thousand dollars per year. WMC, *Annual Report,* 1911–12, 182, Scarritt-Bennett Center; WMC, *Annual Report,* 1914–15; WMC, *Annual Report,* 1912–13, 420–21, Scarritt-Bennett Center.

37. The fourteen-member executive board of the league, vested with administrative powers, actually governed the settlement. This board was composed of three members of the WMC residing in Nashville, three faculty members from Fisk University, two faculty members from the Methodist Training School, and six members from the city at large (three white and three black). The supervisor of the house held an ex officio position on the board, which met monthly.

38. WMC, *Annual Report,* 1913–1914, 155–56, Scarritt-Bennett Center.

39. WMC, *Annual Report,* 1929–1930, 81, Scarritt-Bennett Center.

40. *Missionary Voice* 1, no. 9 (Sept. 1911): 24, 25, Scarritt-Bennett Center.

41. While it is difficult to uncover a clear picture of the educational qualifications of kindergarten teachers working in these settlements, it appears that they were fairly well educated for the time. See *Missionary Voice* 4, no. 7 (July 1914): 406–7.

42. WMC, *Annual Report*, 1917–18, 314, Scarritt-Bennett Center.

43. WMC, *Annual Report,* 1916–17, 354, Scarritt-Bennett Center.

44. WMC, *Annual Report,* 1911–12, 428.

45. WMC, *Annual Report,* 1912–13, 383.

46. WMC, *Annual Report,* 1918–19, 291, Scarritt-Bennett Center.

47. *Missionary Voice* 5, no. 9 (Sept. 1915): 406.

48. *Missionary Voice* 1, no. 6 (June 1911): 7.

49. WMC, *Annual Report,* 1918–19, 289; 1912–13, 378.

50. WMC, *Annual Report,* 1913–14, 184.

51. WMC, *Annual Report,* 1918–19, 277.

52. *Missionary Voice* 3, no. 4 (Apr. 1913): 208.

53. *Missionary Voice* 6, no. 6 (June 1916): 257.

54. WMC, *Annual Report,* 1916–17, 111.

55. WMC, *Annual Report,* 1913–14, 374; Martha Nutt, "Bethlehem Center, Nashville, Tennessee," *Southern Workman* 53 (Sept. 1924): 403. The Nashville Bethlehem Center was located at three different sites before 1923, when the new building, its present location, was erected.

56. WMC, *Annual Report,* 1913–14, 375.

57. WMC, *Annual Report,* 1914–15, 319; WMC, *Annual Report,* 1916–17, 315.

58. WMC, *Annual Report,* 1920–21, 213, Scarritt-Bennett Center.

59. WMC, *Annual Report,* 1925–26, 205–6, Scarritt-Bennett Center.

60. WMC, *Annual Report,* 1915 to 1925.

61. Mary Helm, *From Darkness to Light* (New York: Fleming H. Revell, 1909), 154–55.

62. Mary Helm, "A Fair Attitude Toward the Negro," *Missionary Voice* 2, no. 4 (Apr. 1912): 201.

63. Paine College in Augusta, Georgia, was sponsored by southern black and white Methodists and designed originally for black males. In 1901, in response to Belle Bennett's request, WMC members agreed to establish an industrial department for African American girls at the school. Methodist women continued to support this work for black girls well into the twentieth century. Sara Estelle Haskin, *Women and Missions in the Methodist Episcopal Church, South* (Nashville: Smith & Lamar, Agents, 1920), 195.

64. Lily Hammond, *In Black and White: An Interpretation of Southern Life* (New York: Fleming H. Revell, 1914), 44–45.

65. Hammond, *In Black and White,* 204.

66. In her explanation of the usage of the term "interracial cooperation," Glenda Gilmore contends that white interracialists were not integrationists, nor did they advocate abolishing segregation, yet she also argues for the importance of personal contacts, usually on a local level, between black and white women in effecting change in race relations. Gilmore, *Gender and Jim Crow,* 177–78.

67. WMC, *Annual Report,* 1914–15, 319.

68. WMC, *Annual Report,* 1914–15, 320.

69. Report of George E. Haynes to Executive Board of the National League on Urban Conditions Among Negroes, Dec. 15, 1915, File 3, Charles S. Johnson Collection, Fisk University, Nashville; Haynes to National League, Mar. 11, 1917, Charles S. Johnson Collection, Fisk University, Nashville; WMC, *Annual Report,* 1917–18, 299.

70. WMC, *Annual Report,* 1917–18, 299–300; WMC, *Annual Report,* 1924–25, 197; WMC, *Annual Report,* 1925–26, 205.

71. Haynes to National League.

72. WMC, *Annual Report,* 1919–20, 35.

73. WMC, *Annual Report,* 1927–28, 142, Scarritt-Bennett Center.

74. McDowell, *Social Gospel in the South,* 86.

75. WMC, *Annual Report,* 1920–21, 153.

76. MacDonell, *Belle Harris Bennett,* 139.

77. WMC, *Annual Report,* 1920–21, 153–54 .

78. McDowell, *Social Gospel in the South,* 89; Alice Knotts, "Race Relations in the 1920s: A Challenge to Southern Methodist Women," *Methodist History* 26 (July 1988): 201.

79. WMC, *Annual Report,* 1921–22, 23.

80. WMC, *Annual Report,* 1919–20, 47.

81. Jacquelyn Dowd Hall, *Jessie Daniel Ames and the Women's Campaign Against Lynching,* rev. ed. (New York: Columbia Univ. Press, 1993).

Chapter 2

To Teach, to Preach, and to Heal: The Women's Missionary Society at Konnarock

Jean S. Hamm

> *"Mountain Schools are of various kinds. In all of them, however, one finds the same purpose—a twofold ideal—a purpose to help the students who are enrolled in the school and a purpose to help the communities from which the children come and in which the school is located."*
>
> —Mary Phlegar Smith, 1926

The Women's Missionary Society of the United Lutheran Church opened a small school for girls in the mountain community of Konnarock, Virginia, in 1923 at the intersection of the Appalachians of Virginia, West Virginia, Kentucky, North Carolina, and Tennessee. In the tradition of northern benefactors' contributions toward reconstruction of the South and in the twentieth-century Progressive spirit of the reform work of mountain settlement schools, the goals of the Women's Missionary Society were to help toward the social, moral, and economic rehabilitation of the southern mountain poor, among other mission projects. Acting on the Social Gospel tenets of social Christianity, Lutheran women determined to invest in the material elevation of the southern Appalachians, to educate and prepare young women in the mountains for better lives and financial independence, to represent the Lutheran faith in the mountain South, and to elevate the overall quality of life of the highland people within communities surrounding the school. Toward these ends, the Women's Missionary Society (WMS) turned faith into action in the mountains of northeastern Tennessee and southwestern Virginia. Through their club, church, and educational service, the women who developed and operated the Konnarock Training School (KTS) were women whose work in the public sphere contributed directly to the lives of mountain women and their neighbors in the towns and valleys of Appalachia, and through their efforts they also contributed to, more broadly, the visibility and futures of American women. Lutheran women's roles in East Tennessee and the southern Appalachian Mountains have been largely unnoted historically. The recovery of the work of the Women's Missionary Society of the United Lutheran Church at Konnarock, in the late Progressive period, develops the complexity of southern religious history and culture and expands the record of Progressive women's work in the East Tennessee mountains.

Lutheran women, as with other denominations' missionary societies, were increasingly called to action through the late nineteenth and early twentieth centuries, when progressivism built momentum in philosophy, politics, social reform, and education and as women began to assert themselves in the public sphere through their commitments to social progress. Historically, the women of national preeminence who were instrumental in advancing women's positions in American society during the Progressive period, as significant as they were, were singled out (in earlier decades) as exceptional, not as examples of the widespread involvement of large numbers of women in culture change. Through their decisions and personal actions, it was, of course, the ordinary women of American history who experienced that they had the power to effect significant changes in the societal settings in which they operated and whose impacts were far-reaching across Tennessee, the South, and the United States as a whole. And Lutheran women were among them.

In the sixty years following the Civil War, when women participated in their intense period of institution building, in the "social feminism" of women's clubs and associations founded by women who had been denied access to male institutions, the public work of the Lutheran women matured. Originally formed by women as support networks and social organizations such as sewing or Bible study groups, women's associations saw ways in which their members might work for meaningful reforms in their cities and neighborhoods. Comprised typically of middle-class, educated women interested in causes and sometimes careers outside the home, many women's clubs functioned beyond church circles and expanded their social programs in scope and impact to engage issues such as prostitution, temperance, poverty, and child labor. In their actions beyond the home, clubwomen of the late nineteenth and twentieth centuries emerged as new women in the safe public sphere of charitable work toward the improvement of society and, within the structures of their organizations, found the support they needed to build public lives and develop capabilities they may not have been aware they possessed.[1]

Even within the patriarchal confines of the church, which had so often suppressed them, women established themselves and their reform work as essential to the overall mission of the church. Women's meetings and circles within churches, often formed as women's missionary societies, developed first on local levels and then enlarged into state and national women's organizations. The intensity and capacity of church women to reflect on, articulate, organize, and carry out their beliefs increased as their groups grew. When the ideas of the Social Gospel spread through nineteenth-century churches, women took leadership roles in putting faith into practice to correct social injustices.

In 1908, the national Women's Missionary Society of the United Lutheran Church was formed from three smaller groups of women and undertook a variety of tasks to put Christian faith into action in the world of politics, economics, and society. The effort of the Lutheran WMS to build Konnarock Training School in the mountains of Appalachia was one such project. The society's school at Konnarock, located in an isolated community in the southwestern corner of Virginia, drew students from Tennessee, Virginia, North Carolina, West Virginia, and Kentucky. The establishment and operation of the school exemplify the efforts and accomplishments of these Lutheran new women, and the women they recruited to work with them in the mountains, as they put their faith into social action.[2]

In choosing Appalachia as the location for the school, the national women's group followed the needs of the Lutheran Church, which had historic roots in the especially poor and difficult geographical region of the mountain South. The church had established a presence in Appalachia early on in the history of the country.[3] German Lutherans had moved down from Pennsylvania through the Shenandoah Valley into the southern Appalachians of Virginia and Tennessee even in the 1700s. St. Paul's Lutheran Church in Wythe County, Virginia, was chartered in 1776, and in 1803, the Evangelical Lutheran Synod of North Carolina was organized among churches in North Carolina, Virginia, and Tennessee.

At the time of settlement across the Appalachians and with the Second Great Awakening, a strong ecumenical movement arose among the Protestant denominations to create a "general union" of Christian faiths, brought about in part by the necessity of serving the religious needs and providing adequate church services to Christians in widespread but sparsely populated regions west of the Appalachian Mountains.[4] Cross-ordinations were not uncommon during this period, when, for example, a minister of one denomination would be ordained by another church and when a community church would welcome a circuit rider of any faith. The spirit of general Christian unity, however, broke apart due to disagreements over specific tenets, as differences in biblical interpretation flared religious passions. Even within the individual Protestant denominations, splits over doctrinal issues divided churches into subdivisions within their own religious traditions, resulting in churches fracturing into separate congregations committed to specific precepts of faith.

Within Lutheranism in 1820 in the southern Appalachians, only seventeen years after the church became affiliated with the North Carolina Synod, a group of churches broke away and formed the Evangelical Lutheran Synod of Tennessee. The "Synod of Tennessee" is a misnomer, however, for the Tennessee Synod churches were as widespread as Greene County in East Tennessee, the site of the first annual meeting of the group, to the sites of subsequent meetings, at Staunton, Virginia; Davidson, North Carolina; and Lexington, South Carolina. The Tennessee Synod felt that the general Synod of North Carolina had "departed from the primitive doctrines and usages of the Lutheran Church" to the point of becoming anti-Lutheran and anti-Christian.[5]

Around 1870, the history of Tennessee's and Virginia's Lutheran churches was further complicated by the formation of the Holston Synod, with churches from the eastern half of Tennessee, western Virginia, northwest North Carolina, and some West Virginia congregations. Organizational twists and turns make it difficult to isolate the work of Tennessee women specifically. Therefore, the mission at Konnarock Training School is considered within the context of church women of these southern mountain synods as a whole, and of the national northern Lutheran organizations that contributed their support, whose contributions focused on providing education that would improve the lives of the people in upper East Tennessee, southwestern Virginia, and the Appalachian Mountains.

Just as they did for general historic works, men wrote the histories of the early southern mountain congregations and synods with little concern for women's work for the church. Lutheran Church historian Socrates Henkel's 1890 work documents the history of the Tennessee Synod for the seven prior decades without mention of the women in the church, except occasionally as the wives of ministers.[6] Women must have felt their voices were not being heard in the church and beyond. Developing their own organizations could give them collective power they did not have as individuals, and men would not object to women getting together to help widows and orphans or to save the souls of heathens in far-off lands. Missionary societies that had organized for these purposes became, in short order, deeply involved in not just foreign missions and helping the poor, but the total church ministry. Even though women were still excluded from church hierarchy, mission group work empowered them to bring their own experiences into the life of the church. Progressive women's church groups, while not ready to articulate it as such, laid the foundation of contemporary feminist theology and the modern church's work toward greater justice in society.[7]

The work of women's missionary societies in general[8] corresponds to the Progressive reform work going on in other segments of society, which manifested both as the forward-thinking, socially liberal progressivism of social justice and, sometimes paradoxically, as the conservatism that also characterized progressivism, calling for social controls, rational management, and reliance on professional expertise.[9] Liberal Progressives wanted to dramatically alter the entire social fabric in ways that benefited all people. Thus rights for minorities, labor laws that protected women and children, education, and care for the sick and mentally ill all became important agendas. The ideals of social Progressives parallel those of the Social Gospel advocated in many churches. Depending upon the methods and results of its application, the Social Gospel, as with progressivism, may be viewed as agency for positive social change or as meddlesome intrusion, especially when combined with sociological and scientific principles. Progressives also relied heavily on science and technology as means to effect the social transformations they were seeking. The rapidly changing, industrialized world produced modern, efficient systems that they sought to use for public good. If Progressives could logically and rationally show reasons for change, using newly developed scientific theory and pragmatic instruments, they believed social constructs would be altered for the better.

Both varieties of progressivism helped shape the curriculum, pedagogy, and administration of Konnarock Training School. The school was an institution that sought to bring social justice not only to its students but also to the larger world, and it was an institution that applied modern scientific and sociological techniques to its program in order to provide the best possible educational model. Liberal progressivism and the desire for social justice characterized much of the work of the Women's Missionary Society in its founding and running of Konnarock. The WMS form of social justice included providing educational opportunities that would improve women's place in the world.[10] The Lutheran women's mission to educate women, especially by the twentieth century, was a socially acceptable course of action into public work.

Although the Progressive Era classically dates from the end of the nineteenth century into the first two decades of the twentieth century, the influences of the period began much earlier and the work, particularly in the South, continued long after.[11] The founding of KTS reflects the long chronology of Progressives' work in the South. In 1922, a woman from Marion, Virginia, Laura Scherer Copenhaver, and her cousin, lay minister Kenneth Killinger, journeyed to Philadelphia to speak to the women gathered for the national convention of the United Lutheran Church's Women's Missionary Society in Pennsylvania.[12] Killinger and Copenhaver believed the ninety-seven foreign missions supported by the national WMS group were essential ministries, but, they argued, there were additional opportunities for good works within the United States, especially in southern Appalachia.[13]

Many other mission schools organized by churches had already been established in Appalachia, working toward the education and betterment of the lives of rural hill people. Among those were the Baptist Harrison-Chilhowee Institute in Sevier County, Tennessee, in 1887; the Presbyterian Vardy Community Mission School of Hancock County, Tennessee, in 1892; the Methodist Episcopal Church Pittman Community Center Mission School in Emerts Cove, Tennessee, in 1920; and the Christian Mountain Mission School in Grundy, Virginia, in 1921, to name only a very few just in that montane intersection.[14] In fact, in 1923, Hamblen County, Tennessee, had five mission schools.[15]

And with the urban settlement house movement of the Progressive Era, the settlement school idea had been translated for application into the rural South to address the needs of the hardscrabble communities of southern Appalachia. Different from urban settlements, rural settlements emphasized children's and young people's education. Comparable in process if not content with some of the issues tackled by urban settlements, rural settlements also took on issues of social uplift, human health, and economic development within the Appalachian communities served by the schools. A number of settlement schools had been established in the mountains by various organizations and individuals, including the Hindman Settlement School in Hindman, Kentucky, in 1902; the Pi Beta Phi Settlement School in Gatlinburg, Tennessee, in 1912; and the Pine Mountain Settlement School in Harlan County, Kentucky in 1913.[16]

The problems confronted when establishing mountain schools paralleled the challenges faced by Progressive reformers and educators in building schools throughout the rural South. Despite and because of communities' poverty and restricted economic opportunities, poor health perpetuated by lifestyle patterns, and traditionalism with an often dogged resistance to change, dedicated Progressive reformers embraced education as the foundational and fundamental solution to social change.[17] Work on systematically developing public schools and adequate county educational structures, essentially starting over completely, throughout the rural counties of Appalachia would take prolonged efforts by state educational systems across all of the southern Appalachian states and would encompass most of the early and middle decades of the twentieth century.[18] The very notion that education would lift mountain people out of entrenched patterns of thinking and behaving and that the ideas to which the local people would be exposed through schooling would be brought to them by professional programs and expertise developed externally, from organizations, colleges, or cities far away from the communities being served, went without saying; it was understood by Progressives, educators, social reformers, northerners, city people, and church missionaries alike that backward rural southern life had to change and that those changes must be addressed through both school curriculum and outreach to families and neighbors.[19] Needed throughout the rural South, change was all the more pressing in the hills and hollows of the Appalachians. Until state-run public education could be adequately emplaced, supported by public roads and transportation, mission schools and settlement schools served many rural communities and undertook the ground-up work of educating the mountain youth and their communities. All programs of the era defined their tasks as important, altruistic, and contributing to local life. But some also brought ideals of social justice to the mountains, intending to provide students with skills they could employ to support their families and with which to empower their local communities to develop themselves socially and economically.

Back in Philadelphia and intrigued by the reports of Copenhaver and Killinger, the Lutheran Women's Missionary Society engaged two young women to study the area around northeast Tennessee, southwest Virginia, and northwest North Carolina. Both were exemplary of the new women of their era: They were young, career oriented, interested in reform, and well educated. The Lutheran Church had long supported education for women. At the time of the 1922 convention, there were 897 women enrolled in Lutheran colleges in the United States, many receiving financial support from the WMS.[20] Most of these women were trained for the jobs that were considered acceptable for women: nursing, teaching, social work, and music. Many, however, went into other fields. They were readied to assume leadership positions within their careers and their communities, even though not many of those positions were open to them.

The WMS chose Mary Phlegar Smith, a Pennsylvania native, to set up a small mission in Currin Valley, about five miles from Marion, in southwestern Virginia. When she arrived, Smith not only set up Sunday schools but also began to teach children during the day and local adults at night.[21] When the Konnarock Training School was established in 1923, Smith accepted the position as its first principal. She went on to receive her doctorate, became a dean at Hollins College in Roanoke, Virginia, served on the Board of Visitors of Virginia Tech, and was state education committee chair for the AAUW. Smith was active throughout her life in educational research and published widely, including the article "Legal and Administrative Restrictions Affecting the Rights of Married Women to Work" and *Special Legal Relations of Married Women in North Carolina as to Property, Contracts, and Guardianship* in 1928.[22]

The second woman selected by the Lutheran WMS to study the needs of Appalachia, Cora Pearl Jeffcoat, resigned her post as superintendent of schools in Davidson, North Carolina, to move to the mountainous area around Boone in the western part of her state. She too worked with local children and adults in a variety of capacities, including literacy instruction. Jeffcoat was a graduate of Greensboro College and did graduate work at Peabody College, Mississippi State College, the University of North Carolina, and Columbia University. She would work full time for the WMS educational efforts in the Appalachians, taking a post at the Watauga Mission in Boone, North Carolina, which the Women's Missionary Society also would fund over the next years. Jeffcoat remained with the mission until she suffered a stroke in 1939.

Shortly into their work, both Jeffcoat and Smith realized the need for a school specifically for mountain girls.[23] In 1922, most mountain schools were one-room establishments for grades one through six, located close enough to the children's homes for them to walk to it over the mountain trails. Throughout the Appalachians, roads were almost nonexistent until the 1930s and were not paved until much later. The small local schools were in session each year only about six months or less because of the difficulty of winter travel. Some mountain children received no education at all, and the possibility of a girl receiving a high school education or beyond was practically inconceivable. Girls worked hard in the home and married young. For most families in the mountains, "book learning" was not only unnecessary for girls, it was sometimes considered sinful, especially to read anything except the Bible. Many mountain children had little exposure to the outside world. Electricity and indoor plumbing were almost unknown. Only a few households read a newspaper or books, which were available only infrequently.

The WMS had to decide, if a school for the education of girls were to be built, where it would be best positioned. The need was widespread. Located about thirty miles from Jeffcoat's mission in Boone and twenty from Smith's mission in Marion, Virginia, the small village of Konnarock, Virginia, was selected as ideal. In the southwest corner of Virginia, Konnarock is also near Tennessee (eighteen miles), Kentucky (forty-five miles), and West Virginia (forty-five miles). In addition, and of pragmatic importance, Konnarock was an economically thriving village of more than three hundred people and was connected to cities and universities by railways that had been built by the lumber companies that harvested the mountains. The village already had a small high school for the children of the company employees. When the Women's Missionary Society groups of Southwest Virginia, Virginia, and the Holston Synod merged in 1923, the local group members continued to contribute their support toward foreign missions, scholarships for Japanese students, and a mission in Greeneville, Tennessee, but Konnarock became central to efforts of the regional WMS in Virginia, North Carolina, and Tennessee.[24]

Businessman and philanthropist Luther Hassinger became personally interested in the Konnarock work. His lumber company was the major employer in the community of Konnarock, and he owned a vast amount of land there. Hassinger cut virgin timber from the surrounding mountains and shipped it via the Virginia Creeper Railway to Kingsport, Tennessee, for distribution. He agreed to donate a tract of land and to help with construction of the building itself.[25] In 1924, the very first students—five small girls from Jeffcoat's and Smith's missions—arrived at Konnarock, living with their teachers in a house rented from the sister of Theodore Roosevelt, Corrine Roosevelt Robinson. Mary Phlegar Smith became the first principal at the school; Jeffcoat remained in North Carolina, encouraging local girls to attend the boarding school. That first year about fifteen day students also attended elementary classes at the school.[26] Meanwhile, a modern, three-story building with central heat, indoor plumbing, and generators to provide electricity was under construction on the Hassinger property not far away.

Luther Hassinger oversaw the actual building of the Konnarock school and donated much of the lumber and labor. The active support he received from the general community in the form of donated labor speaks to the community members' desire to see their children and others from surrounding areas educated. Even with the immense local support, the school received significant help from Women's Missionary Society groups from far beyond the area. Lutheran women's groups throughout the nation—Tennessee, Virginia, Pennsylvania, Indiana, Illinois, Minnesota, Wyoming—donated dishes, cooking utensils, curtains, classroom desks, an organ, beds, and whatever else might be needed. These were delivered by the same train that carried Hassinger lumber out of the mountains. A library containing about fifteen hundred volumes was part of the new school, and magazines and newspapers arrived with every train, again many paid for by women. Students from five states lived at the school, ate their meals in a large dining room with white table linens, and were taught by resident teachers from places as far away as Pennsylvania, Indiana, Illinois, and Minnesota. No girl was ever turned away because of the inability of her parents to pay. The national WMS continued to support the school in its budget, as did the regional WMS, and individual women gave scholarships and girls' parents contributed what they could.

If the students' families had no money, they brought bushels of potatoes, beans, apples, or other crops to the school. The girls themselves also worked at the school during the year and for two weeks during the summer.[27] Every student, whether or not her family could pay, was expected to perform routine duties such as setting or clearing tables, dishwashing, laundry, or sweeping floors. These duties rotated so that no girl had the same chore all the time and each understood the importance of all the jobs. The girls' educations were as close to real life as possible; they learned to participate in their community and became prepared to be contributing members of society.[28]

By the second year the school was in operation, the new building, a combination of classrooms and a dormitory, was ready for occupancy. By the third year, the second year in the new building, thirty-five girls boarded at KTS. Most were from Virginia and North Carolina, but two were from Tennessee and two from Kentucky.[29] Those who were high school age boarded at KTS but took their classes at the local secondary school. Increasing numbers of elementary day students attended classes at KTS. There were so many day students, in fact, that Washington County, Virginia, paid a teacher's salary to provide an extra classroom for them at KTS.[30] The openness with which the mountain people welcomed the idea of the new school and the women who came with it belies the traditional stereotype of Appalachian xenophobia.

The new women who established and operated Konnarock Training School brought both liberal and conservative progressivism to the school. Liberal progressivism is reflected at KTS in the building itself, which brought better living conditions to the children, and is also seen in the total school program. The school's second principal, Catherine Cox Umbarger, wrote about the attempts that were made in curriculum improvement in the July 1930 issue of *Lutheran Woman's Work,* the national publication of the Women's Missionary Society:

> We were only doing stereotypical public school work. . . . We felt the need of knowing our children better, in their homes as well as our school. Our grade education was not vital. It took only half an eye to see that "lessons" were only "books to go through," and then at the beginning of another, another set of "books to go through." The old rote type of work seemed to be [the students'] idea of good work. Words were words to be memorized and given back to the teacher. . . . The old system of forcing a child to take all classes in the same grade was broken up . . . [such that] each child was placed in a group where [s]he could do the best work. . . . The idea of failure was abolished except where a student showed plainly that [s]he was unwilling to try. But this was not enough. We needed to break up the idea of "English" as a study all to itself; and "History" as having no connection with anything in our present day existence; and "Hygiene" as the study of health. We undertook a number of studies combining all the [disciplines]. One class spent several weeks studying Early American History. Reading material was supplementary history material. English lessons were stories and letters and finally a play on the "Landing of the Pilgrims.". . . With all this, our state course of study has been very closely fol-

lowed. We use state textbooks—but we use others in addition. We give the required number of hours to each subject—and often more.

We do believe that we are on the right road to helping our girls and perhaps other mountain girls to live a "more abundant life." A definite effort has been made to give each child what she needs to strengthen her weak points, to teach her to think and reason, to broaden her background and vision, and to make her school work vital and of some practical present value to her as an individual.[31]

Umbarger's words echo the vision of educational reformer John Dewey: an integration of disciplines in a child-centered curriculum, educational experiences that are of value in the student's present world, concern for the whole child, a deemphasis on rote learning, and a focus on the idea of education as real life so that the student can participate in her community at school and become a contributing member of her society outside of school.[32]

To further that end, Umbarger appealed to the readers of *Lutheran Woman's Work* for increased vocational education programs for not only the girls of the Konnarock school but also the local women of the nearby communities. She emphasized the critical need for the female mountain population to be able to be economically independent and self-sustaining, to be able to earn a living and provide for themselves and their families. But Umbarger was aware that the faculty and staff of KTS were dedicated primarily to the academic education of the girls and that to enlarge the mission of KTS would require increased personnel trained in industrial education and greater outside funding: "Our staff, as well as our time and budget, do not permit this well-rounded program at present—but we must have it, if we are to serve our girls in the best way."[33] Progressive women advocated education that prepared women to support themselves, insisting that the ability to achieve financial independence was a vital component of women's equality in the larger community.

The longer the Konnarock school served its mountain communities, the more those who operated it realized what yet needed to be accomplished and the more their scope and vision necessarily expanded to respond to pressing needs in the mountains. That enlarged realization, along with liberal progressivism's desire to transform social conditions and

Dewey's emphasis on the school in the community as the agent of social reform, resonate in an article by later KTS principal Helen Dyer:

> Konnarock Training School began with what looks like a simple enough problem—supplying good elementary, vocational, and religious training to children who otherwise would not get even these minimum essentials. . . . [But over time our w]orkers [became] more than ever conscious of the needs of the homes as well as in the pupils themselves. Local needs are so similar to those in the homes and communities from which boarding students come, that it has come to be felt that the more our center could reach out to help this community, and the more it could enter into community life instead of being just a sheltered group of girls who were being given very special educational and living privileges, the more lasting would be the effect.[34]

An earlier article in *Lutheran Woman's Work* also stressed this pressing need to expand the school's role to serve the community: "[In] Mountain Schools . . . one finds the same purpose to help the students who are enrolled in the school and a purpose to help the communities from which the children come and in which the school is located."[35]

Shortly after the school's opening, another group of Progressive women became interested in the Konnarock Training School and had an impact on the lives of the girls of KTS. The Southern Woman's Educational Alliance, primarily a group of university women, operated from 1920 to 1936 for the purpose of researching and promoting women's educational and vocational opportunities throughout the South. Orie Latham Hatcher was a pioneer in the field of women's education and the founder of Bryn Mawr's Department of Comparative Literature. She and her sister Edith were two of five children born in Richmond, Virginia, to a wealthy and well-educated family. The parents and siblings published at least twenty-one books and were all involved in education. In 1915, Edith founded Harcum College in Pennsylvania.[36] Both Edith and Orie believed that women, even those from wealthy families, should be trained for a vocation. In 1914, Orie Hatcher founded the Virginia Bureau of Vocations for Women, which became the Southern Woman's Educational Alliance in 1920. The association embarked on a study of Appalachian schools in 1924.[37]

To begin the study, Mary Phlegar Smith, Konnarock Training School's first principal, was given a year's leave of absence and a grant from the alliance to receive training in research, along with "a Ford car, two assistants, an itinerary and schedules to be used in interviewing."[38] After Smith and her assistants visited twenty-three public and private schools and colleges in six southern states, the alliance chose Konnarock as the site of a more intensive study. A formal study of the school began in November 1926 and lasted through the 1928–29 academic year, utilizing all the modern, scientific tools the researchers could obtain. Case studies that included personal interviews, personality/interest inventories, aptitude and achievement tests, home visits, and discussions with school personnel were completed on thirty-eight girls attending KTS. Two other women, both of whom were trained social workers, Catherine Cox (later Umbarger), who became the second principal, and her sister Cordelia Cox, were heavily involved in the school study, especially in the creation of the case studies. The study's findings were published in *A Mountain School: A Study Made by the Southern Woman's Educational Alliance and Konnarock Training School* in 1930.[39] By engaging Konnarock and its educators in the study, the research furthered the conservative Progressive values of scientific expertise at Konnarock, but the results of the study ultimately embraced a liberal Progressive, social betterment agenda in its community-wide recommendations for implementation in the mountains.[40]

One of the recommendations to come out of the study was that KTS adopt a program of standardized testing. The list of tests was extensive: The Pintner-Cunningham Primary Mental Test, Otis Group Intelligence Scale, Tribune Mentimeters, Stanford Achievement Test, National Intelligence Test, Terman Mental Ability Test, and Iowa High School Contest Examination were all administered to KTS girls.[41] All these assessments had gained popularity in American education after World War I in an effort to bring schools into the modern era. Devotees of the tests argued their value in determining the best avenue for meeting individual needs, while critics pointed out that testing serves to exclude some children from educational services.

Interestingly, at the same time that modern, scientific testing was implemented in this tiny corner of the mountains, Hatcher and others were clearly aware that "scholarship and science can not always measure human well being and the ingredients of human happiness."[42] Therefore, it is not surprising that the Woman's Educational Alliance study would also produce recommendations to further support vocational education programs that could positively impact the larger community.

Hatcher was a leader in women's vocational education, which had gained momentum nationwide during the 1920s, along with the idea of comprehensive high schools. In 1918, a bulletin from the National Education Association (NEA) titled *Cardinal Principles of Secondary Education* called for schools to implement academic master plans that would include programs for the development of "health, command of fundamental processes, worthy home membership, vocation, citizenship, worthy use of leisure, and ethical character."[43] Areas of emphasis for the mission of the comprehensive high school were based on the tenets of social engineering that had gained acceptance with many educational reformers. Their hope was that by using efficiency principles to train educators and administrators, schools could become a sorting bin where, through testing and guidance, students' strengths and weaknesses could be determined in order to find the most fitting adult positions for them. Although it does not seem that KTS adopted the social efficacy model of education, the general aims of the *Cardinal Principles* are echoed both in the list by Hatcher of needs for mountain schools and in a list by KTS titled "Things We Want in Our Curriculum."[44] The latter document targets homemaking, carpentry, care of the person, the right use of leisure, good citizenship, reading, writing, and clear thinking—paralleling the goals set for comprehensive high school as delineated by the *Cardinal Principles* of the NEA.

The work at Konnarock Training School as originally commissioned by the Women's Missionary Society had a threefold purpose: to preach, to teach, and to heal. Konnarock Training School understood the work to be not for the students only, but for the entire mountain community. The southern Appalachian region was the school's classroom. Mission workers quickly identified a critical pressing need of the population surrounding Konnarock: "A trained health worker [is required]. Housing conditions, home sanitation, the care of expectant mothers, the feeding of children, and home care of the sick are subjects upon which instruction is most woefully needed. The opportunities for the community nurse are limited only by her physical endurance."[45]

Not only was there a shortage of educational opportunity in the mountains, but there was a shocking lack of medical care. When KTS opened, one of the first staff members hired was a nurse, and the school continued to hire nurses even after a doctor was brought into the community in 1939.[46] The first duty of the nurse was of course to attend to the KTS students, both boarding and day. The school nurse conducted the state-mandated physical examinations for public school students, and she cared for students through illnesses, seeking the services of a physician when the children were beyond her care. In addition, the nurse taught health and hygiene classes and soon instituted a school lunch program for day students. Without telephone service in the area and with the nearest physicians fifteen to twenty miles away, the work of the school nurse took on greater and greater importance. Soon a dispensary was set up in the basement of the school building, and local residents could come there when they needed care. Not only did the nurse see patients on site, but she also conducted clinics and gave immunizations throughout the area.[47]

When Amy Louise Fisher became the school nurse in 1927, she and Principal Catherine Cox prevailed upon the church women to fund and have constructed a separate dispensary building next to the school. On the completion of the new building in 1928, it was furnished with examination tables, a dental chair, and other medical equipment by women's groups throughout the nation. Fisher was sometimes able to convince doctors and dentists to donate their time to the clinics, but the lack of a full-time doctor still plagued the school and community.[48] In some cases, the school bore the expense of medical treatment even for children who did not attend KTS, seeing to it that the ill children saw doctors or had needed operations. Principal Cox reported to the Women's Missionary Society that during the winter of 1928 there were outbreaks of scarlet fever and flu that swept through the school and community. She made unbudgeted expenditures of $715.28 for the services of physicians and $122.31 for medicines and supplies for dispensary patients, both students and community members.[49]

Nurse Ida Twedten was provided with a car to travel to local homes and with a horse for times when the people who needed her were too far from passable roads for her to reach them. She also was given a large shepherd dog as company and protection when she traveled, a dog adopted by all the children at KTS. During the winter of 1936–37, Twedten treated or helped to treat 339 influenza cases and 15 pneumonia cases.[50] She proudly reported that none of the individuals died from these illnesses, which were often fatal in the mountainous region.

In 1939, Konnarock Medical Center was erected through gifts from the Luther League, a youth organization within the church. H. C. Meyer, a physician, and his wife, a registered nurse, both refugees from Nazi Germany, came to the mountains to work. Meyer, working with Tennessee Valley Authority grants of ten thousand dollars a year, conducted an influential five-year nutritional study of Appalachian residents. Meyer continued his service to patients in the mountains for more than thirty years. He was aided in this work by Lutheran deaconess Sister Sophia Moeller, a registered nurse who also traveled throughout the mountains giving medical care to the residents for more than thirty years. Sister Sophia attended the births of hundreds of mountain children and ministered to the physical and social needs of countless individuals.[51]

Another aspect of community outreach supplied by KTS staff and students was the wide-ranging series of Bible schools held during summer vacations. Volunteers from throughout the United States were also solicited to live in the various communities for several weeks in the summers to help with the efforts. The sessions were generally three weeks long and lasted the entire day. Part of each day of Bible school was devoted to "Opportunity Classes" for those students who needed tutoring in basic language and mathematics skills, helping prepare them for success in their public schools when they returned. Additionally, the school nurse provided health screenings, well-baby clinics, and parenting classes in the outlying communities during Bible school sessions. At the height of the Bible school activity in 1930, there were 40 adult volunteers, 650 students, and 162 mothers who took part in the nine Bible schools and accompanying clinics.[52]

The school's program emphasized the total development of its students. Like many other mountain schools of the period, the school was founded by "outsiders," primarily northern women whose Social Gospel and humanitarian leanings had led them to become involved in home as well as foreign missions. But their work at Konnarock Training School was deeply rooted in the place and traditions of the mountains. Local craftsmen using local hardwoods built the structure of the school and sided the building with the bark of the now almost extinct American chestnut, a tree that once covered the Appalachians. Teachers, many of whom came from throughout the nation, often chose to stay in the area. The emphasis on education and encouragement of training beyond what KTS could provide also encouraged students to return to their home communities and make a difference there. Graduating senior girls all took a leadership class that helped them develop skills they could use wherever their lives might lead them. KTS welcomed the community inside its doors and stepped out to become a part of the larger community in many ways. The belief that all people had dignity and deserved a good education, a decent job with a fair wage, health care, and a voice in their own world underlay the school's efforts in all it did.

In 1958, following the pattern by the mid- to late-twentieth century experienced by many of the mountain mission and settlement schools, Konnarock Training School was closed. Citing better roads and improved area schools, the Board of Missions of the United Lutheran Church in America announced its decision to terminate Konnarock, a decision that was never fully explained to those interested in the school. Rose Cox Kirby, both a graduate of and teacher at KTS, said she felt "if Konnarock had continued, if it had been [supported by the broader church] . . . it could have survived."[53] Another graduate, Peggie Baldwin, said, "They said financial problems. But I thought that right up until closing time they had a great group; maybe not a full house, but enough [students] to keep it running, but I've heard they had financial problems. . . . I always felt the Lutheran Church gave freely, and I felt they could have kept it open. I understand that . . . their enrollments were down and everything, but I do feel it could have been built up to be just a booming school again. You've got to work at anything like that, and I think maybe that had died."[54] A third graduate and teacher, Emily Umbarger, had another view of the closing, that which was voiced by Luther Hassinger of Bristol, formerly the head of the Hassinger Lumber Company: "Somebody lost the vision along the way."[55]

The effects of the mission work carried out in preaching, teaching, and healing by the women affiliated with Konnarock Training School are impossible to adequately quantify. Yet the ripples and waves caused by those efforts are still being seen today. Rose Kirby, who was both a student and teacher at KTS, said this of the work of the Konnarock mission school: "Those ladies of the church—and it was the *women*—they just took that on their shoulders, [and knew] that they could do something that would make an impact on the communities. There's no way to assess the impact made by the [women of] the church."[56]

The Konnarock Training School left a powerful imprint on the mountain people and the entire region touched by the school. Through the efforts of the women lay missionaries, teachers, nurses, and fundraisers, and through the young women educated at the school, Konnarock taught and uplifted, and, beyond its educational curriculum, provided direct, hands-on, caring answers to a wide range of social, economic, and health problems embedded in a corner of the Appalachian South. Because of their work with young mountain women, the Lutheran Women's Missionary Society had an impact on not only the girls but also their homes and their wider rural communities.

NOTES

The opening epigraph refers to Mary Phlegar Smith, "Our Mountain Work," *Lutheran Woman's Work* 19 (July 1926): 272.

1. Estelle Freedman, "Separatism as Strategy," in *Feminism and Community,* ed. Penny A. Weiss and Marilyn Friedman (Philadelphia: Temple Univ. Press, 1995), 90; Mary Field Belenky, Lynne A. Bond, and Jacqueline S. Weinstock, *A Tradition that Has No Name: Nurturing the Development of People, Families, and Community* (New York: Perseus Books, 1997), 200; cf. Tennessee Federation of Women's Clubs, *Woman's Work in Tennessee* (Memphis: TFWC by Jones-Briggs, 1916); Karen J. Blair, *The Clubwoman as Feminist: True Womanhood Redefined, 1868–1914* (New York: Holmes and Meier,

1980); Anne Firor Scott, *Natural Allies: Women's Associations in American History* (Urbana: Univ. of Illinois Press, 1991); Marsha Wedell, *Elite Women and the Reform Impulse in Memphis, 1875–1915* (Knoxville: Univ. of Tennessee Press, 1991).

2. For history of the women of the United Lutheran Church in America (ULCA), see L. DeAne Lagerquist, *From Our Mothers' Arms: A History of Women in the American Lutheran Church* (Minneapolis: Augsburg Publishing House, 1987); Nona M. Diehl, *United Lutheran Church Women: Heritage and History, 1879–1959* (Philadelphia: United Lutheran Church Women, 1961); and General Council of the Evangelical Lutheran Church in North America, *Women's Missionary Society, History 1902–c. 1919* (bulk 1902–1911), box 1, folder 1, Archives of the Evangelical Lutheran Church in America, Chicago, Ill. For the Missouri Synod of the Lutheran Church, see Ruth Fritz Meyer, *Women on a Mission: The Role of Women in the Church from Bible Times Up to and Including a History of the Lutheran Women's Missionary League during Its First Twenty-five Years* (St. Louis: Concordia Publishing House, 1967). Magazines published by Lutheran church organizations provide the most detailed accounts of Lutheran women's involvement in social issues, for example, *Lutheran Woman's Work* (ULCA) and *Women's Missionary Outlook* (Evangelical Lutheran Church in America).

3. Paul K. Conkin, "Evangelicals, Fugitives, and Hillbillies: Tennessee's Impact on American National Culture," *Tennessee Historical Quarterly* 54 (Fall 1995): 249.

4. Socrates Henkel, *History of the Evangelical Lutheran Tennessee Synod* (New Market, Va.: Bell, 1890), 17.

5. Ibid., 18, 102.

6. Ibid.

7. For a discussion of feminist theology, see Rebecca S. Chopp, *Saving Work: Feminist Practices of Theological Education* (Louisville: Westminster John Knox Press, 1995); also Gary Dorrien, "Society as the Subject of Redemption: The Relevance of the Social Gospel," *Tikkun* 24, no. 6 (Nov.–Dec. 2009): 43.

8. For women's missionary work of the Methodist Episcopal Church, South, see Janice M. Leone, this volume.

9. Wayne J. Urban and Jennings A. Wagoner, *American Education: A History,* 2nd ed. (Boston: McGraw-Hill, 2004), 198. "Liberal" and "conservative" are used here in their social historical context, reflective of the often contradictory manifestations and methods of the progressive impulse and progressive actions to achieve reform; they are not references to political ideology. For a discussion of the liberal and conservative aspects of progressivism, see William A. Link, *The Paradox of Southern Progressivism, 1880–1930* (Chapel Hill: Univ. of North Carolina Press, 1992); Maureen A. Flanagan, *America Reformed: Progressives and Progressivisms* (New York: Oxford Univ. Press, 2007); Nancy Cohen, *The Reconstruction of American Liberalism, 1865–1914* (Chapel Hill: Univ. of North Carolina Press, 2002); and Dewey Grantham, *Southern Progressivism: The Reconciliation of Progress and Tradition* (Knoxville: Univ. of Tennessee Press, 1983).

10. Freedman, "Separatism as Strategy."

11. For the long chronology of progressivism, see Elisabeth Israels Perry's chapter, this volume.

12. Sherree R. Tannen, *Kenneth Killinger: Mountain Missionary* (Lynchburg, Va.: Warwick House, 1995).

13. Ibid.

14. Russell Hall, "Pittman Center: A Typical School of the Southern Appalachian Mountains" (BD thesis, Vanderbilt Univ., 1937).

15. Austin P. Foster, *Counties in Tennessee* (Nashville: Department of Education, Division of History, State of Tennessee, by Clearfield Company, 1923).

16. Margaret D. Binnicker, "Settlement Schools," *Tennessee Encyclopedia of History and Culture,* http://tennesseeencyclopedia.net/imagegallery.php?EntryID=S020/ (accessed Jan. 10, 2011); Jess Stoddart, *The Story of the Hindman Settlement School* (Lexington: Univ. of Kentucky Press, 2002); Nancy K. Forderhase, "Settlement Schools," *Kentucky Encyclopedia,* ed. John E. Kleber (Lexington: Univ. of Kentucky Press, 1992), 810; Mary Rogers, *The Pine Mountain Story* (Pine Mountain, Ky.: Pine Mountain Settlement School, 1980).

17. Mary S. Hoffschwelle, *Rebuilding the Rural Southern Community: Reformers, Schools, and Homes in Tennessee, 1900–1930* (Knoxville: Univ. of Tennessee Press, 1998), 14; William A. Link, *A Hard Country and a Lonely Place: Schooling, Society, and Reform in Rural Virginia, 1870–1920* (Chapel Hill: Univ. of North Carolina Press, 1986).

18. Robert H. White, *Development of the Tennessee State Educational Organization, 1796–1929* (Kingsport, Tenn.: Southern Publishers, 1929); Andrew David Holt, *The Struggle for a State System of Public Schools in Tennessee, 1903–1936,* Contributions to Education 753, Teachers College, Columbia University (New York: Teachers College, Columbia Univ., 1938); Charles H. Ambler, *A History of Education in West Virginia: From Early Colonial Times to 1949* (Huntington, W.Va.: Standard Printing & Publishing, 1951); Charles William Hackensmith, *Out of Time and Tide: The Evolution of Education in Kentucky* (Lexington: College of Education, Univ. of Kentucky, 1970); Clinton B. Allison and Chipman G. Stuart, eds., *History of Education in the South* (Norman: Univ. of Oklahoma Press, 1983); Link, *Hard Country*; James L. Leloudis, *Schooling the New South: Pedagogy, Self, and Society in North Carolina, 1880–1920* (Chapel Hill: Univ. of North Carolina Press, 1996).

19. Hoffschwelle, *Rebuilding the Rural Southern Community,* 17.

20. "Convention Report, 1929," Archives of the Virginia Synod of the Evangelical Lutheran Church of America, Roanoke College, Salem, Va.

21. Ibid.

22. Mary Phlegar Smith, "Legal and Administrative Restrictions Affecting the Rights of Married Women to Work," *Annals of the American Academy of Political and Social Science* 143 (1929): 255–64.

23. Mrs. W. F. Moorehead, "Fund for Mountain Missions," *Lutheran Woman's Work* 19 (Apr. 1926): 155.

24. "Convention Report, 1929."

25. "Minutes of the Fifth Biennial Convention of the Women's Missionary Society of the United Lutheran Church in America," *Lutheran Woman's Work* 19 (Nov. 1926): 458–77.

26. Ibid.

27. A. K. Hewitt, "Our Work in the Mountains," *Lutheran Woman's Work* 37 (June 1944): 194–95.

28. Joel Spring, *The American School, 1642–2004* (Boston: McGraw Hill, 2005).

29. "Minutes of the Fifth Biennial Convention."

30. Ibid.

31. Catherine Cox Umbarger, "Report," *Lutheran Woman's Work* 23 (July 1930): 305–10.

32. Spring, *American School.*

33. Catherine Cox Umbarger, "Report," *Lutheran Woman's Work* 20 (July 1927): 279.

34. Helen Dyer, "The Mountain Mission: A Mountain Teacher's Observations," *Inner Mission Work* 2 (Dec. 15, 1934): 3–5.

35. Smith, "Our Mountain Work," 272.

36. "History," Harcum College, http://www.harcum.edu/PS_ABO_History.aspx/ (accessed July 29, 2009).

37. Orie Latham Hatcher, *A Mountain School: A Study Made by the Southern Woman's Educational Alliance and Konnarock Training School* (Richmond: Garrett and Massie, 1930), xix.

38. Ibid.

39. Ibid., xx.

40. Urban and Wagoner, *American Education,* 198.

41. James E. Gay, *Konnarock Training School: Its Spirit Lives On* (Lynchburg, Va.: Warwick House, 1998); Hatcher, *Mountain School.*

42. Hatcher, *Mountain School,* xvii.

43. National Education Association of the United States, Commission on the Reorganization of Secondary Education, *Cardinal Principles of Secondary Education,* Bureau of Education Bulletin 35 (Washington, D.C.: Government Printing Office, 1918), as cited in Urban and Wagoner, *American Education,* 198.

44. Document in collection from Helen Dyer's principalship of KTS in the 1930s, Archives of the Virginia Synod of the Evangelical Lutheran Church in America, Roanoke College, Salem, Va.

45. Smith, "Our Mountain Work," 272.

46. Gay, *Konnarock Training School.*

47. Ibid.

48. Ibid.

49. Catherine Cox Umbarger, "Medical Needs at Konnarock," *Lutheran Woman's Work* 22 (Mar. 1929): 121–22.

50. C. H. Butler, "Konnarock, Virginia and Other Places," *Lutheran,* Sept. 15, 1937, 25.

51. Tannen, *Kenneth Killinger.*

52. Gay, *Konnarock Training School.*

53. Rose Cox Kirby, personal communication, 2001.

54. Peggie Baldwin, personal communication, 2001.

55. Emily Umbarger, personal communication, 2002.

56. Kirby, personal communication.

Chapter 3

Tomato Clubs as Salvation: Canning Clubs for Girls and the Uplift of Southern Rural Society

Minoa D. Uffelman

When tomatoes are ripe we begin our canning.
First result of all our planning.
Can away, can away, can away, Tomato Club Girls!
When the cans are sold and the prizes are given,
We receive the award for which we have striven—
Can away, can away, can away, Tomato Club Girls!

—Canning Club song, 1914

Modern Americans might consider women who taught lessons about canning and domestic production as irrelevant or old fashioned. Indeed, today it is even difficult to imagine canning as an innovative, labor-saving technique. However, Virginia P. Moore and her contemporaries who formed girls' canning clubs in agricultural communities throughout Tennessee in the early twentieth century were new women and revolutionaries who brought education, economic improvement, and forward-thinking ideas to daughters and farm wives in rural southern homes during an era of Progressive reform in American cities.

Until recently even most historians did not see southern agricultural reformers as Progressives.[1] However, examination of the early days of female "demonstration" shows just how foreign and radical their policies were. Agricultural reformers wanted to uplift southern farm families by transforming the farm into a modern, efficient operation capable of earning maximum profits. Some policy makers, including the esteemed

Seaman Knapp, supported inclusion of programs for women led by men agents. Knapp was the well-respected agriculturalist who pioneered experimental farming stations that disseminated practical scientific knowledge to farmers. In the early twentieth century the invasion of the boll weevil into Texas threatened cotton production. Knapp established a demonstration farm to convince farmers to use practices of crop rotation, deeper plowing, fertilizers, and improved seed selection. With the farm's successful results, the U.S. Department of Agriculture (USDA) appropriated money to expand and develop demonstration programs.

Knapp, realizing the success of a family farm depended on female labor as well as male, advocated that women be included in agricultural policies. Many in the Washington power structure, which had accepted the concept of spending money to educate male farmers, were resistant to the concept of using federal dollars to help the newly formed female organizations. Despite their opposition, reform-minded USDA officials convinced Congress that organizing female demonstration programs and organizing women and girls into clubs would benefit rural America. The newly recruited female "demonstration agents," partially funded by the USDA, began to travel the rutty roads and hollows of the South, completely convinced of the righteousness of their cause, ready to demonstrate new ways to improve farm life.

The rather benign names of these groups—"Canning Clubs" and "Tomato Clubs"—belie the lofty and transformative goals reformers who organized them in small southern towns felt these clubs could achieve in southern society. Indeed, the goals of the agents were nothing short of lifting the rural South out of poverty and creating an educated female population. By the mid-1910s these original tomato clubs and canning organizations would take on the more familiar names of "home demonstration" and 4-H clubs, two institutions that became synonymous with southern rural life so that subsequent generations could not imagine a time when they did not exist.

At the helm of establishing canning clubs in Tennessee was a dynamo named Virginia P. Moore. She worked tirelessly, traversing the state and organizing females into clubs to spread the gospel of efficiency, mechanization, and improved profit. Extremely influential in the early development

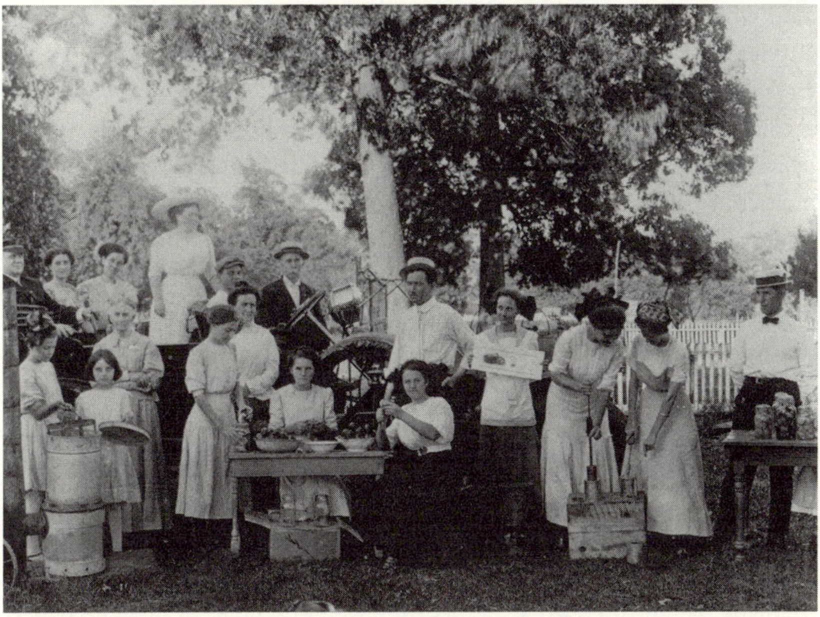

Virginia P. Moore at the first Canning Club demonstration in Manchester, Tennessee, in 1911. Moore, in the rear, is standing on the wagon. Courtesy of the Virginia P. Moore Collection, University of Tennessee Libraries, Knoxville.

of Tennessee farm demonstration agencies, she also spoke effectively to policy makers in other states, urging them to improve their communities by establishing canning and tomato clubs, as were proving successful in Tennessee. At the national level Moore consistently pressured the USDA for programs for women. She coordinated policy between national, state, and local levels and worked to professionalize the field of home demonstration by lobbying politicians to pass legislation providing retirement benefits for the female agents.

Moore's long career, spanning from 1908 to 1946, embodies the almost piecemeal nature of the development of agricultural policies. She began working in rural education coordinating state programs with local school districts, then moved to forming women's branches of the Farmer's Institute, an organization dedicated to improving farm life, which led her to organizing canning and tomato clubs. Passage of the Smith-Lever Act in 1914 created federal programs and provided matching funding for states to establish outreach or "extension" programs associated with land-grant universities. Moore moved to the University of Tennessee Extension School in Knoxville until 1919.[2] She returned to Gallatin to care for her ailing mother, and after her mother's death, Moore worked in home demonstration in Florida from 1923 to 1946.

Moore *knew* she was an active participant in this transitional period in southern history. Viewing herself as a Progressive reformer, she was cognizant and proud of her role in improving rural America. As the various agencies she worked for celebrated milestone anniversaries, she often wrote the history of those organizations, touting the successes and mentioning the hardships of the early days. She kept much of her professional correspondence to use in writing her autobiography. Although Moore died before penning her memoir, her papers are preserved at the University of Tennessee Archives. Her letters, bulletins, and pamphlets tell much more than the straightforward accounts they were intended to be. The papers reveal the stated goals of the agricultural agencies to improve the southern farm and, more important, offer insights into the almost naïve belief in the transforming nature of scientific methods and the missionary zeal of the early agents in spreading the message. Indeed, to compare one of the early agents to an itinerant minister at a brush arbor revival meeting is not much of a stretch. Virginia P. Moore made most of her early demonstrations under large shade trees to the whole community after the neighborhood had been notified of the public meeting. These early "collaborators" (as they were first called) worked just like preachers converting nonbelievers, in this case to the modern ways of canning.

Commercial canneries began to appear in the United States in the early nineteenth century. Late in the century the new technology made home canning possible with the invention of small, portable hot-water canners and cast-iron steam-pressure cookers. USDA agents quickly realized canning provided an excellent way to maximize food production and feed the family nutritious meals during the lean winter months. Moore was eager to demonstrate the advantages of canning and to educate people in rural communities in Tennessee. She was undeterred by the difficulties of travel and took whatever mode of transport was available. When she made her initial trip to mountainous Unicoi County in easternmost Tennessee in 1911, there was no road to her destination, only a creek bed. She hitched a ride with a mailman. She remembered, "I had to hold on with all my might and barely escaped falling on the mules' tail and heels. I was exhausted after traveling that twenty-eight miles." She asked the driver how long his buggy could last. He replied, "Well, it will last you two months if you take care of it."[3] While this may have been an extreme example, many homes only had contact with others on weekends when the men went to town and Sundays when the family attended church.

Considering the roles Moore played in the development of modern agriculture expands our understanding of southern rural history and challenges some of the generally accepted concepts of the "government agent." In the 1980s important historical studies of agricultural policies challenged the celebratory interpretations of the Department of Agriculture and argued that traditional folkways were lost as extension agents tried to force urban middle-class values on farm families.[4] Nevertheless, farm women, far from being passive subjects who accepted wholesale government policies, actively picked and chose which demonstrations to implement or reject.[5]

Rural women's lives were framed around coping, in their efforts to survive the extreme difficulties of farm life in the early decades of the twentieth century. In recent years several historians have provided illuminating works about the lives of rural women and government programs aimed at improving their lives. Melissa Walker studied rural women in the upcountry South from the end of World War I until World War II, and she chronicles the transformation of a local economy based on subsistence farming that changed as agricultural policies increasingly transformed the nature of their communities.[6] Women saw increased opportunities for employment off the farm and often took advantage of wage labor. Women used various resourceful adaptations to accommodate to the changing economic climate. Rebecca Sharpless used oral histories and written memoirs to reconstruct the lives of poor women on Texas cotton farms.[7] Sharpless argues that women living on the Blackland Prairie in the second and third decades of the twentieth century had "narrow choices" to improve their families' lives because of the economic conditions of the period. Yet they contributed to "fertile ground" by the various roles they performed as mother, food producer and preserver, housekeeper, and participant in commercial cotton farming. Lu Ann Jones further expands our understanding of farm women in the first half of the twentieth century.[8] She interviewed scores of women throughout the southern states, most of whom were born between 1900 and 1920, to uncover farm lives that were neither static nor unchanging. Families adapted to economic changes and eagerly employed strategies they viewed as beneficial to their well-being.[9] Mary S. Hoffschwelle focused on Tennessee's efforts to improve schools, homes, and farms in *Rebuilding the Rural Southern Community.*[10]

While these women's historians focused narrowly on specific regions in the South, Daniel T. Rodgers used a wide-angle lens to examine the international aspect of agricultural reformers as European and American Progressives crossed the Atlantic to learn from each other. One southerner in particular, Clarence Poe, editor of the *Progressive Farmer,* was eager to observe European agricultural projects and to see if their implementation in his native region (North Carolina) would benefit the beleaguered southern farmer.[11] Additionally, Jeannie Whayne persuasively applies colonial subaltern theory to the southern black extension service. Subaltern theory originated in colonial studies as a way to understand the interaction between imperials and indigenous people. Wayne argues that U.S. government agricultural extension agents were not unlike colonial representatives in that they were charged with contradictory governmental goals: educating poor rural blacks to improve their lives but also ensuring the continuation of the racial hierarchy that enabled white landowners to maintain control of cheap labor. Black agents were able to negotiate the official goals stated by the USDA and yet also managed to help black families.[12]

Subaltern theory does not as aptly fit the study of white female extension agency but can be another useful approach in examining southern white demonstration work. While African American extension work was essentially the bottom rung of the USDA's ladder, white female extension was only the next rung up. White female agents like Virginia Moore navigated within a gendered hierarchy of male politicians, USDA policy makers, and the very husbands of the women they wanted to help. Politicians at both the state and local levels rarely wanted to appropriate money for female demonstration, policy makers saw women's work important only as it extended the goals of bringing farm women into the market, and rural husbands failed to see the need to adapt technologies that might benefit their wives because it would use already sparse discretionary income. Female agents had to negotiate among these various interest groups in order to address the real needs of farm women.

In the tradition of all these approaches to southern rural history, Moore's papers offer a unique chance to expand understanding of southern rural history by adding a voice of a female extension agent. Her documents describe an understudied region of the South, the entire state of Tennessee. She also participated internationally, speaking at an international conference in 1937 in Paris, where representatives from forty-two countries attended and translators from the League of Nations translated her speech into French and German.[13] Moore navigated subaltern waters by working to convince politicians to include women in Smith-Lever extension programs, learned to argue the benefits of women's demonstration to southern society to skeptical legislatures, and tried to disarm husbands less than enthusiastic about her radical new technology.

Moore was a true believer in the value of knowledge and of her role as expert to dispense new information that would alleviate some of the hardships of farm women. Practically all of the documents that survive in the University of Tennessee's Moore Collection are professional. Only one personal letter slipped through the censoring hand of her devoted great niece (who knew Moore would not want anyone to know her personal business). Regardless, the image that emerges from the collection is of a dynamic, talented, intelligent, self-confident, politically savvy, proud, and ambitious woman. She was an exceptionally skilled organizer, effective at public relations and very resourceful with the meager monies put at her disposal for women's work.

She was born to a respectable middle-class family in Gallatin, Tennessee, in 1880. In 1908 she graduated from Peabody Normal School in Nashville (now part of Vanderbilt University), winning a prestigious art award for her ability in painting. This unusually talented young woman attracted the attention of P. P. Claxton of the Rockefeller Foundation Southern Education Board, who recruited her for school improvement work. By the spring of 1912 Moore had organized fourteen counties. Eventually she worked with forty-five different school improvement associations, striving to improve the sorry condition of most rural schools and making valuable contacts throughout the state.

In 1909 Moore attended a meeting that proved to be one of the most important inspirational moments of her life. She heard a speech on rural improvement by Seaman Knapp, and forever after Moore referred to Knapp with reverence, even taking the time to edit and copy some of his most pithy and inspiring quotes.[14] Knapp said when educating rural people it was "wisdom" to start with the girls first and later with the mothers because the "mothers would learn from the girls."[15] In the fall of 1910 Moore eagerly accepted an invitation by Thomas Early of Shelby County to organize Tennessee girls into tomato clubs.

Early, a protégé of Knapp, had organized Shelby County boys into "Corn Clubs" in 1910. Extension agents in Aiken County, South Carolina, had recently started the first tomato club modeling the male corn clubs. Rural reformers saw the possibility of emulating the success of the Palmetto State throughout the South. Early certainly did not know how to can, and Moore recounted that she had not been trained in canning at the "home Science course I'd taken in the North." Together they studied a USDA canning pamphlet and practiced late into the night and early the next morning in preparation for their first "Canning Party." That initial experiment in canning was successful. Moore writes, "I can yet remember the thrill I had upon discovering the beautiful clear glass round quart jars which were hermetically sealed." Moore used these first cans of tomatoes throughout the fall of 1910 in demonstrations.[16]

Canning as a form of food preservation was a vast improvement over previously used methods, such as drying, smoking, salting, and potting.[17] Canning is basically a catchall phrase for the process of food sterilization. To can tomatoes involved washing, dipping in boiling water, which helped remove the skin, then coring. The person canning then packed the cored tomatoes in a clean jar and filled it with water, leaving half an inch between the lid and the liquid. Tomatoes, because they are high in acidity, can be preserved with a water bath. Most vegetables and meats, however, needed a pressure cooker to reach the high temperatures necessary for sterilization.[18] Initially, women could obtain only glass jars, which had the disadvantage of breaking, but later metal cans became available.

Obviously, this groundbreaking new technology held huge implications for the rural population. Now food could be preserved to ensure a nutritious supply out of season, throughout the entire year. The possibility of improving southerners' health fit perfectly into the Progressive goals of the agricultural agents. As word spread of this new technology in food preservation, Moore became a much sought after speaker at various educational meetings. The Tennessee legislature earmarked a scant four hundred dollars for Moore to initiate the formation of girls' and women's canning clubs. Using connections made during her school improvement days, Moore convinced eight county school boards to contribute one hundred dollars to her fifty dollars. She creatively tripled her budget, allowing organizations to begin in these eight counties.[19]

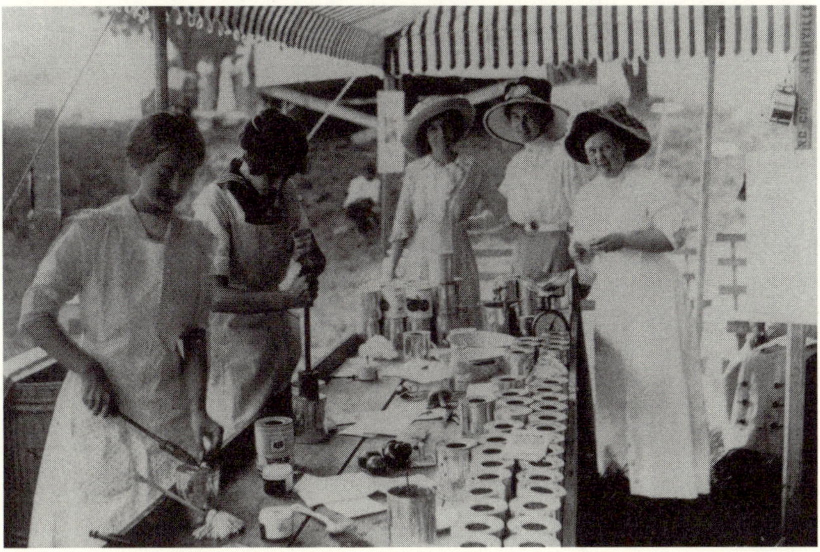

Virginia P. Moore, standing on right, demonstrates canning in metal cans. Courtesy of the Virginia P. Moore Collection, University of Tennessee Libraries, Knoxville.

In August 1911 Moore was ready for her first public canning demonstration in Coffee County in a grove near Manchester. She had coordinated with the superintendent of schools to provide tables, chairs, water buckets, extra glass jars, and sugar. He also told the community to bring peaches and tomatoes to can. Moore had heard of an "outdoor canning machine" in Chattanooga, so she wrote ahead to have it shipped to Manchester. She arrived with her canning kit, consisting of "measuring spoons, cups, a peach seeder, paring knives and a peach peeler and seeder." She directed the boys in attendance to build a furnace for the "boiler" canner.[20]

Surprisingly, more men than women attended this first demonstration for the new technology of canning. The tradition of men socializing in the public sphere held sway because most of the women stayed home.[21] Southern society had yet to be educated to the concept of public demonstrations

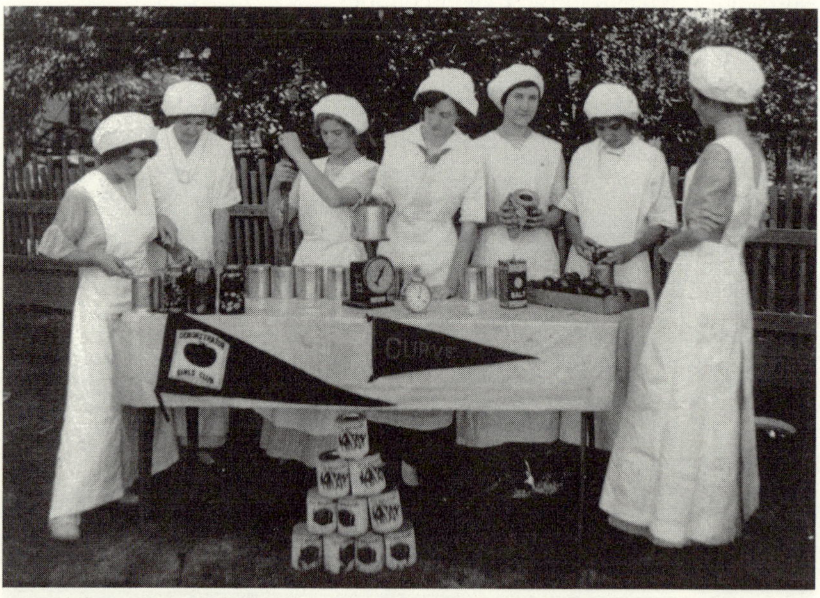

Virginia P. Moore encouraged canning club uniforms, which denoted professionalism, sanitation, and modernity. The table contains both metal and glass containers, a timer, and a scale. Cans are labeled and arranged as they would be in a store. Courtesy of the Virginia P. Moore Collection, University of Tennessee Libraries, Knoxville.

designed for women; on this day in 1911 the old attitudes still prevailed. During the demonstration men "jollied" with each other and joked that they did not do this kind of work at home.[22]

Moore wrote that after the demonstration a long, lanky man came up to her and asked if she was the agent for the seeder and peeler. She replied no, but volunteered the address of the company. She further asked to speak to his wife. The man replied that she was not there because "she felt porely [*sic*] most of the time."[23] Moore was disgusted that farm men saw the value in labor-saving devices for themselves, such as the incredible advancements in farm machinery that had improved American farming technology in the nineteenth and early twentieth centuries, but were uninterested in methods that would benefit their wives. Some poor farm women themselves also needed convincing of the advantages of new technologies. As Moore built her program in other counties, she continued to encounter these same attitudes. In a rare criticism of farm women she wrote, "Women were not in the habit of 'getting out.' They were a resigned, hard-working class, with a dull, hopeless look—feeling a pride in being 'porely' and feeling 'broken down.' They took it as part of their duty as a good wife, it seemed."[24] Moore was determined to radically change these attitudes. She told the men "that next time they must stay home and let the women come to the 'canning party' but if the children were large enough to bring the whole family." Eventually the canning parties became "stylish." Moore worked with local teachers and volunteered as the canning club state leader, working without a salary.[25]

Moore went to extraordinary means to educate anyone interested. In the early 1910s she carried on a correspondence with a young girl named Mary Presswood from Polk County in southeastern Tennessee, sending detailed correspondence on all aspects of growing tomato plants and how to mark off her one-tenth acre plot and prepare the soil. Moore also sent explicit instructions on how to can. Finally, Moore was able to travel by train to the "lone box-car station" to meet Mary and her family. The local women, most of whom "were dipping snuff, eagerly greeted Moore." After going "up and over" the mountain by foot, the group reached Mary's home. Moore realized her long-distance canning instructions had been completely successful when the family proudly showed her their five hundred cans of produce. However, Moore still felt she had much more to do when she was served less than perfect biscuits:

> There were several things I wanted to correct; one was the yellow, thick, "doughy" biscuits that we had for breakfast. So I made cream of tomato soup, I told Mary that crackers or croutons should be served with the soup. I told her to bring me some cold biscuit and I would show her how to make croutons. I mostly wanted to get her interested in making better biscuits. . . . I talked to her, but the mother and neighbors were standing around. . . . [A] biscuit should be thin and thoroughly done. Mary was pleased and tried out my recipe, and her biscuits turned out quite nice.

When Moore finished her demonstration, everyone thought the new biscuits tasted better, except for Mary's father, who declared he preferred the "'thick' and 'yellow'" ones. Moore's account of this incident demonstrates how skillfully she could act as a subaltern agent. Using canning demonstration as an entry into a family's kitchen, she taught several women how to make better bread while ostensibly teaching only the daughter, and she was able to disarm if not completely convince the resistant head of the household.[26]

The women thoroughly enjoyed her stay, and as she was leaving a maiden aunt told Moore that her departure was so sad it was as if a "corpse" was leaving the house: "There is no sadder time for a mountaineer than when a death comes to the home and when the corpse is taken away."[27] This statement in mountain vernacular is a powerful indication of the deep bonds and appreciation rural women felt toward Moore, proof that this marginalized segment of southern society deeply appreciated the efforts made to improve their lives.

Moore recruited the best teachers to become club organizers and even said that "a matured woman of education and culture" would be suitable to this new career. Her summary of the job requirements might as well have been a description of herself: "They must be practical, must have 'gumption,' must be able to see a situation quickly, act quickly for the good of the work and not for selfish reasons must have initiative and leadership . . . must love girls and rural women . . . see their needs but never pity them or appear to 'stoop down,' but always work 'with [them].'"[28]

Apparently local Tennessee men were not the only ones who had to undergo a paradigm shift. Moore wrote, "Men in authority in Washington held up their hands in 'Holy horror' over having women agents of the Government." Perhaps the "men in authority" could not stop the tide of women agents, but they also did not compensate female agents very handsomely. The General Education Board, an organization endowed by John D. Rockefeller to fund programs that improved conditions in the South, paid the women's salaries and expenses, to which the USDA contributed a token one dollar a year.[29]

By 1912 Moore had resigned from school improvement work to devote all her energies to canning and tomato clubs. Her office remained in the Tennessee Department of Education, enabling Moore to continue her close coordination of the educational goals of the tomato clubs with local educators. Teachers tailored lesson plans to include the vocabulary, geography, arithmetic, and science needed to be successful tomato growers, canners, and sellers. For example, each girl used exactly a one-tenth acre plot. The plots varied in shape, so girls needed math skills to figure the length and number of rows. The agents took a truly interdisciplinary approach in educating the girls.

The geography and language lessons were brought out in the history and story of the tomato: where the tomato was first known, the countries to which it migrated, the kinds of people who lived in those counties, and so on. Nature study was linked around the tomato plants. Children were taught to think about the tomato, where it got its food—how it breathed, the good of the sun and rain, insect friends and enemies.[30]

Additionally, club work provided an avenue to provide several other important lessons and ways to improve rural life. The meals prepared in demonstrations "paved the way for a hot dish supplement" to the traditional cold lunch eaten by rural school children. Agents stressed the advantages of improved nutrition. Lessons in sanitation were provided when the ubiquitous flies swarmed around demonstrations. Female agents used the opportunity to show the "marvels" of homemade fly traps.

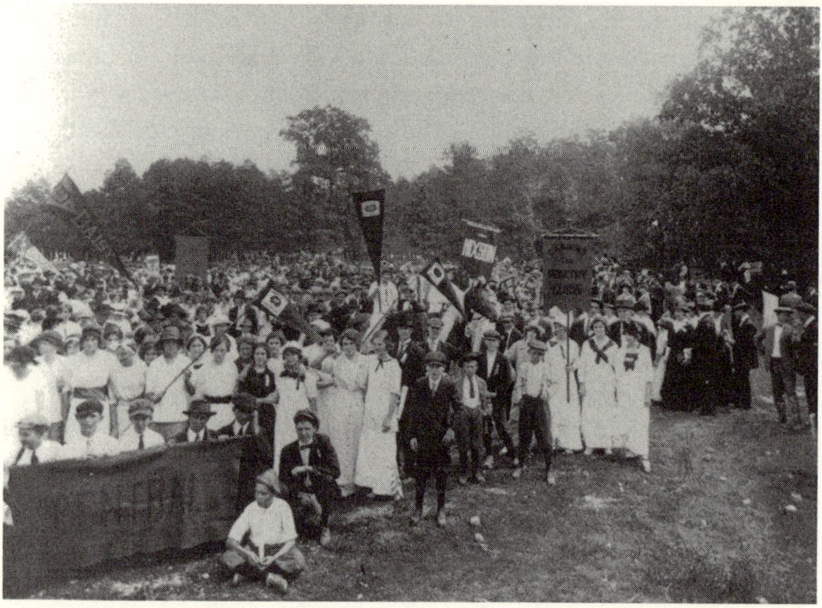

A Demonstration Club rally, presumably near Chattanooga, Tennessee. The banners read "Soddy," "Daisy," "Hixson," and "Central." Courtesy of the Virginia P. Moore Collection, University of Tennessee Libraries, Knoxville.

It was important not to lose sight of a primary goal of earning profits. The extra money earned by farm wives and girls could be used in any number of ways to improve the lives of their families. In tomato club competition, fully 20 percent of the competitive score was based on amount of income garnered by the small plots. Other criteria consisted of "history and written report, quality of products, and quantity." As the program matured, agents added more requirements, thereby expanding the types of training agents administered.

To increase profitability, judges evaluated girls on record keeping and management, creating a type of rudimentary business curriculum. The agents also added another requirement, recipes using tomatoes, ever trying to increase the ways in which the red fruit could be marketed. All of these tomato dishes tasted good with freshly made bread, so baking also became part of the demonstration. Girls sewed caps, aprons, potholders, and hand towels and created a type of Tomato Club uniform, allowing agents to teach sewing and tailoring skills. In the fall the participants and the whole community celebrated all the hard work by holding "Tomato Club Rallies." These festivals in small southern towns became popular community activities complete with exhibits, "speakings," and a parade.[31]

Girls were eager to be members of the new tomato clubs. The opportunity to win valuable prizes for cash-strapped southerners certainly proved effective at recruiting members. Local winners would win a trip to the state fair. State fair winners might win a trip to Washington, D.C. In addition, demonstration agents often teamed up with local merchants to provide prizes. In a rural world of few extras and rare travel opportunities, these prizes enticed girls to go to great lengths to participate. One girl at the 1914 Mississippi State Fair, lacking standard glass canning jars, exhibited her goods in ink bottles and Vaseline jars. This club girl won first place, used the prize money to purchase standardized jars, and came back the next year to win another first prize. Another girl overcame transportation difficulties by crossing a bayou in a skiff, then walked several miles, carrying her canned tomatoes in a basket. Happily, she won a pink parasol from a local merchant. Sometimes, local businessmen provided cash prizes.[32]

In a 1913 report, Moore detailed just how much profit a successful Tomato Club girl could garner in a year. She used the example of Katie Gunther of Samaria, South Carolina, on her one-tenth of an acre plot:

Cost of yield in canning	\$35.33
Canned products	770
Net cost per can	4 cents
Purchased home canner	\$6.25
Net profit for season	\$78.37
Sold some fresh tomatoes	\$47.90
Profit on acre basis	\$783.70[33]

Each girl farmed precisely one-tenth of an acre to ensure standardization and fair competition. Ironically, Moore took the time to recalculate and report the profit of one full acre, although the girls were limited to one-tenth. Perhaps she wanted officials in the Agriculture Department as well as the prospective young members to recognize the girl's profit

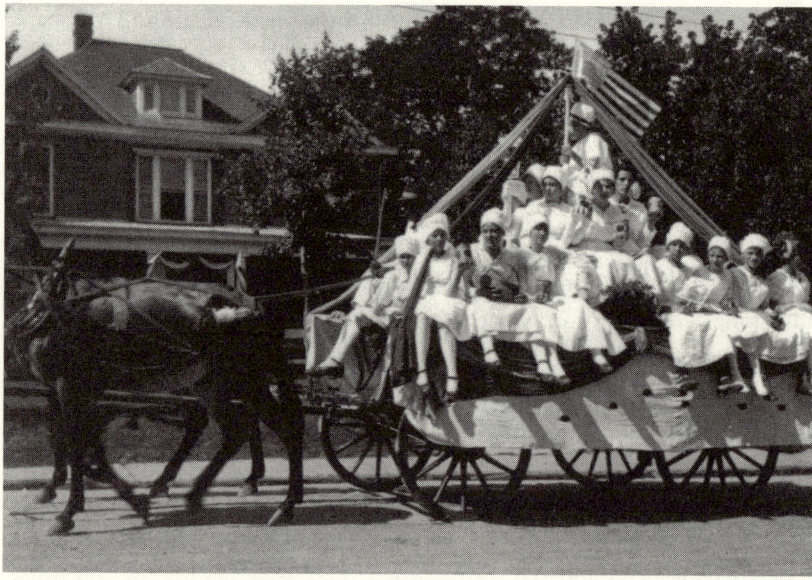

A Demonstration Club parade in Putnam County, Tennessee. The girls are wearing canning club uniforms and displaying an American flag. Courtesy of the Virginia P. Moore Collection, University of Tennessee Libraries, Knoxville.

potential. Additionally, perhaps Moore hoped the USDA would realize the financial significance to both the rural families who participated in canning club programs and communities that supported club work.

Everywhere the agents started canning demonstrations, girls and men eagerly adopted the new food preservation technologies. One Lake County, Tennessee, agent complained that women were not interested in any demonstrations other than canning: "They think this is all there is to learn."[34] When Texas began tomato clubs in 1917, women there enthusiastically adopted the new form of canning. However, the cost of pressure cookers was prohibitive for many poor women of the Lone Star State. In her study of Texas cotton farms, Sharpless demonstrated how some of these women creatively shared resources to take advantage of the new technology they could not individually afford. One woman in the neighborhood owned a pressure cooker. Other families provided all the vegetables and half the jars. The owner provided the other half of the jars, did the actual canning, and kept half the canned vegetables for payment. No doubt similar kinds of arrangements happened throughout the rural South.[35]

Demonstration agents were master tabulators. They tallied every kind of demonstration, every type of canned vegetable, and even recorded the types of cans used. The first four years of club work showed impressive results. Tennessee had 3,551 girls enrolled. Agents made 2,132 various demonstrations. Girls had canned an amazing 205,610 cans of tomatoes, 109,274 cans of beans, and, additionally, over 78,000 miscellaneous items, including soups, fruits, peppers, and tomato sauce. Moore calculated the total value of club products as $47,109.55, with each girl averaging a profit of $23.00. To further professionalize the canning culture, agents taught girls how to sew their own Tomato Club uniforms. Girls sewed 66 canning club dresses, 856 aprons, and 828 caps, plus hundreds of holders and towels.[36] These were impressive numbers given the scant budgets with which agents had to work. The high numbers reveal the eagerness with which rural women and girls adapted to a new technology they viewed as improving their lives.

Moore believed club work also cured other ills of southern society. She said that in Unicoi County in the mountains of East Tennessee people forgot their "feuds" when they ate together at club activities. She also thought that club work mediated some of the class difference within southern society. Moore was proud that girls of both landowners and tenants attended meetings, proclaiming the tomato club "a truly democratic organization."[37] Meetings were usually held in the back yards of club members to encourage interaction between social classes. However, she made no mention of sharecropping girls participating in tomato clubs. Moore was also a firm supporter of demonstration work for African American women and helped organize the initial "negro agents." The Tennessee state director of agriculture asked her to organize a program for African American agents and she visited Hampton and Gloucester Counties in Virginia to see their programs. Three black agents worked directly under Moore and she worked within the segregated system.[38] This democratic organization had its limits.

In an annual address to the East Tennessee Farmers' Convention in 1913, Marie Willoughby of the USDA acknowledged the tremendous contribution Moore made toward educating local communities: "She did all the work from the cold frame to the canner, canning sixty-six varieties of tomato products and making a net profit from her plat of over $100. Furthermore, she worked out 126 tomato recipes and compiled them in a nicely designed and illustrated booklet. The story of 'How I Made My Crop of Tomatoes' forms a fourth booklet, making in all four well-written and nicely illustrated essays."[39] Moore strived to develop many different ways to create tomato products as evidenced by her compiling 126 different recipes for the women and girls to use. She wanted the information to be easily accessible so she designed and published booklets to disseminate knowledge throughout the state.

Canning Club work was already well established in eighteen Tennessee counties when the Smith-Lever bill, to federally support extension work within land-grant universities, was before Congress in 1914. Walter Hines Page, a member of the Rockefeller-funded General Education Board, was worried that politicians were not going to include rural women in this landmark legislation. Page asked Moore and other agents to go to Washington to lobby the secretary of agriculture and members of the agricultural committee for the inclusion of rural women. Congressmen heeded her pleas and work for women was indeed included, guaranteeing the continuation of demonstration work. Because of Moore's groundbreaking work with school improvement, tomato and canning clubs' implementation of Smith-Lever was easily integrated into the existing club network.

At every opportunity Moore stressed the need for both governmental and public support for female demonstration. While working with the U.S. Food Administration during World War I, she sent letters to "All Home Demonstration Agents and Food Chairmen, Women's Committee, Council of Defense," in part stating, "If your county goes over the top it will be on account of the women doing their part, the food chairmen and food administrators, and farm and home demonstration agents; this means a long pull, a hard pull, and a pull together." This 1918 letter listed local women's contributions first and foremost and concluded with female demonstration agents.[40]

One account of an address Moore made to a Hamilton County, Tennessee, public school meeting states that she "was given a rousing ovation as she delivered an address full of praise and encouragement. She is no stranger to Hamilton County." She told briefly some of the goals hoped for in the way of future training "along domestic arts and canning and breadmaking lines and prophesized a still greater success for Hamilton County." Other speakers addressing the crowd that day included several prominent politicians, a professor, two editors of newspapers, a judge, and a certain Mrs. Sam Divine, a champion bread-baking winner. Certainly, being included in this well-respected group of powerbrokers in Hamilton County indicates Moore's influence.[41] She was the only female policy maker given a public voice that night, highlighted by the fact that the only other woman there gained access by winning a bread-baking contest.

Moore was one of a cadre of early demonstration agents who created modern female home demonstration. The numerous letters between Moore and the early collaborators reveal the active role they took with information they shared and the mutual training they conducted at an interstate level. They lobbied politicians for funds for their programs and later for retirement benefits. While creating a profession for themselves, the agents never forgot the women they dedicated their lives to help. One colleague, Jane S. McKimmon of North Carolina, said, "I like to reach the forgotten woman, the woman who once had ambition but who has had it taken out of her by drudgery, by poor equipment, by work in the field, by many children. The spark is there, and we can rekindle that old ambition by showing her first [that if] she can do something well [she] can dispose of it to the profit of her family. . . . I want to reach such women and I want to keep little girls from becoming forgotten women."[42]

Moore and the other agents both male and female shared the reformist Progressive ideology of Seaman Knapp and Clarence Poe, editor of the most popular farm publication, the *Progressive Farmer.* The journal strongly supported home demonstration and extension programs and frequently published articles written by agents. Moore's friend and colleague Susie Powell of Mississippi regularly contributed to the magazine. Editors and writers for agricultural publications considered themselves partners with the agents working with farm men, women, and children with the goal of improving the rural South.

Moore believed in improvement and progress. But how would she have defined those terms? Was she trying to encourage farm women to fit into changes in high-technology commercial agriculture? Or was she keeping a place for women based on traditional expectations only pursued with more technological expertise? Moore was a contradiction. She pursued a career at a time when southern women traditionally had not worked outside the home. She engaged in activities, such as traveling alone and speaking in public, which would have been shocking just a generation earlier. In those ways, she was the embodiment of the new woman of the era. However, she did not seem to comprehend a time when family farms would exist in other than the traditional form of husband and wife partnership. Therefore, she wanted to alleviate the arduous work of farm women by implementing new technologies. She pursued new markets for female production. For example, she used her connections to sell berry juice canned in Tennessee to the Willard Hotel in Washington.[43] She relished the fact that farm girls might have a brighter future through money earned selling their agricultural products. One Putnam County Tomato Club girl, in a moment of enlightenment, said to Moore, "A girl don't have to marry if she can make some money for herself."[44] No longer would a girl *have* to marry in her teenage years. To Moore the ability to improve earnings led to the sort of structural change in southern society that improved girls' options in life.

The three pursuits of efficiency, mechanization, and improved profits were almost a holy trinity that would lead to salvation for southern rural society. Moore published a report of canning clubs' progress in 1913. Her concluding paragraph sounds like an agricultural benediction: "May the spirit of that great apostle, Dr. Seaman A. Knapp, live in the hearts of each of us and encourage us to do our part in helping to train the girl and woman for efficiency and to develop her outlook on life."[45] In many ways, Moore seems like an educator who hoped to develop new skills females might use in a variety of ways. Thus she was teaching the women of Tennessee lessons that would improve their lives within the traditional expectations for women while also opening up new opportunities for others.

Near the end of her life Moore wrote simply, "I felt a 'call' to do rural work." She continued her life's mission, interrupted only for a short period when she returned to her family's farm to care for her mother who had suffered a stroke. She remained unmarried and completely devoted to her work. She once became engaged to a man, but family tradition holds that her betrothed confided to his aunt that he felt a married woman should not work outside the home. When Miss Moore heard his opinion concerning career women, she promptly ended the engagement.[46] Moore embodied the new woman of the twentieth century in that she was educated, a good public speaker, an impressive organizer, and unlike women of a generation earlier. Southern society had changed enough to allow her a career perfectly suited to her many talents.

On June 28, 1929, Moore sat down to pen a reflective letter to her four-year-old great niece. The letter was never finished nor mailed. The intended recipient read it only in 1988 after finding it in a cedar chest. The letter adequately describes how Moore felt about her role in history. She did not just place herself in southern or even American history, but in the context of the world. She wrote, "Fifty years from now you may be glad that I have recorded some of the things I shall write because in all this big 4-H movement it was my privilege to have been one of the pioneers of this movement. I was one of the first five Home Demonstration agents in the world." Indeed, Virginia P. Moore was so proud of this honor that she had her tombstone in Gallatin, Tennessee, engraved to read, "One of the First Five Home Demonstration Agents in the World."[47]

NOTES

The opening epigraph refers to "Canning Club Song," *Carroll County Consevative*, Aug. 15, 1914.

1. See William A. Link, *The Paradox of Southern Progressivism, 1880–1930* (Chapel Hill: Univ. of North Carolina Press, 1992).

2. Mary S. Hoffschwelle, *Rebuilding the Rural Southern Community: Reformers, Schools, and Homes in Tennessee, 1900–1930* (Knoxville: Univ. of Tennessee Press, 1998), 23–24, 30, 31, 32–33, 107, 111, 112, 144, 159n41, 163n70, 196n41.

3. Virginia P. Moore, "Tennessee's Early Tomato Club and Home Demonstration Work, from 1911–1919," 7, Virginia P. Moore Collection, Hoskins Library, University of Tennessee, Knoxville (hereafter cited as Moore Collection).

4. See Jack Temple Kirby, *Rural Worlds Lost: The American South, 1920–1960* (Baton Rouge: Louisiana State Univ. Press, 1987); Pete Daniel, *Breaking the Land:*

The Transformation of Cotton, Tobacco, and Rice Cultures since 1880 (Urbana: Univ. of Illinois Press, 1986); Abbe L. Karmen, "Putting the House in Order," *Maine Historical Quarterly* 32, no. 1 (1992): 30–50.

5. Kathleen R. Babbit, "The Productive Farm Woman and the Extension Agent," *Agricultural History* 67, no. 2 (Spring 1993): 83–101.

6. Melissa Walker, *All We Knew Was to Farm: Rural Women in the Upcountry South, 1919–1941* (Baltimore: John Hopkins Univ. Press, 2000).

7. Rebecca Sharpless, *Fertile Ground, Narrow Choices: Women on Texas Cotton Farms, 1900–1940* (Chapel Hill: Univ. of North Carolina Press, 1999).

8. Lu Ann Jones, *Mama Learned Us to Work: Farm Women in the New South* (Chapel Hill: Univ. of North Carolina Press, 2002).

9. Walker, *All We Knew Was to Farm*; Melissa Walker, *Country Women Cope with Hard Times: A Collection of Oral Histories* (Columbia: Univ. of South Carolina Press, 2004); Sharpless, *Fertile Ground, Narrow Choices*; Jones, *Mama Learned Us to Work.*

10. Hoffschwelle, *Rebuilding the Rural Southern Community.*

11. Daniel T. Rodgers, *Atlantic Crossings: Social Politics in a Progressive Age* (Cambridge, Mass.: Belknap Press of Harvard Univ. Press, 1998).

12. Jeanne Whayne, "'I Have Been through Fire': Black Agricultural Extension Agents and the Politics of Negotiation," in *African American Life in the Rural South, 1900–1950,* ed. R. Douglas Hurt (Columbia: Univ. of Missouri Press, 2003), 152–88.

13. Virginia P. Moore, "Miss Virginia Moore Makes Talk in Paris," undated copy held by author, given by Elizabeth Virginia Dameron.

14. Virginia P. Moore, "Gleanings from the Sayings of Dr. Seaman A. Knapp, the Agricultural Profit who Founded Home Demonstration Work," in possession of Elizabeth Virginia Dameron, Memphis.

15. Virginia P. Moore, "A Review of a Few Steps in Home Demonstration Work, 1908 to 1936," 2, in possession of Elizabeth Virginia Dameron, Memphis.

16. Moore, "Tennessee's Early Tomato Club," 3–4.

17. On the development of food preservations, see Sarah F. McMahon, "Laying Foods By: Gender, Dietary Decision, and the Technology of Food Preservation in New England Households, 1750–1850," in *Waste Not, Want Not: Food Preservation from Early Times to the Present Day,* ed. C. Anne Wilson (Edinburgh: Edinburgh Univ. Press, 1991); Sue Shepard, *Pickled, Potted and Canned: The Story of Food Preserving* (London: Headline Book, 2000).

18. U.S. Department of Agriculture, *Canning in Glass Jars in School and Institutional Kitchen, Fruits and other Acid Food* (Washington, D.C.: U.S. Government Printing Office, 1951).

19. Moore, "Tennessee's Early Tomato Club," 3.

20. Ibid.

21. See Ted Ownby, *Subduing Satan: Religion, Recreation, and Manhood in the Rural South, 1865–1920* (Chapel Hill: Univ. of North Carolina Press, 1990).

22. Moore, "Tennessee's Early Tomato Club," 3.
23. Ibid.
24. Ibid., 4.
25. Ibid., 11–12.
26. Ibid., 12.
27. Ibid.
28. Moore, "Review of a Few Steps," 8.
29. Ibid.
30. Ibid., 15.
31. Moore, "Tennessee's Early Tomato Club," 7.
32. Danny Moore, "'To Make the Best Better': The Establishment of Girls' Tomato Clubs in Mississippi, 1911–1915," *Journal of Mississippi History* 63, no. 2 (2001): 101–18.
33. Virginia P. Moore, *Tennessee Agriculture* 1, no. 1 (May 1912): 186.
34. Quoted in Mary S. Hoffschwelle, "'Better Homes on Better Farms': Domestic Reform in Rural Tennessee," *Frontiers: A Journal of Women Studies* 22, no. 1 (2001): 51–73.
35. Sharpless, *Fertile Ground, Narrow Choices,* 128–29.
36. Annual reports, 1910–17, Farmers Cooperative Demonstration Work and the Division of Extension Work States Relation Service, U.S. Department of Agriculture, 148–49.
37. Moore, "Review of a Few Steps," 15.
38. Ibid., 2; Melissa Walker, "Home Extension Work among African American Farm Women in East Tennessee," *Agricultural History* 70, no. 3 (Summer 1996): 487–502.
39. "What Is the Best Method of Getting Homemaking in the Public Schools and Rural Communities," *Tennessee Agriculture* 2, no. 7 (Aug. 1, 1913): 272.
40. Letter, Box 1, Folder 6, Moore Collection.
41. Account of Moore address to a Hamilton County public school meeting, Box 1, Folder 7, Moore Collection; "Epsilon Sigma Phi" undated copy held by author, given by Elizabeth Dameron.
42. "She 'Lifted' Sixty-Six Counties: The Story of Jane S. McKimmon's Work in North Carolina," *Country Gentleman,* June 29, 1918.
43. "A Brief Review of Tomato Club, Girls Canning and Poultry Club from 1910–1939 Inclusive," handwritten draft, Box 2, Folder 2, Moore Collection.
44. Moore, "Tennessee's Early Tomato Club," 10–11.
45. "The Girls' Industrial Club Work," *Tennessee Agriculture* 1, no. 4 (1912): 186.
46. Elizabeth Virginia Dameron, interview conducted by the author, Sept. 24, 1999.
47. MS-1546, Box 1, Folder 2, Moore Collection.

Chapter 4

Shall the Women Be Silent? A Tennessee New Woman's Challenge to Southern Church Patriarchy

Carole Stanford Bucy

> *Men may change with the changing conditions of modern life, but when women find themselves trying to keep step with their fathers, brothers, and husbands in the new order of things, the brethren stand in front of them with a drawn sword and demand a halt, because, they say, the Bible forbids, when it does nothing of the kind.*
>
> —Silena Moore Holman, 1913

The social order of nineteenth-century America confined women to the private sphere of hearth and home and denied them participation in the public spheres of business, politics, and religion, where American males conducted affairs. Although women made up the majority of worshippers in southern Protestant churches, the hierarchy of these churches remained exclusively male until late in the twentieth century. While society and custom assigned the responsibility for moral development of children and the maintenance of religious values to women, women had no voice in the affairs of most churches. Herein lay a great paradox: Women were the keepers of morality, yet they had no authority in the church, the moral institution of society. The "cult of domesticity" limited opportunities for women and allowed all labor to be divided by gender function. It provided clear messages for women about how to be feminine. The home was considered to be feminine; the world of work, masculine. Women established a sense of femininity through proper subordination to duty and service to others. The doctrine of separate spheres created gendered boundaries

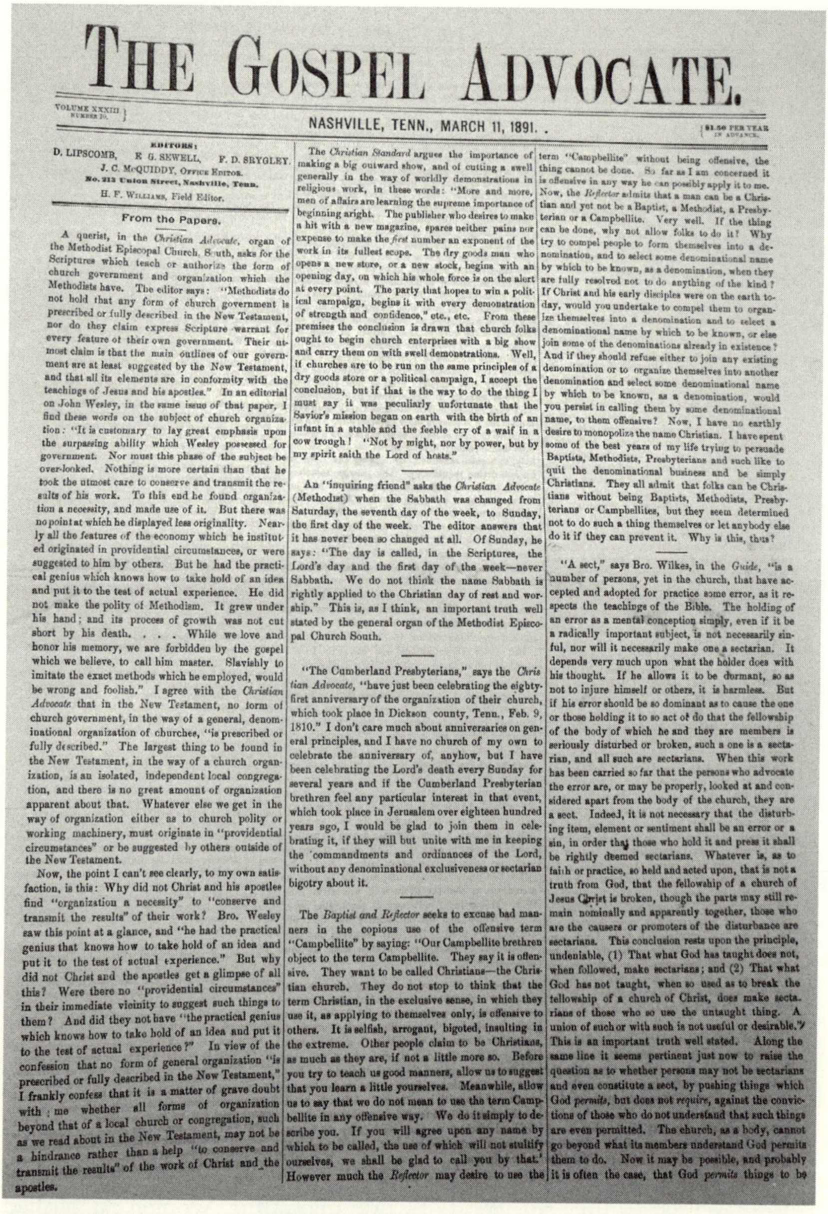

THE GOSPEL ADVOCATE.

VOLUME XXXIII. NUMBER 10. NASHVILLE, TENN., MARCH 11, 1891. $1.50 PER YEAR IN ADVANCE.

EDITORS:
D. LIPSCOMB, E. G. SEWELL, F. D. SRYGLEY.
J. C. McQUIDDY, OFFICE EDITOR.
No. 213 Union Street, Nashville, Tenn.
H. F. WILLIAMS, Field Editor.

From the Papers.

A querist, in the *Christian Advocate*, organ of the Methodist Episcopal Church, South, asks for the Scriptures which teach or authorize the form of church government and organization which the Methodists have. The editor says: "Methodists do not hold that any form of church government is prescribed or fully described in the New Testament, nor do they claim express Scripture warrant for every feature of their own government. Their utmost claim is that the main outlines of our government are at least suggested by the New Testament, and that all its elements are in conformity with the teachings of Jesus and his apostles." In an editorial on John Wesley, in the same issue of that paper, I find these words on the subject of church organization: "It is customary to lay great emphasis upon the surpassing ability which Wesley possessed for government. Nor must this phase of the subject be over-looked. Nothing is more certain than that he took the utmost care to conserve and transmit the results of his work. To this end he found organization a necessity, and made use of it. But there was no point at which he displayed less originality. Nearly all the features of the economy which he instituted originated in providential circumstances, or were suggested to him by others. But he had the practical genius which knows how to take hold of an idea and put it to the test of actual experience. He did not make the polity of Methodism. It grew under his hand; and its process of growth was not cut short by his death. . . . While we love and honor his memory, we are forbidden by the gospel which we believe, to call him master. Slavishly to imitate the exact methods which he employed, would be wrong and foolish." I agree with the *Christian Advocate* that in the New Testament, no form of church government, in the way of a general, denominational organization of churches, "is prescribed or fully described." The largest thing to be found in the New Testament, in the way of a church organization, is an isolated, independent local congregation, and there is no great amount of organization apparent about that. Whatever else we get in the way of organization either as to church polity or working machinery, must originate in "providential circumstances" or be suggested by others outside of the New Testament.

Now, the point I can't see clearly, to my own satisfaction, is this: Why did not Christ and his apostles find "organization a necessity" to "conserve and transmit the results" of their work? Bro. Wesley saw this point at a glance, and "he had the practical genius that knows how to take hold of an idea and put it to the test of actual experience." But why did not Christ and the apostles get a glimpse of all this? Were there no "providential circumstances" in their immediate vicinity to suggest such things to them? And did they not have "the practical genius which knows how to take hold of an idea and put it to the test of actual experience?" In view of the confession that no form of general organization "is prescribed or fully described in the New Testament," I frankly confess that it is a matter of grave doubt with me whether all forms of organization beyond that of a local church or congregation, such as we read about in the New Testament, may not be a hindrance rather than a help "to conserve and transmit the results" of the work of Christ and the apostles.

The *Christian Standard* argues the importance of making a big outward show, and of cutting a swell generally in the way of worldly demonstrations in religious work, in these words: "More and more, men of affairs are learning the supreme importance of beginning aright. The publisher who desires to make a hit with a new magazine, spares neither pains nor expense to make the *first* number an exponent of the work in its fullest scope. The dry goods man who opens a new store, or a new stock, begins with an opening day, on which his whole force is on the alert at every point. The party that hopes to win a political campaign, begins it with every demonstration of strength and confidence," etc., etc. From these premises the conclusion is drawn that church folks ought to begin church enterprises with a big show and carry them on with swell demonstrations. Well, if churches are to be run on the same principles of a dry goods store or a political campaign, I accept the conclusion, but if that is the way to do the thing I must say it was peculiarly unfortunate that the Savior's mission began on earth with the birth of an infant in a stable and the feeble cry of a waif in a cow trough! "Not by might, nor by power, but by my spirit saith the Lord of hosts."

An "inquiring friend" asks the *Christian Advocate* (Methodist) when the Sabbath was changed from Saturday, the seventh day of the week, to Sunday, the first day of the week. The editor answers that it has never been so changed at all. Of Sunday, he says: "The day is called, in the Scriptures, the Lord's day and the first day of the week—never Sabbath. We do not think the name Sabbath is rightly applied to the Christian day of rest and worship." This is, as I think, an important truth well stated by the general organ of the Methodist Episcopal Church South.

"The Cumberland Presbyterians," says the *Christian Advocate*, "have just been celebrating the eighty-first anniversary of the organization of their church, which took place in Dickson county, Tenn., Feb. 9, 1810." I don't care much about anniversaries on general principles, and I have no church of my own to celebrate the anniversary of, anyhow, but I have been celebrating the Lord's death every Sunday for several years and if the Cumberland Presbyterian brethren feel any particular interest in that event, which took place in Jerusalem over eighteen hundred years ago, I would be glad to join them in celebrating it, if they will but unite with me in keeping the commandments and ordinances of the Lord, without any denominational exclusiveness or sectarian bigotry about it.

The *Baptist and Reflector* seeks to excuse bad manners in the copious use of the offensive term "Campbellite" by saying: "Our Campbellite brethren object to the term Campbellite. They say it is offensive. They want to be called Christians—the Christian church. They do not stop to think that the term Christian, in the exclusive sense, in which they use it, as applying to themselves only, is offensive to others. It is selfish, arrogant, bigoted, insulting in the extreme. Other people claim to be Christians, as much as they are, if not a little more so. Before you try to teach us good manners, allow us to suggest that you learn a little yourselves. Meanwhile, allow us to say that we do not mean to use the term Campbellite in any offensive way. We do it simply to describe you. If you will agree upon any name by which to be called, the use of which will not stultify ourselves, we shall be glad to call you by that." However much the *Reflector* may desire to use the term "Campbellite" without being offensive, the thing cannot be done. So far as I am concerned it is offensive in any way he can possibly apply it to me. Now, the *Reflector* admits that a man can be a Christian and yet not be a Baptist, a Methodist, a Presbyterian or a Campbellite. Very well. If the thing can be done, why not allow folks to do it? Why try to compel people to form themselves into a denomination, and to select some denominational name by which to be known, as a denomination, when they are fully resolved not to do anything of the kind? If Christ and his early disciples were on the earth to-day, would you undertake to compel them to organize themselves into a denomination and to select a denominational name by which to be known, or else join some of the denominations already in existence? And if they should refuse either to join any existing denomination or to organize themselves into another denomination and select some denominational name by which to be known, as a denomination, would you persist in calling them by some denominational name, to them offensive? Now, I have no earthly desire to monopolize the name Christian. I have spent some of the best years of my life trying to persuade Baptists, Methodists, Presbyterians and such like to quit the denominational business and be simply Christians. They all admit that folks can be Christians without being Baptists, Methodists, Presbyterians or Campbellites, but they seem determined not to do such a thing themselves or let anybody else do it if they can prevent it. Why is this, thus?

"A sect," says Bro. Wilkes, in the *Guide*, "is a number of persons, yet in the church, that have accepted and adopted for practice some error, as it respects the teachings of the Bible. The holding of an error as a mental conception simply, even if it be a radically important subject, is not necessarily sinful, nor will it necessarily make one a sectarian. It depends very much upon what the holder does with his thought. If he allows it to be dormant, so as not to injure himself or others, it is harmless. But if his error should be so dominant as to cause the one or those holding it to so act or do that the fellowship of the body of which he and they are members is seriously disturbed or broken, such a one is a sectarian, and all such are sectarians. When this work has been carried so far that the persons who advocate the error are, or may be properly, looked at and considered apart from the body of the church, they are a sect. Indeed, it is not necessary that the disturbing item, element or sentiment shall be an error or a sin, in order that those who hold it and press it shall be rightly deemed sectarians. Whatever is, as to faith or practice, so held and acted upon, that is not a truth from God, that the fellowship of a church of Jesus Christ is broken, though the parts may still remain nominally and apparently together, those who are the causers or promoters of the disturbance are sectarians. This conclusion rests upon the principle, undeniable, (1) That what God has taught does not, when followed, make sectarians; and (2) That what God has not taught, when so used as to break the fellowship of a church of Christ, does make sectarians of those who so use the untaught thing. A union of such or with such is not useful or desirable." This is an important truth well stated. Along the same line it seems pertinent just now to raise the question as to whether persons may not be sectarians and even constitute a sect, by pushing things which God *permits*, but does not *require*, against the convictions of those who do not understand that such things are even permitted. The church, as a body, cannot go beyond what its members understand God permits them to do. Now it may be possible, and probably it is often the case, that God *permits* things to be

The *Gospel Advocate* was widely read and distributed by Disciples of Christ members across the nation during the years following the Civil War. On its pages the debate between Silena Holman and David Lipscomb took place. Courtesy of the Disciples of Christ Historical Society, Nashville.

and became a bedrock of southern culture. Nowhere were the boundaries more defined than in southern churches, where preachers called for a return to the patriarchy of antebellum days.[1]

By the time of the Civil War, northern women had begun to stretch the accepted boundaries that confined women by working within all-female voluntary associations to establish independent identities. In the South, however, expansion of women's roles came far more slowly. Southern preachers in evangelical churches continued to define gender boundaries in terms that had been used before the Civil War. When the war ended, evangelical preachers called for a return to the prewar patriarchy that had been established to protect the institution of slavery. Across the South there was a yearning for the past. Evangelical preachers reflected the desire to resume the societal structure of the prewar South and called for the return to clear lines of gender responsibility and biblical male authority. However, among the southern women who could envision a new, different future for women, one independent-minded Tennessean, Silena Holman, a doctor's wife and mother, challenged the accepted interpretations of Scripture of her era concerning the role of women in the church by publicly initiating a correspondence with David Lipscomb, a highly influential evangelical preacher and writer, on the pages of Lipscomb's publication, the *Gospel Advocate.* Through intensive self-study, Holman developed an alternative feminist interpretation of New Testament verses that differed from the accepted views of Lipscomb on the role of women, and while not denting her church's intractable conservatism, Holman early on voiced the wisdom of the new woman and laid out a vision for the potential involvement of women even in fundamentalist Christianity.

Evangelical Christianity dominated the South in the nineteenth century. Congregational churches could be found in cities, towns, and rural areas of the states that had seceded from the Union. When the Civil War ended, these churches reestablished their congregations and returned to their teachings of female submission and silence in the church. Evangelicals placed a great emphasis on a crisis-like conversion or rebirth experience and held their members to a nonworldly standard of personal holiness and moral purity. Evangelical Protestantism came closest of all elements of culture to providing a unifying force among southerners. The southern churches, however, unlike their northern counterparts, reenforced existing kinship networks rather than providing a separate identity for female members. Women's organizations within some southern churches developed slowly, and some preachers continued to preach that women could not have a voice in church affairs.[2]

One of the most outspoken opponents of any kind of role for women within the church was David Lipscomb, a well-known Nashville preacher, teacher, and writer. Lipscomb, a biblical literalist who believed in the inerrancy of the Scriptures, had been converted as a college student and baptized by Tolbert Fanning, a follower of Alexander Campbell. Like Fanning, David Lipscomb believed that there was no room whatsoever for any interpretation of the Bible, failing to acknowledge that his own views were interpretation. When Lipscomb succeeded Fanning as editor of the *Gospel Advocate,* the conservative newspaper of the southern Disciples of Christ (the Christian Church and later Church of Christ) that was published in Nashville, Tennessee, in 1866, he created a following of like-minded evangelicals.

Baptists, Methodists, and Presbyterians dominated religion in most southern towns, but the "Christians" or "Churches of Christ" or "Disciples of Christ," as their congregations were variously known—they are referred to herein simply as Disciples of Christ—were a congregational-style denomination that had grown out of the Stone-Campbell movement of the Second Great Awakening and could be found in towns across Kentucky, Tennessee, and Alabama. Because congregational independence was a characteristic of each Disciples church, the denomination flourished especially in rural areas after the Civil War. As editor of the *Gospel Advocate,* David Lipscomb wielded considerable influence over late-nineteenth-century Disciples, extending from Nashville into the Deep South states and west into Texas. Lipscomb refused to support the service of women in any position of visibility or leadership in the church, which he believed directly contradicted the Bible. He expressed his views in print regularly.

Silena Moore Holman, a member of her local Disciples of Christ congregation in Fayetteville, Tennessee, in rural Lincoln County, began to test the boundaries of the women's sphere by challenging David Lipscomb for his patriarchal views about the role of women in the church beginning

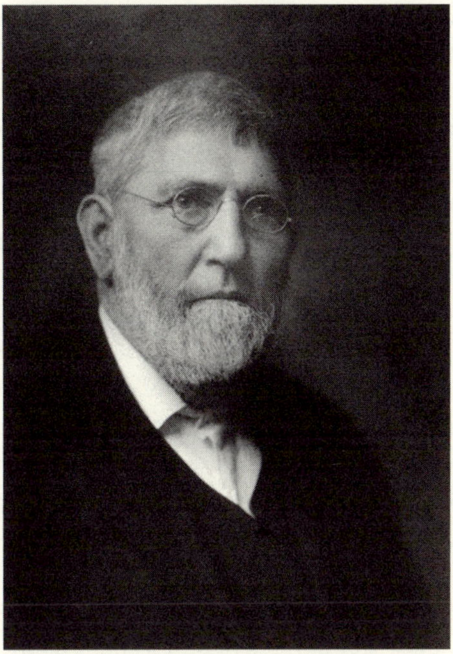

David Lipscomb, editor of the *Gospel Advocate*.
Courtesy of the Disciples of Christ Historical Society, Nashville.

in the 1880s. Although Holman in her time did not oppose the "cult of true womanhood," she saw a new woman growing out of the accepted view of women.[3] For Holman, this new woman occupied an expanded position of activism within the church as well as the larger community. Like Frances Willard, the national president of the Women's Christian Temperance Union (WCTU), Holman realized that women could engage in service work in the larger community if their activities did not conflict with the domestic sphere or threaten the accepted place of women in American society. As Holman matured and became active within the WCTU, she increasingly came to realize that there was no reason women should not have greater voices within their own churches. To openly express a new woman perspective, she began, tentatively in 1880 and then with dedication starting in 1888, to write letters to the *Advocate* in response to Lipscomb's articles about women. While David Lipscomb and Silena Holman agreed completely on the need to promote temperance and other moral reforms, they differed about how visible the actions of women should be toward public support of moral purity in the community and in church. The debate that ensued between them lasted for more than thirty years through the pages of the *Gospel Advocate.* Neither ever backed away from the debate and neither moderated his or her differing position about women in the church.[4]

The Civil War created a crisis in gender in the South. The position of southern women changed during the war years as men left the plantations and farms of the South to fight in the Confederate army.[5] Women singlehandedly ran farms, large and small, and held positions of authority when men went off to war. But by war's end, endlessly repeated tales of northern atrocities toward defenseless southern ladies flourished. The unspoken conclusion to the stories was that Confederate men were guilty of failing to protect their women, deepening the offense that the South's military loss represented southern men's greatest failure to protect their loved ones. Across the South, these overall feelings of powerlessness manifested themselves in the creation of male-only organizations such as the Pale Faces and the Ku Klux Klan. Men had to reassert authority over families, ex-slaves, and all of southern society.

As the South considered how the Civil War and the South's defeat would be interpreted by future generations, southerners created explanations that omitted the consequences of a society based on the brutality of the institution of slavery. The myth of the Lost Cause was one such interpretation, which provided southerners an explanation for why the war occurred. The war had not been about slavery; it was about states' rights. Confederate soldiers had fought for a noble cause.[6] Southerners forgot the deep divisions in the population about secession and replaced the events leading up to the war with a history that was filled with imagery of courageousness, great personal sacrifice, deep religious conviction, patriotism, and martyrdom. The Lost Cause provided a rationale for the restoration of the patriarchy in the South. Southern society expected its women, who had been left as heads of households during the war, to return to the private sphere because southern manhood needed to be restored.

Nowhere was the unquestioned acceptance of the patriarchy more evident than within churches of the South, in which preachers reinforced the ideology of the Lost Cause from pulpits across southern states. During the years following the war, David Lipscomb became one of the most highly visible leaders of the Disciples of Christ. After graduating from Franklin College in Nashville, a school founded by Tolbert Fanning as an agricultural school, Lipscomb moved to Georgia to manage a plantation. He held that position for two years but soon returned to Tennessee, where he farmed and preached. In 1855, Lipscomb joined his mentor Fanning in founding the Disciples of Christ periodical the *Gospel Advocate.* Although the Civil War forced the *Advocate* to cease publication, publication resumed in 1866 with Fanning and Lipscomb as its editors.

Fanning's decision that same year to withdraw from the *Gospel Advocate* to pursue educational interests permitted the ascendency of Lipscomb to sole editorship of the journal, a preeminent position from which to express his opinions widely across the South.[7] Growing in reputation and influence because of his articles and editorials, Lipscomb became the "Editor Bishop" of his church, a reference to a Disciple's statement that "we don't have bishops; we have editors."[8] Lipscomb's position of authority greatly affected denominational affairs within the loosely organized, nonhierarchical Disciples of Christ congregations.

The Civil War had a profound effect on the thinking of David Lipscomb. He developed a pacifist philosophy, believing that the Bible forbade violence and warfare.[9] He also developed strong views about the relationship between Christians and civil government and opposed any activities other than yielding to the civil structure of government. "We will never come closer to these governments than submission to their authority," he wrote after the war.[10] His literal interpretation of the writings of Paul supported his opposition to even the act of voting in elections. Lipscomb observed the many changes in southern society that had been brought on by years of war. As men left home to fight, women and their roles within the domestic arena had changed; women had had no choice but to assume responsibilities that men had previously shouldered.[11] Lipscomb witnessed this shift in women's positions with some alarm. He also saw the women's movement developing in the North as a threat to traditional society. The boundaries of the private sphere for women had to be confined, and he used theology and the circulation of the *Advocate* to restore the social order.[12]

In the North, the women's movement that had begun at Seneca Falls, New York, in 1848 resumed its activities after the war. Susan B. Anthony was outraged that the Fifteenth Amendment excluded women and provided the right to vote exclusively to African American men. In the years following the ratification of the amendment, Anthony's National Woman Suffrage Association (NWSA) worked tirelessly for the vote, but the organization remained a relatively small group of women, viewed by many as radical and unfeminine. The crusade Anthony's women's rights advocates launched for woman suffrage would not end until the ultimate ratification of the Nineteenth Amendment in 1920, a powerful victory for women.

Women's voluntary associations flourished after the Civil War as men worked together to provide social services and charity work in towns and cities. The creation of the Woman's Christian Temperance Union in 1874 provided women new opportunities to work together and stretch the gendered boundaries of the private sphere. The WCTU became a far more acceptable organization than the NWSA, and later NAWSA, because it did not directly challenge the "cult of domesticity" and thus it radically altered the character of the temperance movement. Women, particularly southern women, could participate in the WCTU without undermining their gendered position in society. Large numbers of southern women quickly became involved. By 1892, the national organization had almost 150,000 members.[13] The WCTU provided women a way to combine activism with their religious convictions. Church women across a broad spectrum of religious denominations saw their participation in the temperance movement as an extension of their church membership. However, since prohibition required laws to be changed, women's benign temperance work ultimately led them to political activity, producing "stealth feminists" early on, before the Progressive Era really got underway.[14]

Although numerous chapters of male-dominated temperance societies could be found in Tennessee, the WCTU was the organization that finally brought the issue of prohibition to the forefront of Tennessee politics.[15] Could women's participation in the WCTU threaten the reestablished patriarchal society of the South? When a group of concerned Tennessee women founded the state branch of the WCTU in 1881, it provided women from various religious faiths an opportunity to work together. A visit by Frances Willard the following year gave the organization visibility and name recognition. Tennessee newspapers carried accounts of Willard's revivalistic speech at a mass meeting in Memphis. Willard called for women to join the cause of prohibition to rid the nation of alcohol. Eleven local chapters quickly organized across the state.[16] WCTU growth surged again a few years later under the dynamic leadership of Lide Smith Meriwether of Memphis, an energetic and effective public speaker. By the end of 1887, Tennessee cities and towns had 116 unions for white women and 14 unions for black women. All the activities of the Tennessee WCTU had a strong religious component; Scripture readings and hymn singing accompanied every meeting.[17]

Tennessee's WCTU had much to celebrate in 1887. The state organization's campaign to convince the members of the general assembly to strengthen the legislation known as the Four-Mile Law to prevent the sale of liquor within four miles of any school in Tennessee was successful. Both houses passed the bill and the governor quickly signed it. The 1887 session of the Tennessee General Assembly also imposed a heavy tax on liquor dealers, an important step toward the state union's ultimate goal of an amendment to the Tennessee Constitution prohibiting the manufacture and sale of liquor across the state. The WCTU persuaded both the Tennessee Democratic and Republican parties to include a state prohibition amendment in their platforms. Throughout the summer Lide Meriwether campaigned from West to East Tennessee in support of the amendment, giving impassioned lectures in churches and homes in anticipation of the referendum, set for September 29, 1887. On election day, WCTU members went to the polls throughout the state, not to vote, but to pray, serve coffee, and urge men to cast their ballots for the state amendment outlawing alcohol. When the votes were counted, 118,000 Tennesseans favored of the amendment, but 145,000 did not.[18] David Lipscomb, an opponent of drinking, had urged Tennessee readers of the *Gospel Advocate* to boycott the election altogether because he did not believe that Christians should become involved in politics, even by voting.[19] In spite of the defeat, the visibility of the campaign increased WCTU membership in Tennessee. The decision by the national WCTU leadership to hold its national convention at the Ryman Auditorium in Nashville in November of that year was further indication that the movement had survived the local loss and would become reinvigorated.

In response to the visibility of the WCTU in Tennessee in 1887, Silena Moore Holman became a WCTU member in her home county in the spring of that year. Like Lide Meriwether, Holman had leadership skills as well as enthusiasm for the cause of prohibition. Silena Holman joined the Band of Good Templars, a small local temperance organization in Mulberry, Tennessee, outside of Fayetteville, where she and her husband, Thomas P. Holman, a physician who had once treated her for an illness, lived with their eight children. Holman herself was the oldest of five children whose father had died from wounds received while serving in the Confederate army when she was fourteen years old. Because her childhood family was forced to sell its home for indebtedness, young Silena went to work, finding a teaching position. She taught school for ten years, during which time the determined Silena earned enough money to repurchase the Moore family home for her mother.[20]

After her marriage to Holman, Silena gave birth to and raised eight children, and through the decades of her mothering years and married life she became increasingly committed to the cause of prohibition. It became her "consuming passion, and nothing daunted her or ever turned her aside from this great work."[21] The WCTU provided Holman an outlet for her intellectual energy and allowed her to develop writing skills that she used to articulate her views about womanhood. Almost immediately after joining the WCTU in 1887, Holman became her local WCTU's department superintendent for state work and then began serving as Tennessee reporter for the *Union Signal,* the journal of the national WCTU. She became a prolific writer for the *Union Signal,* with regularly published articles about the state chapters' activities. The WCTU also provided Holman with educational opportunities through her association with like-minded women with Progressive ideas. Her temperance work allowed Holman to develop and articulate her ideas about the role of women in society and must have influenced and furthered her views about the role of women in the church. She felt that she was a better wife and mother because of her prohibition activism, but others viewed her activities outside the home with less enthusiasm.

Even before Holman became involved in the WCTU, however, she had begun writing to the *Gospel Advocate* about the position of women in society. Holman and her husband were members of the Washington Street Disciples of Christ congregation in Fayetteville. At the time of her first published letter to the editor in 1880, Silena Holman was the mother of three young boys under the age of four. In her letter, she responded to a newspaper article about a woman who had identified her occupation in court as "wife and mother." The newspaper reported that on hearing the woman's occupation, "the court smiled." Holman's two-thousand-word letter to the editor of the *Gospel Advocate* was a defense of motherhood.[22] While accepting the understood position of motherhood, she argued for training for mothers. Progressive women would later take up this idea for scientific housekeeping. "Where in all our broad land are the means of equipping the young women who enter the matrimonial field for the practice of this royal profession?" Holman asked. She called on women to study parenting before they gave birth. In her letter, Holman also articulated what would be a theme in all of her writing: It was time to accept "the new woman," whom she described as "awake, alert, thoughtful, up-to-date, and well informed." While Holman did not suggest that women leave the private sphere of the home, she began to consider the expansion of the boundaries of the private sphere.

Editor David Lipscomb did not respond to or acknowledge Holman's first letter on the position of women, although he printed it.[23] However, in the years that followed Holman's initial letter in the *Gospel Advocate,* Lipscomb did respond. That first letter was but a start of a regular exchange between Silena Holman and Lipscomb on the editorial pages of the church journal that lasted until Holman's death and was read by women and men all across Tennessee and the South.[24]

When the *Gospel Advocate* published a letter to the editor in March 1888 asking for an interpretation of 1 Corinthians 14:34, "Let your women keep silence in the churches," editor Lipscomb replied in print that "women must teach privately or be condemned."[25] In his mind, the book of Acts in the New Testament clearly proscribed women's public voice in church.[26] Silena Holman quickly wrote a rejoinder to Lipscomb's response. Holman's letter, "A Peculiar People," criticized the practice of taking verses of Scripture out of context for use in church policy.[27] She then went on to give her own interpretation of the passages quoted in Lipscomb's article. She believed that the Bible was open to interpretation and went on to cite numerous verses where the interpretation of a single verse could be considered in different ways. "The Bible says 'children obey your parents,' 'wives obey your husbands,' does any person living believe that passage is ALWAYS to be interpreted literally?" Holman asked. Holman wanted to know how a woman or child should respond "when commanded or asked to do anything sinful." For Holman, there could not be a literal interpretation for every verse in the Bible. In her opinion, if Lipscomb's logic about women was followed, women could not even "GO TO CHURCH AT ALL." Holman's letter demonstrated insight and the depth of her knowledge of Scripture, which in part came from her scholarly study of the Bible, another activity opposed by Lipscomb. She went on to say confidently that "woman's emancipation began" with the teachings of Jesus.[28]

A month after the *Gospel Advocate* published Holman's May 1888 letter, it published a response to Holman with a letter from A. A. Bunner that criticized Holman's views on women.[29] Thus the debate began. Bunner accused Holman of looking at Paul's admonition that women should be silent in the churches "from a woman's standpoint" rather than from a scriptural standpoint. Bunner believed that women could work in the church without being "public proclaimers of the gospel" in many ways. While Bunner disagreed with another writer who had left a church when it began to allow women to teach children in Sunday School, he continued to affirm that there was no public role for women in the church. Again he referred to 1 Corinthians 14:34, "Let your women keep silence in the churches for it is not permitted unto them to speak." At the heart of the debate was the question of interpretation. Bunner did not think that women should interpret Scripture. He believed Holman took Scripture out of context and accused her of inappropriately linking verses together, such as 1 Corinthians 14:3, "He who prophesies speaks to men for their up-building and encouragement and consolation," with Acts 21:9, about Philip's four daughters who prophesied. While Bunner agreed with Holman about the number of women who followed Jesus, he felt that Paul's instruction, "Let your women keep silence in the churches," was the final word.[30]

Holman's return to Bunner came quickly, and the *Gospel Advocate* published it a few weeks later.[31] Holman titled it "Let Your Women Keep Silence" and stated that she was now "making a study of the 'woman question'" and wanted "to look at it from every possible standpoint." She wanted to know what the role of widows and unmarried women in the church should be. She specifically asked "Brother Bunner" to respond to several questions concerning Scripture, including Paul's injunction to men "to keep silence in the church." Holman believed that if readers took the First Corinthians verse literally, women could not even sing congregational hymns in church. She continued questioning Paul's writings on women. When Paul said that "every woman that prayeth or prophesieth with head uncovered dishonoreth her head," did Paul intend for a woman to cover her head when praying by her bedside at home? And "what is meant by the word church?" Holman asked. Is it a building or an "organized body of Christian people?" If women should not pray, should women not speak out on any subject such as "literature or science or temperance?"[32] By this time, Holman had begun to write for the WCTU's *Union Signal* on the subject of temperance. Soon she would be speaking publicly across the state in support of prohibition, as she quickly rose through the ranks of the state organization to become a highly visible WCTU leader in Tennessee.

In the October 1888 *Gospel Advocate,* Silena Holman again addressed the scriptural status of women and their exclusion by the church. This time, she referenced Galatians 3:28: "There can be no male and female; for ye are all one man in Christ Jesus." Here she compared the exclusion of women from an active role in the church to "the status of women in the heathen world where women were not even allowed to read scriptures or sacred texts."[33] She identified Hindus, the ancient Greeks, and Jews as among the heathen. "Heathen prejudice has debarred woman from legal rights, from intellectual culture, from religious instruction," Holman wrote, but "Christ and the Christian religion has [*sic*] been woman's best friend." "Slowly, surely, she has emerged from the darkness of heathenism into the full light of the perfect day of a Christian civilization." Holman's writings demonstrated that she was a well-read woman even though she lived in a small country town in Tennessee. In her letters, she quoted a variety of biblical scholars and their views about women. Here she pointed out that several biblical commentators thought "women should do public work in the gospel" and that that number was "growing larger and larger every day."[34] Lipscomb dismissed any scholarly interpretations of the Bible that contradicted his own entrenched views.

Holman also brought up the subject of prophesying, an activity she saw as another unpopular and controversial aspect of women doing public work. She had discovered three Old Testament biblical prophecies related to the prominence of women in the "propagation of the religion of Christ." Here she quoted a translation of Psalms 68:11: "The Lord giveth the word. The women who publish the tidings are a great host."[35] In her October 1888 letter, she made a reference to the use of the feminine gender as used in the Hebrew participle in a verse in Isaiah. Holman had studied various translations of the Bible and preferred to read Isaiah 40:9 as "O daughter that bringeth good tidings to Zion, get thee up into the high mountain! O daughter that tellest good tidings to Jerusalem, lift up thy voice with strength and say unto the cities of Judah, behold your God!" Holman then went on to discuss the role of New Testament women who had contact with Jesus. "I never could understand how a man could say that woman shall not tell the story of the cross, when she received her commission to do so from the Savior's own lips," she wrote. Holman believed that if Paul did not want "woman to teach or usurp authority over a man," he completely prohibited women from teaching in private as well. She closed her letter with a comparison of women "to the least of these" and asked for understanding of her views.[36]

David Lipscomb replied to Holman's letter in the very same issue of the *Gospel Advocate* with a lengthy refutation of her arguments.[37] He felt that women were too emotional to have leadership positions in the church. This time he directly criticized Holman. "She [Holman] cannot see that the Holy Spirit is telling, 'I suffered you to take the lead once; your strong emotional nature led you to violate God's word and to shipwreck a world, I cannot again trust you to lead,'" Lipscomb wrote. To him, a woman in any position beyond the private sphere of wife and mother demonstrated "unnatural, unwomanly, ungodly ambition."[38] Lipscomb's strong response, however, would not be the end of the discussion.

Remarkably, Silena Holman noticed that Lipscomb himself had taken on the personal task of contradicting her opinions, instead of A. A. Bunner. Silena Holman's next letter appeared in the *Advocate* the following month. In this letter, Holman wanted to defend her views about women and make it clear that she did not challenge the position of men as the head of the family. Apparently some readers had immediately concluded from her earlier letters that Holman thought "women should 'usurp authority over man.'" She apologized for any misunderstanding that this could have caused but then returned to her earlier themes about the role of women. This time she referred specifically to Frances Willard as a woman "with the genius of a Napoleon, who has led two hundred thousand women to battle with success."[39]

Here Holman responded to critics of the WCTU who suggested that the alcohol problem had been caused by the "failure of Christian mothers to do their duty."[40] Holman believed that if Christian mothers had a voice in public policy related to the sale of alcohol, "no licensed saloon or other school of crime would stand." Again, she reiterated her firm view that "a woman might take interest in other than domestic affairs." She simply did not believe that the Bible made "any distinction between public and private teaching, or preaching." Knowing that her barrage of letters had begun "to try any editor's patience," she closed this letter with a reaffirmation of an earlier statement she had made that if the Bible commanded women to be silent in the church, women should not be allowed "to sing in church, or partake of the Lord's supper" because there was not "the faintest allusion in the Bible as to [women] having ever done either."[41]

Immediately, Lipscomb responded again. "We think our sister should not excite or encourage a desire in other women that is so repugnant to her own womanly instincts and feelings," he began.[42] His letter reaffirmed for Holman and his readership his intractable conclusion that women should not have leadership or voices in the churches. For Lipscomb, women who engaged in public life would be hindered from childbearing. Here he quoted divorce statistics from New England, which he interpreted as proof that this would happen in other parts of the country if the status of women changed. Then he asked the question, "Do you not come to the conclusion that Satan is engaged in mighty industries?" Lipscomb addressed the work of Frances Willard in his article and made a distinction between Willard and Holman since Willard had not married. "Paul said an unmarried woman could devote her time to God with more undivided consecration than the married one," but for Lipscomb the Bible "commanded" women to marry. "A woman may devote herself to the work of the church today and never make a public speech. Thousands do," he wrote. "Our sister [Holman] seems to have the idea that no service can be done for God except by public harangue."[43]

In the years that followed, Holman continued to challenge David Lipscomb's position on women. Her increasing activities in the WCTU, however, undoubtedly limited the amount of attention that she gave to keeping her published debate with Lipscomb alive. From 1888 to 1892 no letters from Holman appeared in the *Gospel Advocate,* but when in 1892 the *Advocate* published an article by Lipscomb on "Women and Her Work," Holman once again felt compelled to write. Lipscomb's article commenced with six New Testament quotations from the letters of Paul whose meanings Holman and Lipscomb had already debated.[44] Lipscomb's same arguments supporting wifely submission and silence in church that he had used in his earlier letters then followed. "There can be no doubt of the teaching of the Bible on the subject of women's work and position," Lipscomb said. "God prohibits to her [a] public position." He then went on to describe what had happened in New England when women "entered the public arena." "The result is, religiously, New England has almost become infidel. It is threatened with a relapse into paganism."[45] By connecting the notion of women's rights, whether the right to vote or rights for equality in religion, to northerners, Lipscomb's readers would make the connection that equality in religion was unacceptable.

Holman's response came the next month. "A Protest," the title of her letter, was an angry defense of her own activities as well as those of the members of the WCTU.[46] As she interpreted Lipscomb's remarks, he blamed women for a long list of societal problems beginning with the decline in male church attendance and then going on to "the growing infidelity in the country, loose marriage, easy divorce laws, the indisposition of women to bear children, with all the attendant social impurity, the threatened extinction of a great race, the spread of Roman Catholicism," and other evils of society. Paragraph by paragraph, Holman dissected Lipscomb's article. "Where is his proof?" she asked the readers. Surely by this time she must have known that Lipscomb's response would be "The Bible." She closed with the following support of the work done by woman: "It would be more charitable and much nearer the truth I should think to say that women everywhere have seen the Lord's work not done because there are not enough laborers in the field and in their desire for the advancement of his kingdom, have gone out to labor with their own hands, than to say that the work is not done because women have undertaken to do a part of it."[47] The *Gospel Advocate* printed an anonymous response in the same issue, undoubtedly written by Lipscomb himself or one of the *Advocate* staff. The writer wanted to tie Holman's views to those in the North, where "the decrease of the puritan race" could now be seen. "The masses of the churches North are now managed by women. They frequently use the pastor through whom to work. The same condition is rapidly working its way South. The only reason I object to it is, it is unscriptural, and I am sure will soon work the same irreligious condition among the men here that so greatly exists there."[48]

Lipscomb responded to Holman personally in the next issue. Again, he quoted lengthy passages in the New Testament arguing that women should not have visibility in church. "It is no violation of these restraints thrown around woman for her to take a class of children, or old persons, and quietly, in the Bible school, teach them. There is privacy in publicity. When all sing there is not publicity attached to one singing. When one sings alone, there is publicity."[49] Lipscomb could not understand why Holman would not be content with the position in which his interpretation of the Scripture placed women.

Holman, for her part, steadfastly continued to defend the rights of women to work for causes that benefited the public good. She criticized Lipscomb's assertions that women's preaching and praying in public caused "growing infidelity in the country" and "the spread of Roman Catholicism," a fear among southern evangelicals. She opposed households in which men controlled the purse strings and demanded that responsibility for family expenses be shared. As "an earnest advocate of the higher education of woman," Holman believed that educated women would be better wives and mothers. Furthermore, she addressed other women's issues, calling for dress reform, saying that "so great is my abhorrence of a small waist in women . . . I would like to lead a crusade against it."[50]

Increased industrialization after the Civil War had brought educational opportunities, career options, and choices to many women that antebellum women had not had. As the end of the nineteenth century approached, newspapers began using the term "new woman" to describe females who saw for themselves and their daughters an expanded place in society accompanied by freedoms their mothers had not known. As the concept of the new woman spread, some southerners immediately responded to it as contrary to their ideas of the "southern lady." Many believed that southern men did not desire these "new women" and wanted to see the continuation of patriarchy in both gender and race relations across the South. In 1895, David Lipscomb decided that the time had come to directly confront the new woman in a lengthy diatribe in the *Gospel Advocate.* Lipscomb would not tolerate independent women, and he saw them as antithctical to the laws of God.[51]

After Lipscomb's article appeared, Silena Holman came back with her own: "The 'New Woman': Is There a New Woman; and If So, What Causes Led to Her Creation?"[52] Holman introduced the subject by saying that since Lipscomb's commentary had been published, she had been asked to respond with her interpretation of womanhood. Here she provided a historic survey of the status of women throughout history. Once again, she pointed out the contradictions of Lipscomb's arguments. She clarified that the struggles of women of the late nineteenth century had not simply happened after the Civil War; these societal improvements had moved forward since the earliest days of history. Holman emphasized, however, that historic changes that had taken place in the United States had indeed affected the role of women. "The woman of today differs in many respects from the woman of the past centuries, and even from the woman of one hundred or of fifty years ago," she wrote. "While the comic papers and newspaper paragraphers have failed to discover her—or, if they have done so, they have distorted her features beyond all recognition—yet there is a 'new woman,' in one sense of the word; and she is not only coming, but is come."[53] This would be Holman's thesis. Life for her was now different. A new day had dawned. Holman looked forward to the future; she believed that Lipscomb was mired in the past.

For Silena Holman, women's education was essential. She pointed out that women had been thought to be too "mentally incapacitated," frail, and emotional to endure the rigors of education. On the other hand, as more and more women attended college, they were criticized for being unwomanly, as being women who "would fail to inspire men." Holman disagreed, saying, "The educated man wants an educated wife now and always . . . and he doesn't believe that education has impaired her feminine grade or lovable qualities in the slightest degree."[54]

In the edition of the *Advocate* that published Holman's 1896 "New Woman" article, editor Lipscomb again followed with a personal response. "It gives a body the blues to read Sister Holman's article on man," he countered. He described her summation of history as a gross "caricature of facts."[55] Lipscomb believed that the "terrible struggle" throughout history that Holman described was "all in our sister's imagination." For Lipscomb, Holman's "new woman" was in reality as "ridiculed" by women as by men. Lipscomb said that Holman sounded as if women had not even been permitted to learn to read and write. He pointed out that Silena Holman's grandmother was "a well educated woman, as well educated as her grandfather." Lipscomb did not see the historic struggle for women's rights that Holman described. "The contest now over the rights of woman is not between the men and the women," he concluded.[56] His unwritten message was that a few outspoken women were the ones responsible for any perceived struggle. For Lipscomb, Holman was stirring up trouble where none existed.

The next week's issue of the *Advocate* carried "The New Woman, No. 2: What She Is Not, and Something of What She Is and Will Be," by Silena Holman.[57] Part 1 on "The New Woman" had been published under the name of "Mrs. T. P. Holman." While Holman reiterated her earlier comments about the responsibilities that women had as wives and mothers, she also stated her belief that women had choices. "I think that one of the most hopeful signs of the times is that an unmarried woman's chances in life are now such as the 'new woman' will not have to 'marry for a living,' a thing which is so degrading in thought or fact that no true woman could look on it but with horror," Holman told her readers. Here she drew from her own life experiences when her father died in the Civil War and left her mother as a widow "with a house full of girls, the oldest, myself, just fourteen, and a baby boy." Holman recalled that after her father's death, the neighbors offered her mother condolences not simply for the death of her husband, but at the same time for having so many "girls on her hands" at a time when "boys could have been of so much use" to her. When Holman's father died, her family was left in dire straits. She began to teach to help support the family. "What could we have done if there had been no 'career' open to me but a place in somebody's kitchen, which would not more than have enabled me to support myself?" she asked.[58]

Bicycle riding by women was one of the chief targets of critics of the new woman. By the 1890s, bicycling had become a popular activity. Since a woman had to straddle the bicycle and could not ride a bicycle in the same fashion that she rode a horse, some considered this activity unfeminine. Many women who rode bicycles had taken to wearing clothing similar to Amelia Bloomer's designs and further seemed to threaten masculinity. "Strange—isn't it?" Holman wrote, "that men should place such stress on a little matter of the arrangement of dress and say such vile things of a woman because of it." For Holman, "the girls who dress that way" were "as sweet and lovely and pure and womanly as any of God's creations." Holman saw the bicycle as an invention that would "prove a blessing to the human race." She saw the benefits of exercise for women and believed bicycle riding to be no more "masculine or unwomanly" than horseback riding.[59]

Even though Holman was married, she saw nothing wrong with men who preferred a career to marriage. "If a woman prefers an unmarried life and financial independence, she has Paul's permission to remain unmarried—and who could furnish higher authority?" she asked, referencing Lipscomb's final authority, the apostle Paul. Still, Holman felt a need to repeat her view that "the happiest and best life for a woman is to be happily married with children of her own growing up around her." Nevertheless,

Holman believed that a era had begun for women and society. "I maintain that the average trend of our womanhood is upward in all that is best and most desirable in the human race." She knew that the "days of the clinging vine woman are gone forever" and that a "husband will find walking by his side the bright, wide-awake companion, . . . a helpmeet in the best possible sense of the term." For Holman, there was not only a new woman but also a new man, who "should keep himself as pure as a woman should."[60]

Holman concluded her "New Woman. No. 2" article with a discussion of woman suffrage. "Will the new woman vote?" she asked. "The signs of the times seem to point that way. . . . But this I know: A woman will no more lose her womanliness or purity or goodness because she has the privilege of expressing her opinion at the ballot box . . . than she did in being allowed to receive a higher education."[61] Silena Holman died in 1915, five years before women won the right to vote.

Neither Lipscomb nor Holman's views about women changed during the years of their public correspondence in the pages of the *Gospel Advocate.* In 1913, when both neared the end of their lives, Holman summed up the more than thirty-year debate: "To continue the discussion would be very much like the constant assertion: 'It is,' 'It is not,' 'It is,' 'It is not.' For he would continue to assert that the Bible teaches certain things and I would as surely continue to say that the Bible teaches differently on this question. I think it would be as well to rest the question here and let the readers decide as to which has the best of the argument."[62] Of course, Holman did not end there. She went on with one last lengthy defense of her views.[63]

Historian Fred Bailey has suggested that the struggle over the role of women in the church and society was a major factor in Lipscomb's decision to break with the Disciples of Christ denomination.[64] While the followers of Lipscomb who came to identify their congregations as Churches of Christ do not claim Lipscomb as the founder of their denomination, few will deny the extent of his influence on the growing differentiation between the Disciples of Christ and the Churches of Christ. Although there had been distinctions among congregations for some years, when the Churches of Christ became formally and officially identified in 1906 as a separate denomination,[65] the subjection of women in church affairs was a key tenet of their church. Lipscomb's Churches of Christ forbade the organization of women's missionary societies, as well as the playing of organ music. At a time when the role of women in society had begun to change and open to possibility, Lipscomb and other southerners tenaciously adhered to the "true womanhood" model and to women's confinement to the domestic sphere. For them, no public place, nor public voice in church or on Scripture, was appropriate for a woman.

Ironically, the *Gospel Advocate* continued to publish her pieces, if only to ridicule them. Unrelenting, and not allowing years and public rebukes to silence her commitment to women's equality in the church, in an article titled "The Woman Question Again" in the *Advocate* in 1913, Holman, near the end of her life, once more confronted her church's stance on women's second-class citizenship and inferior status, which remained as unimproved as when she had begun her dialogue with its male patriarchs in the 1880s.[66] In the decades of correspondence in the pages of the church journal, Holman and Lipscomb found no common ground on the subject.

Silena Holman eschewed a submissive, obsequious image of woman and firmly promoted the ideal of the new woman, but neither did she fully embrace all tenets of twentieth-century feminism. Holman became the model for a southern new woman. She raised eight children. She continued to be a faithful church member. She became president of the Tennessee WCTU in 1899 and held that position until her death in 1915. During her presidency, the state WCTU grew from a few hundred members to an organization of greater than four thousand women.[67] It was also during her presidency that the political assassination of Senator Edward Ward Carmack, an ardent prohibitionist, caused Holman to mobilize her extensive membership into action. Led by Holman, the Tennessee WCTU persuaded the Tennessee General Assembly in 1909 to pass statewide prohibition, some ten years before the United States ratified the Eighteenth Amendment to the U.S. Constitution.[68]

As Holman saw her death approaching, she wanted her funeral service to be given by someone who would not disrespect her. She trusted prominent Church of Christ minister T. B. Larimore and was confident he would be able to speak with love and generosity about her. Newspaper accounts of her funeral estimated that more than two thousand people gathered on the lawn of Holman's Fayetteville home on a beautiful autumn Sunday afternoon in 1915 to honor her life and work. H. B. Carre, president of the Tennessee Anti-Saloon League, and Florence Atkins, lecturer of the National WCTU, joined Brother Larimore in eulogizing Silena Holman. Each of the speakers praised her contributions to the state and the nation. Even the Tennessee Baptists, long considered to be in competition with the Churches of Christ, acknowledged Holman's dedication and impact on Tennessee. The *Tennessee Baptist and Reflector* published an obituary for Holman the week after her death that undoubtedly presented how she wanted to be remembered in history: "To the taunt sometimes made by liquor men that it is the business of women to stay at home and

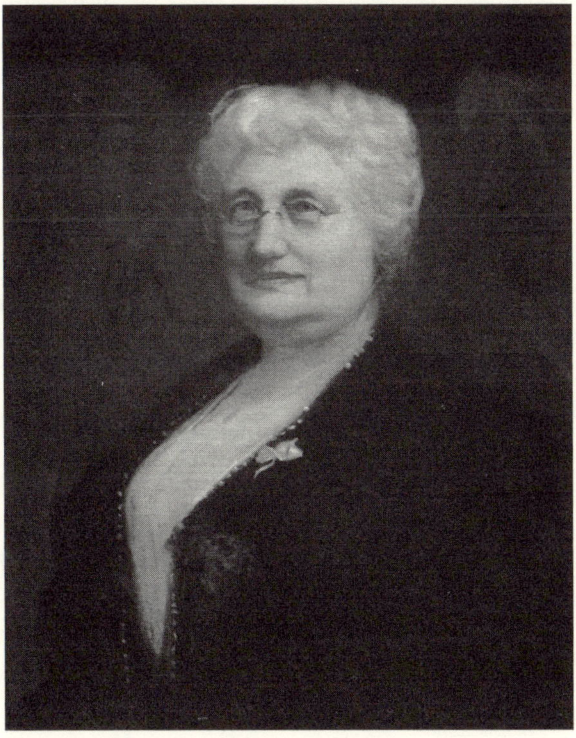

Portrait of Silena Moore Holman commissioned by the WCTU after her death. Courtesy of the Tennessee State Museum, Nashville.

rear their children, she could reply, and sometimes did reply, that she was the mother of eight boys, and it was to protect her boys and the boys of other mothers from the liquor traffic that she was giving her life to the temperance cause."[69]

Following her death, the Tennessee WCTU commissioned a portrait of Silena Holman. When the painting was completed, it was hung in the Tennessee State Capitol, a high honor for a woman or a man.[70] The early tributes to the life of Silena Holman praised her ardent work for temperance, but none recognized her considerable influence as a spokesperson and role model for the new woman who had an active role in shaping society from an expanded position of influence beyond the boundaries of her home.

History often forgets women like Silena Holman. Ultimately temperance, the cause for which she labored so successfully, failed. The Eighteenth Amendment, which was ratified after her death, was repealed by the Twenty-first Amendment. Holman's efforts to create a public role for women in her denomination also failed. Lipscomb remained unmoved by her arguments to the very end. Although the Disciples of Christ did broaden their views of women to become a more inclusive denomination, the Churches of Christ, the congregations influenced by David Lipscomb that had separated from the Disciples of Christ over musical instruments and foreign missions, did not. Holman's home church in Fayetteville became a Church of Christ. David Lipscomb's view on women remaining silent in the church is still held in most Churches of Christ today.

In spite of what would seem like the failures of her life's work, Holman's contributions cannot be dismissed. The visibility that she and her WCTU women received when they convinced the Tennessee General Assembly to pass statewide prohibition legislation undoubtedly was a positive step toward the next battle for women—suffrage. Although Holman was not among the officers of the Tennessee Equal Suffrage League, her legislative campaign paved the way for the suffrage battle to come. From a small town in rural Middle Tennessee, her published arguments for women and her personal model for the expanded participation and voice of women in all arenas of public life were precedent setting.

NOTES

The author of this chapter gratefully acknowledges the work of Professor Ernst Rollmann of Memorial University in St. John's, Newfoundland, for his painstaking efforts to transcribe many of Silena Holman's writings for a website that he maintains on the Restoration movement; Dr. Dwight Tays of Lipscomb University, Nashville, who read an earlier draft of this essay; and Dr. C. Leonard Allen of Abilene Christian University, Abilene, Tex., whose scholarly work on Holman precedes my own. The opening epigraph refers to Silena Moore Holman, "The Woman Question Again," *Gospel Advocate,* Apr. 10, 1913.

1. Barbara Welter, "The Cult of True Womanhood: 1820–1860," *American Quarterly* 18 (Summer 1966): 151–74.

2. Paul K. Conkin, "Evangelicals, Fugitives, and Hillbillies: Tennessee's Impact on American National Culture," *Tennessee Historical Quarterly* 54 (Fall 1995): 249; Jean E. Friedman, *The Enclosed Garden: Women and Community in the Evangelical South, 1830–1900* (Chapel Hill: Univ. of North Carolina Press, 1985).

3. Friedman, *Enclosed Garden*; C. Leonard Allen, *Distant Voices: Discovering a Forgotten Past for a Changing Church* (Abilene, Tex.: Abilene Christian Univ. Press, 1993).

4. Allen, *Distant Voices,* 126–35.

5. Drew Gilpin Faust, *Mothers of Invention: Women of the Slaveholding South in the American Civil War* (Chapel Hill: Univ. of North Carolina Press, 1996); George Rable, *Civil Wars: Women and the Crisis of Southern Nationalism* (Urbana: Univ. of Illinois Press, 1991); LeeAnn Whites, *Gender Matters: Civil War, Reconstruction, and the Making of the New South* (New York: Palgrave Macmillan, 2005); LeeAnn Whites, *The Civil War as a Crisis in Gender: Augusta, Georgia, 1860–1890* (Athens: Univ. of Georgia Press, 1995); Tina Stewart Brakebill, *"Circumstances Are Destiny": An Antebellum Woman's Struggle to Define Sphere* (Kent, Ohio: Kent State Univ. Press, 2006).

6. All biographical sources on David Lipscomb mention his opposition to the institution of slavery. When Lipscomb was five years old, his father, Granville Lipscomb, moved his family to Illinois in order to free his slaves. When his wife died, Granville Lipscomb brought his children back to Tennessee. David Lipscomb's literal interpretation of the Bible led him to become a pacifist.

7. Paul K. Conkin, *American Originals: Homemade Varieties of Christianity* (Chapel Hill: Univ. of North Carolina Press, 1997), 1–56.

8. Elesha Coffman, "A Long Ride on the Mainline: A Hundred Years of the Christian Century," Nov. 14, 2008, *Christianity Today,* http://www.christianitytoday.com/global/printer.html?/bc/2008/novdec/12.20.html/.

9. Robert E. Hooper, *Crying in the Wilderness: A Biography of David Lipscomb* (Nashville: David Lipscomb College, 1979).

10. *Gospel Advocate,* Dec. 11, 1866.

11. Whites, *Civil War as a Crisis in Gender,* 38–39.

12. For further biographical information about Lipscomb, see also Earl Ivin West, *The Search for the Ancient Order: A History of the Restoration Movement, 1849–1906* (Indianapolis: Earl West Religious Publishing, 1950).

13. Alison Marie Parker, *Purifying America: Women, Cultural Reform, and Pro-Censorship Activism, 1873–1933* (Urbana: Univ. of Illinois Press, 1997), 21–31; Ruth Bordin, *Woman and Temperance: The Quest for Power and Liberty, 1873–1900* (New Brunswick: Rutgers Univ. Press, 1990), 3.

14. Sarah Wilkerson-Freeman, "Stealth in the Political Arsenal of Southern Women," in *Southern Women at the Millennium: A Historical Perspective,* ed. Melissa Walker, Jeanette R. Dunn, and Joe P. Dunn (Columbia: Univ. of Missouri Press, 2003), 42–82.

15. Paul E. Isaac, *Prohibition and Politics: Turbulent Decades in Tennessee, 1885–1920* (Knoxville: Univ. of Tennessee Press, 1965), 12–31.

16. *Memphis Commercial Appeal,* Feb. 1882.

17. Isaac, *Prohibition and Politics,* 8–9.

18. Ibid., 11.

19. Ibid., 160. Lipscomb published his views about how Christians should respond to the government in a 1913 book, *Civil Government,* now retyped in its entirety on the Memorial University of St. John's Newfoundland's Restoration movement website, http://www.mun.ca/rels/restmov/texts/dlipscomb/civgov.html/.

20. Isaac, *Prohibition and Politics,* 121–27.

21. Ibid., 123.

22. Silena M. Holman, "Wanted—Mothers," *Gospel Advocate,* Apr. 1, 1880, 4.

23. Ibid.

24. While the *Gospel Advocate* occasionally published letters by other women, no other women were as prolific as Holman. Lipscomb and male readers frequently responded to Holman, but if women did respond, their letters were not published. To date, no published responses by women to Holman's views have been found.

25. David Lipscomb, "Women's Work in the Church," *Gospel Advocate,* Mar. 14, 1888, 6–7.

26. A. A. Bunner, "Woman's Work in the Church," *Gospel Advocate,* June 20, 1888, 5.

27. Silena M. Holman, "A Peculiar People," *Gospel Advocate,* May 2, 1888, 12.

28. Ibid.

29. Bunner, "Woman's Work in the Church," 5.

30. Ibid.

31. Mrs. T. P. Holman, "Let Your Women Keep Silence," *Gospel Advocate,* Aug. 1, 1888, 8.

32. Ibid.

33. Mrs. T. P. Holman, "The Scriptural Status of Woman," *Gospel Advocate,* Oct. 10, 1888, 2.

34. Ibid.

35. John James Stewart Perowne, *The Book of Psalms, a New Translation with Introductions and Notes, Explanatory and Critical* (London: George Bell and Sons, 1883).

36. Holman, "The Scriptural Status of Woman," 2–3.

37. David Lipscomb, "Woman's Station and Work," *Gospel Advocate,* Oct. 10, 1888, 6.

38. Ibid.

39. Mrs. T. P. Holman, "Women's Scriptural Status Again," *Gospel Advocate,* Nov. 21, 1888.

40. Ibid.

41. Ibid.

42. David Lipscomb, "Women in the Church," *Gospel Advocate,* Nov. 21, 1888.

43. Ibid.

44. David Lipscomb, "Woman and Her Work," *Gospel Advocate,* Oct. 13, 1892.

45. Ibid.

46. Mrs. T. P. Holman, "A Protest," *Gospel Advocate,* Nov. 17, 1892.

47. Ibid.

48. Anonymous, *Gospel Advocate,* Nov. 17, 1892.

49. David Lipscomb, "Woman's Work," *Gospel Advocate,* Dec. 1, 1892.

50. Mrs. T. P. Holman, "The Proper Education of Our Daughters," *Gospel Advocate,* Apr. 13, 1894.

51. David Lipscomb, "The New Woman," *Gospel Advocate,* Dec. 5, 1895.

52. Mrs. T. P. Holman, "The 'New Woman': Is There a New Woman; and If So, What Causes Led to Her Creation?" *Gospel Advocate,* July 9, 1896, 438.

53. David Lipscomb, following Holman, "New Woman," 438.

54. Ibid.

55. David Lipscomb, *Gospel Advocate,* July 9, 1896.

56. Ibid.

57. Silena Holman, "The New Woman, No. 2: What She Is Not, and Something of What She Is and Will Be," *Gospel Advocate,* July 16, 1896, 452.

58. Ibid.

59. Ibid.

60. Ibid.

61. Ibid.

62. Holman, "Woman Question Again."

63. Ibid.

64. Fred Bailey, "Disciple Images of Victorian Womanhood," *Discipliana* 40, no. 1 (Apr. 1980): 7–11.

65. In 1907, David Lipscomb made a request of S. N. D. North, director of the federal census in 1906, that the Bureau of the Census begin to list the two groups separately, and thus 1906 is considered an official date of differentiation (David Lipscomb, "The 'Church of Christ' and the 'Disciples of Christ,'": *Gospel Advocate,* July 18, 1907, 457;

"Disciples or Christians," *Religious Bodies:* 1906, Part 2, *Separate Denominations: History, Description, and Statistics, Special Reports,* Bureau of the Census, Department of Commerce and Labor (Washington: Government Printing Office, 1910), 235–41.) The cleavage between the two groups had in fact been coming on for several years. Because of no denominational superstructure, individual congregations chose to refer to themselves in different ways and by different names (Robert E. Hooper, *A Distinct People: A History of the Churches of Christ in the 20th Century* (West Monroe, La.: Howard Publishing, 1993), 40–41; Richard T. Hughes, *The Churches of Christ,* student edition (Westport, Conn.: Praeger, 2001). Holman used Christian, the Christian Church, the church, and disciples in her early writings, but by October 1888 in "The Scriptural Status of Woman," she speaks in the *Gospel Advocate* primarily of the Church of Christ.

66. Holman, "Woman Question Again"; F. W. Smith, "Reply to Sister Holman," *Gospel Advocate,* Mar. 13, 1913; Allen, *Distant Voices.*

67. Allen, *Distant Voices.*

68. Mattie Carson Duncan Beard, *The W.C.T.U. in the Volunteer State* (Kingsport, Tenn.: Kingsport Press, 1962), 122–27.

69. *Tennessee Baptist and Reflector,* Oct. 16, 1915, 9.

70. Beard, *W.C.T.U.,* 127.

Chapter 5

Women Who Fought to Stop Lynching in Tennessee: Progressive Women and the "Fury of the Mob"

Paula K. Hinton

> *Alone and unarmed, the wife of Sheriff J. C. Butler today held back a mob of 100 men that sought to take away a wounded negro prisoner held for shooting a policeman. The negro, Henry Walker, was arrested by Vaughn Pierce, of Humboldt, and locked in the county jail here [Huntingdon, Carroll County, Tennessee]. . . . Mrs. Butler was alone in the living quarters of the jail when she heard the mob gathering in the jail yard. "Where's your husband?" some one [sic] shouted. "My husband's gone," the woman replied evenly, "and you'll get the prisoner only over my dead body." "Rush her," cried a leader of the mob. But the woman's steady stand in the doorway and her calmness broke the ranks of the crowd before they reached her.*
>
> —*Atlanta Constitution*, 1931

In 1931, Mrs. J. C. Butler,[1] with her two daughters, Margaret aged twenty and Maxine aged sixteen, held off a mob determined to lynch a black male. The image of this woman, unarmed yet standing her ground against a hundred angry and violent men, with her two frightened daughters looking on, is both powerful and humbling. What were members of the mob thinking when they were confronted by an assertive white southern lady? And what were her daughters thinking when they saw their own mother model such courage and strength of character? Particularly striking is that Butler, a white female in the Jim Crow South, intervened at all to stop the lynching of a black man. That she did so single handedly is all the more remarkable.

Moreover, Butler, a private and reticent woman, recognized this incident as both personally empowering and as evidence of the growing opportunities available to southern women in the public sphere. When the Commission on Interracial Cooperation (CIC) awarded her a medal usually reserved for sheriffs, she acknowledged that her stance against the mob had deviated from accepted gender norms. She admitted to her own extreme shyness, her lack of knowledge beyond home and family, and her genuine fear and reluctance to speak and act publicly.[2] Yet she had held her own against numbers and racial bitterness.

Butler's stance, however, was not a position taken in isolation. There were women just like her who had staked out the moral high ground against lynching. Butler was emboldened because of the decades-long battle being fought by antilynching activists all over the country and especially by white women in the South who had preceded her in stopping illegal brutality and who continued to challenge societal racial and gender norms. Progressive southern women sought to reshape regional, racial, and gendered paradigms. These women would no longer aid in perpetuating the false image of the weak, passive southern white woman. These new women were destined to endure attacks at the hands of neither the stereotyped brutish black male nor the brutish white male mob. The new image they proffered was woman as altruistic advocate for equal protection under the law.

Certainly African American women in Tennessee, most notably Ida B. Wells, had spoken and written extensively against lynching since the nineteenth century.[3] But southern white women, missionary in their advocacy, had also taken up the crusade in ever-increasing visibility. Although their numbers were comparatively small, these women changed and saved lives even as they pushed the boundaries of what was considered "ladylike" behavior. Many traveled widely, and often alone. They organized, strategized, and were in constant contact with journalists and publishers, urging them to publicize the issue. They were lobbyists, circulating petitions and sending countless letters and telegrams to local, state, and federal government officials. In the spirit and methodology of temperance workers, they urged fellow southerners to sign oaths promising to do whatever they could to prevent lynchings. And the women lectured in public, further eroding the limitations on accepted roles for proper white women.

These activists did all of their work in an atmosphere often charged with hostility and violence. But in the end, southern Progressive women could look back with pride at all they had accomplished. The situation had been dire. From 1892 until 1940, more than three thousand men and men were lynched in the United States. Of those, more than twenty-six hundred were African Americans.[4] Tennessee ranked sixth in lynchings: Between 1882 and 1930, 214 people were lynched, mostly in West and Middle Tennessee. At least 81 percent of the victims were black.[5] Of Tennessee's ninety-six counties, seventy had been the sites of lynchings. Shelby and Obion were the counties with the most egregious records, with eighteen lynchings in Shelby and seventeen in Obion.[6]

Tennessee, however, was unusual in that by 1898 it was one of only three states that had put in place some form of antilynching legislation. The Tennessee General Assembly had passed a law that punished sheriffs if they allowed, purposefully or through negligence, a prisoner under their watch to be lynched. Such an officer could be fined and could lose his position.[7] As a result of such legislation, Butler's act of bravery might be interpreted as having been nothing more than looking out for her husband's job security and her own self interest—were it not for the fact that the Association of Southern Women for the Prevention of Lynching (ASWPL) had had direct personal experiences for years dealing with "fractious . . . complacent sheriffs," unrepentant jail guards, and city officers unwilling to prohibit lynchings within their jurisdictions and under their watch or to investigate the actions (or inaction) of lawmen.[8] Breaking that pattern was considered exemplary and earned Butler well-deserved national recognition.

Progressive southern women were engaged in antilynching activism for several decades beginning in the late nineteenth century, but tracing the influence of any one segment of this movement can be challenging. There is a veritable spider web of organizations, clubs, and individuals from all over the South involved, and the participants rarely accepted credit for their work. Although the largest of the antilynching associations in the South, the ASWPL, dutifully maintained files of correspondence, copies of speeches, newspaper clippings, and minutes of meetings, teasing out the significance of Tennesseans is difficult to isolate as they are often embedded within the social programs and reform missions of Progressives committed to numerous objectives.

Historians disagree regarding how much the Social Gospel and more classic, northern-influenced "progressivism" impacted reformers and reform organizations in the South. Mary Jane Brown joins earlier historians, among them C. Vann Woodward, who argue that progressivism had little impact on antilynching groups in the South.[9] Brown asserts that racism was so dominant and overarching throughout the South that it negated any possibility of successful antilynching strategies and undermined the legitimacy of the South's ability to be Progressive at all.[10] Christopher Waldrep points to the fact that northern Progressives were mainly focused on issues produced by urban industrialization, and since lynching was predominantly a rural phenomenon, antilynching could not be by definition assessed as an element of progressivism.[11] Other historians disagree.

Donald L. Grant maintains that progressivism caused a paradigm shift in thinking about social issues, including lynching. Progressivism emboldened activists. Social ills were no longer inevitable and unstoppable. Progressives argued that social problems could be publicly, actively confronted and eventually ameliorated.[12] Grant asserts that as the number of lynchings decreased, white involvement in the antilynching movement did the same; and as the number of lynchings increased, so did white participation in the movement.[13] Progressive southerners spotlighted the evil among them and stepped forward to address it. There is, in fact, a strong undercurrent of the Social Gospel in the work of white Tennesseans in the movement.

The Social Gospel, calling for people of faith to act collectively to remediate the ills of society and to relieve the suffering of those damaged by circumstances and social structures beyond their control, appears early in the 1800s in the work of the first female missionaries of the Methodist Episcopal Church, South. Through their charitable work in their communities, Southern Methodist women were among those who came to the forefront of social action to act out their faith in the present world through helping the people in need around them, both in body and in spirit. They viewed society as sinful but worthy and capable of redemption and understood intellectually that positively impacting the environments in which people lived could better individual lives and whole communities.[14]

Although northern women embraced Social Gospel doctrine and "municipal housekeeping" earlier than women in the South, a multitude of southern educational, civic, and patriotic clubs sprang up out of church organizations, temperance societies, and Civil War associations and were popular with southern white women. By the 1860s women's religious associations tended to fall into one of three core groups: foreign and home missionary societies, Christian women's temperance advocacy through the WCTU, and Christian organizations like the YWCA. Many southern women attracted to these types of organizations eventually pursued sole proprietorship of their own groups. They wanted to manage their own finances, elect their own leaders, and address issues of their own choosing.[15]

Women combined their energies and resources and worked effectively together, compelled by a Christian spirit of service, often participating at the grass-roots level in social issues that would have been deemed radical without the protective mantle of the designation of "religious" and "church work." Their efforts were imbued with the Social Gospel. Southern clubwomen fought an intransigent public but organized, created, and joined groups dedicated to solving society's problems, actions which over time became expressly more political.[16] Female Progressives in the South, just like their sisters in the North, exposed corruption, utilized connections and networks they had created over time, lobbied for political and social reforms, and cultivated their political awareness and new voting power. Many of these women were bold, formidable, ambitious, and possessed of grand visions of a better society.

Women's missionary unions and women's home missionary societies in several Protestant denominations gave women an opportunity to increase their public presence through church activities.[17] Missionary societies were very successful, and most included subcommittees dedicated to missionary work with "Colored People in the South," "Indians" in the West, and "Illiterate Whites in the South."[18]

Belle Harris Bennett was a key participant in the symbiotic relationship between the Social Gospel and the Methodist Church's Woman's

Missionary Council.[19] She was also vital to the influence of the Social Gospel philosophy in the antilynching movement. Born in 1852 to a Methodist family that owned slaves, through the women's rights movement Bennett became interested in social issues and became very active in the Methodist Church's home and foreign missions.[20] Among the many accomplishments of the Methodist Episcopal Church, South, Woman's Home Missionary Society (later the Woman's Missionary Council) were the financing and operation of Scarritt Bible and Training College when it opened in 1892, initially in Kansas City, Missouri, and when it moved to Nashville in 1924. A college for whites only, Scarritt was responsible for training future social workers for the South, including several leaders in the antilynching movement.[21]

A turning point in Bennett's social consciousness came in May 1901 at the Woman's Board of Home Missions meeting in St. Louis. According to Lily Hammond, another influential leader of that time, Bennett had wanted to address race relations even earlier "but felt that the prejudice must die down somewhat before it was feasible. Finally, in answer to the argument that prejudice would die sooner if somebody fought it, she turned to God for guidance."[22] Bennett began her work the next day when she convinced the board to help fund the women's annex at the Colored Methodist Episcopal Church's Paine College in Augusta, Georgia, an institution that would be significant in the lives of many antilynching activists.[23] In 1913 the Woman's Missionary Council, representing about twenty thousand women, unanimously passed an antilynching resolution.[24] Bennett urged the women to publicize their disgust with lynching and to vote against it whenever and wherever possible. The council agreed and also issued a condemnation of the Ku Klux Klan.[25]

Lynching statistics (collected and maintained by both the NAACP and later the ASWPL) revealed the true scope of the problem of lynching in Tennessee. From 1882 to 1890 there were 54 lynchings; from 1891 to 1899 there were an astounding 105; and between 1900 and 1935 there were 80.[26] An effective argument used to bring more southern white women into the antilynching movement was lynching's impact on black women, white women, and on womanhood in general. Between 1882 and 1927, ninety-two females were lynched, seventy-six of whom were black. Many of these women were pregnant at the time they were murdered.[27]

Southern reformer Lily Hammond was from Augusta, Georgia, and, like Belle Bennett, came from a slave-owning family. Hammond spent years living in northern urban areas where her passion for reform was fueled. A supporter of Paine College and bulwark of the Southern Methodist home missions, Hammond argued that "being a woman goes deeper than being of this race or that, of this or that social station. . . . Women should stand together for the womanhood of the world."[28] In an essay titled "White and Colored Women Too Far Apart in Practical Sympathy," published as part of the 1916 annual report of the Women's Convention of the National Baptist Convention, Hammond argued that the "whole race problem will be quickly and easily solved when white women teach their children around the fireside not to respect white women less, but to respect colored women more. . . . The race problem will never be solved until white and colored women work together for mutual respect and protection."[29] Although many female antilynching reformers shared Hammond's ideals, others believed that helping to improve the lives of African Americans was simply their Christian duty.

Hammond held membership in countless local and national organizations. One of the most active was the Bureau of Social Services, a Southern Methodist organization formed years earlier to aid African Americans.[30] By 1919 the group had integrated and evolved into the Commission on Interracial Cooperation.[31] Founded in Atlanta, Georgia, the CIC, guided for some time by a Methodist minister from Nashville named William W. "Will" Alexander, was created by educators, clergy, and social workers in order to "foster understanding among blacks and whites through conferences, education, and publicity."[32] The CIC also attempted to obtain the backing of law enforcement and helped facilitate reciprocal support by publicizing and rewarding police officers and sheriffs who protected prisoners from lynch mobs.[33]

In 1920, southern white women affiliated with various religious denominations, many motivated by African American clubwomen, organized to investigate race relations. One of the first tasks they set for themselves was to meet with leading African American women. In July 1920, a group of white church women attended a conference of the National Colored Women's Clubs at Tuskegee Institute, where black and white women together discussed the lynching problem and how both groups might work in cooperation to end it.[34] When the CIC learned of the clubwomen's collaboration, they saw an opportunity. The commission developed a conference in Memphis in October of the same year, and it was there in 1920 that the Woman's Division of the CIC first organized. Representatives from the YWCA, women's clubs, and Protestant denominations (ninety-one white women in all), invited four influential black women active in the club movement: Margaret Murray Washington, widow of Booker T. Washington and superintendent of the Industrial Department at Tuskegee Institute; Mrs. Charlotte Hawkins Brown, principal of Palmer Memorial Institute and president of the North Carolina Federation of Colored Woman's Clubs; Mrs. George E. Hanes, secretary of the Department of Social Science for the U.S. Employment Bureau; and Mrs. Jennie Moton, wife of Tuskegee Institute's president. The women were invited to discuss problems in the African American community.[35] There were fifteen Tennessee women who attended, representing the YWCA; Bethlehem House in Nashville; the Nashville Education Department; the Woman's Missionary Council; Scarritt Bible and Training School; the Methodist Episcopal Church, South; Shelby County Public Schools Department of Negro Education; and the Tennessee Synod of the Presbyterian Church. The women wanted to "show to the whole world the power of Christianity to settle racial differences and to meet inter-racial crises everywhere."[36] At the end of the conference they promised to "work with black women 'for a Christian settlement of the problems that overshadow the homes of both races,'" including lynching.[37]

The CIC Woman's Division quickly organized a Woman's Division for each of the state committees. By 1923 there were four hundred auxiliary groups working toward these goals throughout the South, heavily comprised of Methodist women such as Bertha Newell, superintendent of the Bureau of Social Relations for the Woman's Missionary Council (WMC); Estelle Haskin, editorial secretary of the Board of Missions for the WMC; and Louise Young, chair of the WMC's Committee on Interracial Cooperation. In fact, the first three chairs of the CIC Woman's Division were Methodists, including Jessie Daniel Ames.[38]

1930 marked the beginning of another vital phase of the antilynching campaign, the founding of the Association of Southern Women for the Prevention of Lynching. The ASWPL continued the outreach and programs of the woman's work department of the CIC but focused more energy directly and specifically on the antilynching campaign. By 1930, spurred on by with an increase in lynchings, reform-minded women felt that a group separate from the Woman's Division of the CIC was necessary, one that concentrated solely on the blight of lynching in the South. Many women were angered when Will Alexander, director of the CIC, chose only men for the Commission on the Study of Lynching, which he formed in 1930. Alienated, they organized a conference in Atlanta in November 1930 in order to address the increase in lynchings and to carve out a greater role for themselves.[39] With some financial help from the CIC, Texan Jessie Daniel Ames spearheaded the undertaking and was named executive director of the ASWPL. Unlike the interracial composition of the CIC, the ASWPL was made up of white women only, justified on the premise that white women's advocacy of racial progress would have the greatest influence and impact on racist southern whites. Most of the members were middle class and married with children.[40] The organization grew quickly. By 1935 there were thirty-five thousand members.[41] At its peak, the ASWPL numbered more than forty-three thousand members, with connections to well over two million more clubwomen, making it the "largest and most visible group of white women to work against lynching," and Tennessee women were among them.[42]

There were no dues or bylaws, no charter or constitution for the ASWPL, so technically there were no real *members* nor was it an *organization* in the classic sense of the word, but the terminology was still used. Members included "every woman who associates herself with State Associations" of the ASWPL.[43] In other words, there were no barriers to membership. The group was peopled by mostly urban women who had "evangelical backgrounds."[44] The ASWPL organized by states and each state had a director.[45] The vast majority of the association's women also belonged to other groups and spread the ASWPL message through their wider associations. By estimate, more than two million women were exposed to the ASWPL.[46]

The association's mission was a "repudiation of the idea that lynching was necessary for the protection of Southern womanhood; recognition that lynching undermined the Constitution; and the admission that lynching detracted from the credibility of foreign missionary efforts."[47] At the first official ASWPL meeting in November 1931, held at the Piedmont Hotel in Atlanta, those present included the Tennessee representative to the ASWPL, Mrs. R. L. Harris, and a reformer named Estelle Haskin who had accepted the position as an "at large" representative for Tennessee. Harris was president of the Woman's Missionary Union of the Southern Baptist Church and Haskin served on the Board of Missions for the Methodist Episcopal Church, South. Attendees had been asked to obtain a supportive message from the governor of their own state. In a letter from Estelle Haskin to Jessie Ames, Haskin bemoaned the fact that "our governor aint [*sic*] much good but, of course, his telegram might be."[48] Tennessee governor Henry Horton did indeed send a letter in support,[49] and the group received a great deal of backing from other southern governors—at least on paper. The ASWPL adopted a strongly worded resolution, immediately released to journalists, urging governors, public officials, mothers, teachers, religious leaders, and the press, "to use every power at their disposal to protect from mob anarchy the laws of our country."[50]

To accomplish their objectives, the ASWPL employed a myriad of tactics: "Repetition" of facts concerning the causes of lynching, using studies to show that between 1889 and 1929 only 16.7 percent of lynching victims had been accused of rape and 6.7 percent of attempted rape, in other words, that lynching had nothing to do with saving white women from black men; "Investigation" of lynchings and those involved; "Present[ing] Facts" to people in communities; and "'Agitation'—non-stop—even *before* lynchings happen."[51] ASWPL women lobbied state legislators, governors, and county sheriffs, organized annual conferences, submitted articles and letters to newspapers, and created contact lists and a calling system of women who could be used to confront mobs when necessary.[52] They also continued earlier CIC work of obtaining signatures on antilynching pledges and investigated claims of rape that had precipitated lynchings.[53] During election years they sent a questionnaire to every candidate for governor inquiring as to his position on the issue. Members circulated newspaper clippings, bulletins, and declarations.[54] They sent brochures, flyers, posters, maps, and antilynching "kits" to organizations in their area and

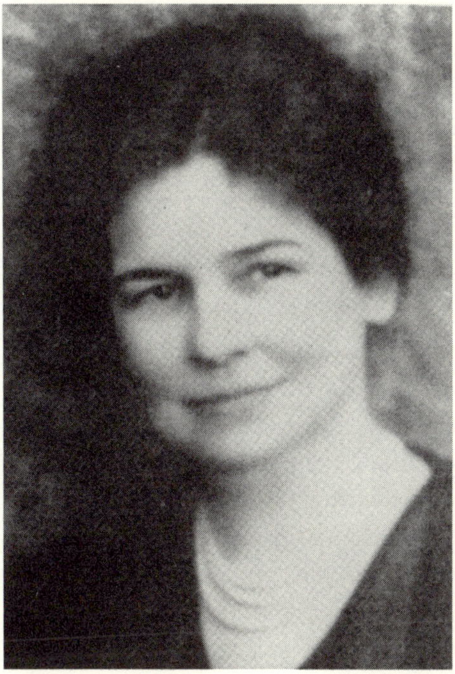

Mrs. R. L. Harris, ASWPL state representative, Tennessee Council, was also active in the Knoxville Woman's Club and president of the Woman's Missionary Union, Southern Baptist Convention, for more than a decade. Courtesy of Mildred L. Iddins Special Collections, Carson-Newman College, Jefferson City, Tennessee.

asked the groups to give the materials to their members.[55] Membership lists for various organizations were gathered and literature was mailed to members on a regular basis.[56]

Women were encouraged to increase their political presence by leveraging their newly won voting power. Mrs. J. W. Mills, president of the Texas Conference of the Woman's Missionary Council of the Methodist Episcopal Church, South, sent a letter to other missionary societies urging them to become "intelligent voters."[57] The ASWPL was highly organized, with frequent conferences and meetings and thousands of communications between members. A "Plan of Action," "Technique for Carrying on the Work," and "Suggested Points in Presenting [the] Purpose of [the] ASWPL" were typed and circulated to all of the state councils for distribution.[58] Progress was measured at least every year, at times more often, by gathering statistics from the states.

Organizers had agreed that the state councils would follow the plan created by the Mississippi council. An executive director, a central council of ten women, and a smaller executive committee were supported by the thirteen state councils. In practice the ASWPL was simply an umbrella of sorts. Organizers believed it would be far more efficient to use organizational structures already in place.[59] Each of the state councils was to be made up of women who were leaders in the various state organizations that had aligned themselves with the ASWPL. The women were encouraged to present information about the ASWPL and its progress at each of the affiliate organizations' yearly conventions and regular meetings.[60]

Organizing the Tennessee chapter of the ASWPL proved challenging at times as the women made a concerted effort to fashion a diverse group, a practice adopted by most of the states. Countless committees, commissions, and other groups were represented. By July 1931 Mrs. F. C. Paschal was made chairman of the Tennessee chapter of ASWPL, replacing interim chair, Louise Young, but there were still vacancies to be filled.[61]

In 1933 Jessie Ames invited a number of leading Tennessee women to attend an executive meeting in Nashville in order to organize the state council: "The ASWPL has completed its permanent State Council organization in each one of the thirteen Southern States except Tennessee. This has not been because of any lack of interest in the women, but because the pressure of other states, where lynchings were so much more probable, required all the time and energy available in the first two months of this year."[62] Leadership in the Tennessee chapter changed frequently, usually because the primary woman in leadership found herself overwhelmed by other committee work or problems at home.[64] The turnover, however, was in some ways positive, as it served to expose more people to the ASWPL message.

Accidents, family crises, deaths, and illnesses proved challenging to many of the women. Chattanooga's Julia Collier Harris, writer and wife of newspaper publisher Julian Harris, had to decrease her work with the organization when she was ill for more than sixteen months. She had suffered a "heart seizure and nervous breakdown" and when released from the hospital remained in a wheelchair for some time.[65] Mrs. K. W. Warden apologized to Ames for missing a deadline: "Having had much serious illness in my family and two deaths during the late summer months, I have not been able to do the intensive work that I had expected to do."[65] Frances Spahr wrote Ames to share some happy news. She would have to miss an upcoming meeting, and "here's the big reason," she wrote. "About the first of March I expect a son (or daughter) and since I've had trouble in the past Dr. Acuff thinks I'd better not risk the trip at this stage of the game." The Spahrs had "hungered for another child for six years and the doctors said there would be no more—[so] I'm willing to forgo any pleasure."[66] "Mrs. John R. Wheeler had family obligations too: "I really would like to attend your conference . . . but I have so many engagements ahead that I cannot leave home another day, and also a good husband that I must consider as I have an engagement with him on that day."[67] Mrs. Warden was out of town for over a month taking care of her seriously ill mother. Kate Trawick had been engaged in field work for a month.[68] Trawick had other problems related to her position with the Department of Health in Nashville. In 1935 Ames wrote Trawick and asked her to serve as state chairman for the ASWPL. After repeated meetings with the administration, Trawick declined; her job had asked her to cut back on her outside activities due to an anticipated heavy work load over the next twelve months.[69]

Occasionally someone just didn't work out, as in the case of Mrs. P. B. Lowrance, a reformer with an outstanding reputation and track record who found herself growing increasingly unpopular with Ames and others. Tensions began in July 1934, when Lowrance wrote Ames to apologize for missing a deadline. She had been on vacation for several weeks, and when she returned her "mail had piled up in piles." In August Kate Davis (South Carolina ASWPL) wrote Ames to update her on her state ASWPL's progress and included what appears to be a non sequitur, although she and Ames may have discussed the issue before: "At Ridge Crest I presented Interracial work at several of the conferences. Everyone is disgusted with Mrs. P. B. Laurence's [*sic*] lack of interest. We had 909 women at Ridge Crest Camp and we expected about 400." Nothing more is discussed during the rest of the letter. In October a letter from Ames to Davis contained another rather cryptic reference to tension between Lowrance and others: "I do wish that Mrs. Lowrance were more active, for the Baptist women are now ready to take more than they are getting. What you write about

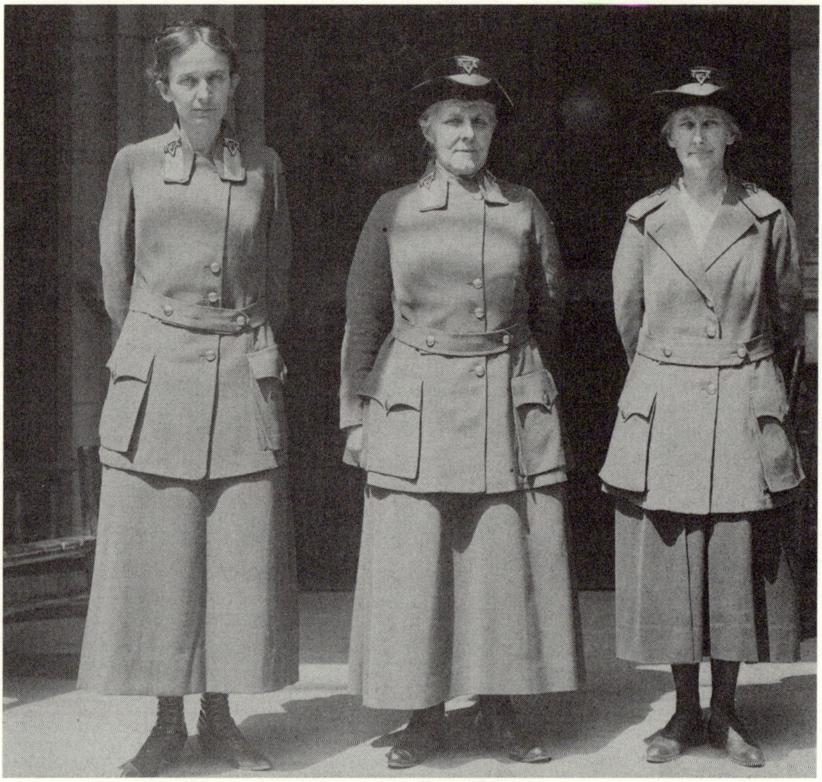

Kate Herndon Trawick (*left*) during World War I in a YWCA uniform. The YWCA was one of many organizations and efforts in which Trawick participated, most notably her dedication to antilynching. Courtesy of the Tennessee State Library and Archives, Nashville.

Ridgecrest is one proof of my statement." In a letter from Ames to Mrs. Robert O'Neal, Ames referred to Lowrance as "so inactive that I am afraid [a] letter would be buried on her desk and no attention paid to it." Two months later Ames received a letter of resignation from Lowrance, who explained that she was "overburdened with difficult activities and [she] realize[d] that I am not the right person for Chairman for Tennessee."[70]

Some women expressed doubt that they could be of any real assistance or that they would be able to make a real difference. Louise Young, West Tennessee's ASWPL representative member from the Woman's Missionary Council of the Methodist Episcopal Church, South, and a teacher at Scarritt College, was one of these women. At an antilynching conference, she "testified" to the power of the Social Gospel message communicated by ASWPL leaders: "While lynching is a terrible thing, it [had] seemed to me to be a thing about which I could do nothing. I should like to express my gratitude to the Commission for convincing me that there is something I can do."[71] Ames herself frequently struggled. In a letter to an ASWPL member she wrote, "You cannot realize what it means to have you assume some of the responsibility of this job that is growing heavier all the time but none the less fascinating." Heavy travel, a daughter with polio, and an invalid mother proved challenging to Ames.[72]

Regardless, Jessie Daniel Ames was always reassuring and supportive; she buttressed the work of the Tennessee ASWPL and provided encouragement. As national ASWPL executive director, Ames made frequent trips to Tennessee to strategize with Tennessee members and leaders and to attend meetings and deliver speeches.[73] She made five trips to the state during the first seven months of 1931, for example.[74]

In ASWPL records there are countless requests for pamphlets and other material from Tennessee members. Tens of thousands of pamphlets were distributed throughout the South by ASWPL members and affiliates, and Tennessee women did their part by circulating more than eight thousand pieces of literature in one year alone.[75] Antilynching kits were also disseminated, not just to organizations but also to thirty-nine libraries, the majority of which were in colleges and high schools.[76] There were five different kits available by 1936: "Appreciation and Understanding"; "Racial Handicaps"; "General Information," including "Recent Trends in Race Relations" and "Realistic Approaches to the Race Problem"; "What Church Women are Doing in Race Relations"; and "Lynching and Christian Citizenship."[77]

Other groups affiliated with the ASWPL did not technically fall under the auspices of the ASWPL itself. Member organizations still operated within their own systems and for their own purposes, but they simply agreed to spread the message of the heinous nature of lynching and to engage women in active support for the cause in their home communities. At the 1935 ASWPL meeting, the relationship between the ASWPL and its constituent groups was clearly stated: "We represent a great many organizations here. Each one of those organizations is at liberty to act as it desires. We simply are a council."[78] Una Roberts Lawrence, mission study editor at the Home Mission Board, Southern Baptist Convention, echoed the sentiment that the "council left every one free to pursue any program or method" appropriate for her own group; "the PTA can do something that the Baptists Convention cannot do," for example.[79]

In the 1940s, at the peak of the reform influence exerted by ASWPL, 109 organizations across the country and throughout the South had officially endorsed the work of the ASWPL,[80] including the Woman's Missionary Council, Methodist Episcopal Church, South (and the Woman's Missionary Society of both Memphis and Tennessee); the Executive Board of the Woman's Auxiliary to the National Council of the Protestant Episcopal Church; the Southern Interstate Conference of the National Council of Jewish Women; the National Council of Jewish Women; the national YWCA; the Woman's Missionary Union of the Southern Baptist Convention; the Business Girls Conference, the YWCA and Camp Nakanawa, in Tennessee; the Methodist Leadership School at Junaluska, North Carolina; and the Methodist Leadership School at Sequoyah, Arkansas.[81] Even more organizations promised to adopt a "Program of Education to Prevent Lynching." Those groups included numerous Parent Teacher Associations; the United Daughters of the Confederacy; the Daughters of the American Revolution; the American Association of University Women; Rotary Clubs; the National Federation of Business and Professional Women's Clubs; the Committee on Woman's Work of the Presbyterian Church in the United States; Woman's Missionary Organizations, Presbyterian Church USA (Synodical Society for Missions, Tennessee); the Woman's Auxiliary to the National Council in the Province of Sewanee, Protestant Episcopal Church, in seven dioceses; the Fifty-first Triennial, General Convention of the Protestant Episcopal Church, 1934; the National Federation of Temple Sisterhoods; Woman's Missionary Societies, Methodist Episcopal Church, South, including two Tennessee conferences; the Methodist Episcopal Church, South; the Disciples of Christ, including Tennessee Women's Christian Missionary Society; the General Federation of Women's Clubs, including the Tennessee branch;

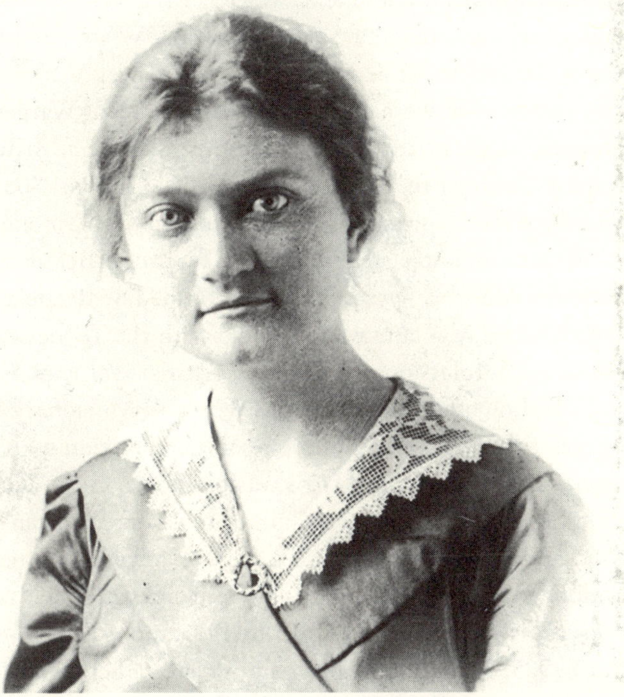

Writer and reformer Una Roberts Lawrence, treasurer and executive committee member of the ASWPL in Missouri and Tennessee, and Home Mission Board editor for the Woman's Missionary Union, Southern Baptist Convention. Courtesy of Una Roberts Lawrence Collection, Southern Baptist Historical Library and Archives, Nashville, Tennessee.

and the Woman's Missionary Union of nine state Baptist conventions, including Tennessee.[82]

A partial listing of ASWPL leaders illustrates the interconnected nature of the organizations. The Woman's Missionary Council, Methodist Episcopal Church, South, was, at various times, represented by Belle H. Bennett, president; Louise Young, chairman, Interracial Cooperation, WMC; and Mrs. J. W. Perry, chairman, Rural Development, WMC. Louise Young also served on both the national and local boards of the YWCA, taught at both Paine College and the Hampton Institute, and taught at Scarritt College in Nashville, as did Miss Mabel Howell, another chairman, Rural Development, WMC. Mrs. W. A. Newell was superintendent of the Bureau of Social Relations, WMC, and superintendent of the WMC itself, while Mrs. J. W. Downs was WMC Home Department's secretary of woman's work. Gladys (K. W.) Warden served as superintendent of Christian social relations, Woman's Missionary Society, Memphis Conference, Methodist Episcopal Church, South. The superintendent of the Tennessee Conference of the WMC at one time was Mrs. E. U. Robinson, and Estelle Haskin chaired the Board of Missions and became the editor of *World Outlook,* published by the board.[83]

Mrs. G. G. McClure was affiliated with the Tennessee Federation of Business and Professional Women's Clubs, as was Mrs. Robert O'Neal. Mrs. P. B. Lowrance served on the Woman's Missionary Union, Southern Baptist Conference, Committee on Cooperation with Negro Baptist Women, while Mrs. R. L. Harris was president of the Woman's Missionary Union, Southern Baptist Church, for more than ten years and also chaired and served on committees of the Knoxville Woman's Club. Kate Herndon (Arch) Trawick was closely affiliated with the Nashville YWCA; she served as president from 1913 to 1916 and as general secretary from 1915 to 1925. Trawick was also an associate in School Health Education for the Tennessee Department of Public Health, on the Fisk University Board of Directors, and vice president of the Woman's Missionary Council, Methodist Episcopal Church, South. Mrs. Neal B. Spahr was a member of Knoxville's Ossoli Circle. Mrs. C. V. Biddle was president of the Women's Christian Temperance Union in Knoxville.[84]

Although men were certainly active in the movement, totals of antilynching pledge signatures highlight the influence of women.[85] By 1936, 35,468 women had signed a pledge against lynching; only 1,799 men had done so.[86] Overall, by 1939, national ASWPL women had managed to obtain the signatures of 1,229 law enforcement officers in fifteen states. The previous year, officers had prevented more than forty lynchings, "saving three white men, forty-nine Negro men and a Negro woman from mobs. In each of these officially recorded cases, the Association of Southern Women for the Prevention of Lynching was on the job, not up front in a dramatic, headline way, but quietly functioning where action counted."[87]

By July 1940 Tennessee women had gathered signatures in seventy-one counties and 208 towns. At that point, 4,071 women and 265 men had signed pledges in Tennessee against lynching. In 1942 Frances Spahr sent in five hundred signatures but was unhappy with her accomplishment: "The women haven't kept up the work as I hoped they would. Very few sheriff signatures have come in. Why do we have to keep after intelligent women. As I write I realize I'm one of the worst offenders."[88]

Tennessee women were most proud of the number of pledges they obtained from law enforcement: 228 by that time.[89] Signatures were obtained by going door to door, via friends and acquaintances, and most often at meetings of other organizations. For example, within a few months' time in Tennessee, antilynching advocates collected signatures at the district conference of the Woman's Missionary Society; meetings of the Woman's Missionary Society, Methodist Episcopal Church, South, in Memphis; "auxiliaries" in the Memphis Conference (members took pledge cards with them to their local sheriffs); the Thompson Station Auxiliary of the Woman's Missionary Society of the Southern Methodist Church; Spring Hill Missionary Society zone meetings; the New Bethel Woman's Missionary Society; the Union Avenue Methodist Church in Memphis; the Murfreesboro District of the Tennessee Conference of the Missionary Society, Methodist Church, Shelbyville; and the Trinity Adult Missionary Society.[90]

Activists worked in an environment often charged with hostility and violence. Louise Young remembered that when she left to go teach in an all-black school, "most of my friends and family just threw up their hands. This was in 1919, this was really a disgraceful thing to do. One young man told me he would rather see me in the penitentiary, he'd rather see me in prisoner's garb than to see me go down there. That's how deeply people felt about it."[91]

Jessie Daniel Ames, executive director of the ASWPL, confirmed that when members began to investigate the details and circumstances of how lynchings had taken place, they encountered more than a little resentment: "Fifteen of us visited towns in which lynchings had been committed. . . . Interviews with preachers disclosed most devastatingly the position of local congregations toward mob violence. Fractious as well as complacent sheriffs and editors were visited. Leading women set forth their attitudes which for the most part were frankly, if confidentially, condemnatory. In one instance we were positive that we were talking to the leaders of a recent lynching."[92]

The disturbing and frightening experiences of the AWSPL women quickly taught them that when addressing an audience for the first time, particular attention had to be paid to their own safety. They learned that large public talks against lynching could be counterproductive. Rather, direct one-on-one personal contacts with key individuals within communities generated better results, allowing their message to be passed along from person to person and woman to woman within any community; this process became "the only safe procedure."[93] In a *Holland's Magazine* editorial, the bravery of the activist women was detailed and celebrated:

> These dauntless women have gone, times without number, to peace officers in charge of prisoners who might become lynch victims, and pleaded for preventive action. They have gone into situations so tense that few men would dare intrude. They have faced threats of all kinds from truculent individuals and even organizations in the South. They have been ridiculed. They have been ordered by municipal officials not to speak. They have gone into community after community, where lynchings had occurred, and patiently and fearlessly searched out the facts of the case for their records. And in every case, they worked, not through a woman from the central office of the Association, but through their local member or members.[94]

Ames pointed out that "women who sought to have officers protect their prisoners from mob violence at any cost found themselves in receipt of anonymous letters conveying nauseating threats in slimy words."[95] Threats were so severe that Ames knew of "women who wouldn't tell their husbands of the threats because they feared their families would insist that the women quit the work."[96] Violence against others who made their antilynching attitudes known must have frightened the women even more. For example, Mrs. Robert O'Neal related that vengeful and racist arsonists torched the house of a local minister in Shelbyville, Tennessee, who advocated against mob rule and lynching.[97]

When a lynching did occur, ASWPL women went into action, gathering information and newspaper accounts, interviewing people involved, contacting the press and other affiliated groups, and writing the authorities. For example, following the 1933 lynching of Cordie Cheek, a young man who was taken from a Nashville jail and killed in Maury County, Tennessee, ASWPL women sent a letter to then Governor Hill McAlister, with copies to the press and other state authorities:

> Honorable Sir:
>
> Nashville is humiliated and indignant because of the double crime committed in the case of the seventeen year old negro boy, Cordie Cheek, who was kidnapped and killed by a mob of lawless men.
>
> The citizens of Nashville have a right to demand that technicalities shall not bar the prompt investigation and the bringing to account of those who took part in the crime which was not committed against a single citizen but against the city of Nashville and the great state of Tennessee.
>
> We commend Sheriff Bauman for all effort made to investigate this unpardonable offense, but urge him to continue to make every effort possible to apprehend and bring to justice those who have brought shame and reproach upon our State and country.
>
> We, the undersigned, implore the Governor of Tennessee to take vigorous action and, if necessary, offer reward for the apprehension and conviction of these criminals.[98]

In the decade between 1922 and 1932 there were 8 lynchings in Tennessee. The total for the entire United States during that period was 232.[99] The ASWPL proudly issued numerous bulletins detailing prevented lynchings in the South. In 1930 there were three prevented lynchings in Tennessee: in Bolivar, Union City, and Lawrenceburg. All three involved black men charged with rape. In 1931 there was one lynching in the state, in Union City: "George Smith, Negro, 20, was hanged in the courthouse jail by a mob of several hundred people at 2:30 P.M. He was accused of attempted criminal assault on a young white girl." However, during that same year, between two and four lynchings in Tennessee were prevented.[100] In one of those cases the ASWPL was pleased and excited to report that a woman in Tennessee, the aforementioned Mrs. J. C. Butler, had physically prevailed against the "fury of the mob" and personally intervened to prevent a lynching. The story of Butler, and how she held a lynch mob at bay with a rifle, telling the violent crowd that "they couldn't put anything like that over on her," spread throughout the South. Newspapers in Atlanta, Tennessee, and as far away as New York highlighted the brave Tennessee woman.[101]

These successes did not go unnoticed. Tennessee governor Henry H. Horton sent a message to Mrs. F. C. Paschal, chairman of the Tennessee ASWPL in 1931:

> I have noticed with interest the efforts of Southern Women to prevent lynchings in the Southern States, and wish to offer my congratulations especially to the group of Tennessee women of which you are Chairman. It is a matter of gratitude that in 1930 there was not a lynching in Tennessee. Several attempted lynchings have been prevented by the heroic actions of individuals, such as that of the wife of the Sheriff at Huntingdon during this year [Butler]. That all offenders in this State should be given the opportunity of trial is a matter of deep concern to me as Chief Executive, as well as to all right-thinking people, and I therefore congratulate you and your Association upon your efforts in this direction.[102]

In 1932 two women escaped lynching in a single incident in Lebanon, Tennessee. Jessie Daniel Ames wrote Mrs. Robert O'Neal; Ames's excitement is apparent in her letter: "Yesterday's *Constitution* carried a story which, if true, we have been longing for in the Association of Southern Women for the Prevention of Lynching. At Lebanon there was an attempted lynching of two Negro women, which was prevented, according to the news story, when the 'Chief of Police Robert Gan pushed his way through and, aided by pleas of a number of women and some men, succeeded in obtaining release of the women and returned them to jail.'"[103]

In 1933 there were two lynchings in Tennessee, one of them the Cordie Cheek murder in Columbia.[104] The following year was a mixed one for those fighting lynching in state; although the ASWPL reported six prevented lynchings in Tennessee, there was one that was carried out.[105] In Manchester, in June of that year, Richard Wilkerson, a black man accused of "striking a white man" was "ambushed by a mob of eight and shot . . . stripped of his clothing, and beaten on the head with an axe."[106]

One of the prevented lynchings, however, gave the association more than one reason to celebrate. In November 1934, a twenty-two-year-old black man was arrested in Shelbyville, Bedford County, in Middle Tennessee, for assaulting a young white girl. A mob began to form, so the officers transported the prisoner to Murfreesboro in neighboring Rutherford County. When a mob became enraged there as well, the officers then took the arrested man to a jail in Davidson County for greater safety. An editorial in the *Tennessean* commended the officers involved.[107] Mrs. Morton King of Shelbyville sent a copy of the editorial to Mrs. Robert O'Neal in Clarksville, along with a letter detailing some exciting news for the association: "Just about two weeks ago, this [Bedford County] sheriff and his deputies signed . . . the declaration which you gave me while in Nashville and I can't help but feel that it had some influence in their way of managing this affair. There was a mob of several hundred gathering here when he took the prisoner away and was able to keep him safe. So maybe our efforts are worth something after all."[108] Ames wrote that although "the women do not assume that if these signatures had not been secured there would have been a lynching, they do believe that an articulate public opinion, as expressed in their activities, help[ed] to strengthen the purpose of [the] officers."[109] Some of the thrill and sense of accomplishment was dampened, though, when violence broke out in Shelbyville and the National Guard had to be sent in to quell it. Although the prisoner was protected from being lynched, three members of the mob were killed and twenty others wounded. The courthouse was also destroyed by fire.[110]

The women immediately began a letter-writing campaign to thank those involved in keeping the prisoner safe even though doing so interrupted their Christmas activities. They wrote to Sheriff T. E. Gant, Deputy Sheriff J. E. Gant, Constable Olie Watson, and Governor McAlister. Ames also urged the women to write to Mrs. Morton King, the woman who had obtained the signatures in the first place, "because it is quite probable that she may also be under fire." Multiple letters were sent, and they were signed by many women.[111]

Louise Young wrote an especially articulate and moving letter to Governor McAlister on that Christmas Day, despite the holiday and the fact that she was confined to her bed with a heart condition. She thanked the governor for his support and brought up an issue of special importance to her and others: "I am especially mindful of the impression that this incident will make on the minds of the young people of our State. When mob rule prevails the incident becomes a part of local history and young children have their imaginations stirred to think that some day they too may participate in similar acts of violence with the approval of their community and without the punishment of law. Similarly, a mob thwarted and, if it may be, members of the mob brought to trial furnish an unforgettable lesson of the majesty of the law and of its orderly processes."[112]

In 1935 Methodist Woman's Missionary Council superintendent Mrs. W. A. Newell sent a report to all of the auxiliary superintendents of Christian social relations. In the letter she urged women to keep fighting, reminding them that ASWPL members still had much to accomplish toward educating the general public on the evils of lynching. She related that there had been fourteen lynchings in 1934 but that, positively, fifty-five lynchings had been stopped that year, due to the leadership, perseverance, outreach, and moral high ground of the women's work.[113]

A Mrs. Greer told a very compelling story at an ASWPL conference about one of those 1934 prevented lynchings, in Cleveland, Tennessee, in Bradley County:

> Every bit of that was the result of one of our women. She went immediately to the sheriff. She was a prominent woman. She went to him and said, "This is a terrible thing. You know me and I know you. I want every step of this to be legal." He knew she had influence, the women were with her. He listened to her and everything was legal. That Negro . . . killed three or four people and yet he was not lynched. I believe every bit of it was due to the woman who had signed this little card . . . [and] if more of our women had the courage, a lot of these lynchings would be prevented.[114]

At the same ASPWL meeting, the number of prevented lynchings for 1935 in the South was proudly unveiled: eighty-nine, more than four times the number of executed lynchings that year.[115] In Tennessee there were four men who were saved from the mob: two in Johnson City, one in Henning, and one in Shelbyville. However, in November 1935, in White Bluff, Dickson County, in Middle Tennessee, Baxter Bell, a black man who had been arrested for allegedly striking a white woman, was forcibly taken from officers by the woman's husband and four other relatives. His body was discovered half an hour later with a bullet through the chest. The men involved were later acquitted.[116]

From January to June 1936, another thirty-eight lynchings were prevented in the South, as seven white men, thirty-one black men, and eight black women were protected.[117] Tennessee's record for 1936 was two people saved from lynchings, including a black man who had attacked a white woman with an axe.[118] The year 1937 saw another lynching in Tennessee, one of eight in the South that year. It occurred in Covington, Tipton County, West Tennessee. A black man who had allegedly killed an officer was "taken from the Sheriff, W. J. Vaughan, who was returning him from Memphis" for trial in Covington. However, in Coffee County in Middle Tennessee, a black man was saved from lynching.[119] The following year two more black men were protected from the hands of lynch mobs, one in Cleveland and the other in Gallatin.[120] In 1939 an eighteen-year-old boy, race not mentioned, was saved from lynching in Nashville.[121] Ames wrote Mrs. McClure in Clarksville that a "nice personal letter of commendation to the sheriff might be one of those instances of a pebble thrown into a pond, and so on. It might prevent a lynching during the next six months."[122]

By 1940 there was a vast reduction in the number of lynchings that occurred annually, although two of the five in 1940 were in Tennessee. In June, after a black man named Elbert Williams attempted to vote, his body was discovered in the Hatchie River in West Tennessee. Two months later another black man, Roosevelt Jones, was shot numerous times by a posse in Dyersburg, also in West Tennessee. Some organizations hesitated to list this incident as a lynching, but it was present in ASWPL records.[123]

Although there were five lynchings in 1940, from that point onward there were no more "double digit years."[124] In 1940 an editorial in the *Chattanooga Times* lauded the decrease in lynchings and argued that in "very large part the credit goes to the women of the South."[125] The ASWPL then had "40,000 members . . . backed by 2,000,000 more women who belong to religious, civic and social groups. Combined, they are perhaps the most powerful of the elements that have lighted the way to an end of this crime against a race of people."[126] Ames set the numbers even higher. She argued that by 1937 "we have aligned with us in our program eighty-one state, sectional and national groups with an estimated Southern membership of over four million."[127] The 1940 editorial in *Holland's Magazine* lauded the "amazing effectiveness of organized womanhood." Specifically, since the ASWPL was founded a decade prior, "the Association has quietly proved again the might of concerted womanhood. The annual average of lynchings in the South from 1922 to 1930 was 25.5. The annual average during the nine years since the Association was organized is exactly 12."[128]

The work of groups associated with the ASWPL slowed and then, in 1942, ceased altogether as the need for them decreased. Another landmark was achieved in 1952, the first year without any lynchings in the United States.[129]

While the antilynching movement failed to obtain federal legislation against lynching, it did force Americans, particularly in the South, to face the problem and see it for what it was—a means of oppression, not punishment for rapists.[130] The women who worked to stop lynching educated the public, alerted Americans to the problem, and helped reduce both the numbers of lynchings and then lynching itself. In fact, the women who fought lynching never backed any federal antilynching legislation, believing that "the slow process of educating society to recognize and abhor the evils out of which lynchings grow is the only sure way to stop lynching."[131] Another reason was, as Ames explained, the fear that "there were some women, particularly in the churches, who are opposed to what would seem to be politics. We would lose almost at once the possible support of the Southern Baptist women, we would lose instantly the support of the Southern Presbyterian women, we would lose the support of the Episcopalian women. We [w]anted it to be interdenominational."[132]

John Shelton Reed studied lynching statistics in areas in which the association was active and those in which it was not. He found that, unequivocally, in counties where the ASWPL engaged and proactively operated, the work of the association's women measurably decreased lynching in those communities.[133] The Tennessee women of conviction who stood up for due process and access to an equitable system of law for all citizens effected legal, behavioral, and attitudinal changes across the state, altering processes within the criminal justice system and having an impact on people, perceptions, and values.

Southern white women, including women from Tennessee, changed their society for the better. Their work is a testament to the power of reform and the passion of the reformers. Perhaps James E. Clarke, Tennessee's state chairman of the Commission on Interracial Cooperation, said it best at the ceremony honoring Mrs. J. C. Butler: "The little woman in the doorway had won a victory, and the majesty of the law prevailed."[134]

NOTES

The opening epigraph refers to the *Atlanta Constitution,* Apr. 19, 1931, Association of Southern Women for the Prevention of Lynching Papers, 1930–1942 (hereafter cited as ASWPL Papers) (Ann Arbor: University Microfilms International, 1983), Reel 3.

1. The phrase "fury of the mob" in the title was already in common usage by 1904; see Clarence Poe, "Lynching: A Southern View," *Atlantic Monthly* 93 (Feb. 1904): 160. Butler's first name is unknown; all references to her refer to her as "Mrs. J.C. Butler." The women antilynching activists researched, except those who were single, rarely used their first names in correspondence or in reference to others. I have identified as many women's own names as possible from other sources.

2. "One Woman and a Mob, July 1932," Reel 4, ASWPL Papers.

3. See Sonya Ramsey's chapter, this volume.

4. Mary Jane Brown, "Eradicating This Evil: Women in the American Anti-Lynching Movement 1892–1940," in *Studies in African American History and Culture,* ed. Graham Russell Hodges (New York: Garland, 2000), 3.

5. Carroll Van West, ed., *The Tennessee Encyclopedia of History and Culture* (Nashville: Rutledge Hill Press, 1998), 560; Margaret Vandiver, *Lethal Punishment: Lynchings and Legal Executions in the South* (New Brunswick: Rutgers Univ. Press, 2006), 20.

6. West, *Tennessee Encyclopedia,* 560.

7. Ibid., 561; Philip Dray, *At the Hands of Persons Unknown: The Lynching of Black America* (New York: Random House, 2002), 262; Christopher Waldrep, ed., *Lynching in America: A History in Documents* (New York: New York Univ. Press, 2006), 135–36.

8. *Southern Women Look at Lynching* (Atlanta: Association of Southern Women for the Prevention of Lynching, Feb. 1937), 7; "These Women and Lynching," *Holland's Magazine,* Feb. 1940, 2.

9. Brown, "Eradicating This Evil," 74; John Patrick McDowell, *The Social Gospel in the South: The Woman's Home Mission Movement in the Methodist Episcopal Church, South, 1886–1939* (Baton Rouge: Louisiana State Univ. Press, 1982), 2.

10. Brown, "Eradicating This Evil," 75.

11. Waldrep, *Lynching in America*, 183.

12. Donald L. Grant, *The Anti-Lynching Movement: 1883–1932* (San Francisco: R and E Research Associates, 1975), 57.

13. Ibid., 56.

14. McDowell, *Social Gospel in the South*, 34–35.

15. Anne Firor Scott, *Natural Allies: Women's Associations in American History* (Urbana: Univ. of Illinois Press, 1991), 85.

16. Ibid.; Anne Firor Scott, *The Southern Lady: From Pedestal to Politics, 1830–1930* (Chicago: Univ. of Chicago Press, 1970), 152–55, 160.

17. Herman A. Norton, *Religion in Tennessee, 1777–1945* (Knoxville: Univ. of Tennessee Press, with the Tennessee Historical Commission, 1981), 86.

18. McDowell, *Social Gospel in the South*, 8.

19. For more on Belle Harris Bennett, see Janice M. Leone's chapter, this volume.

20. Jacquelyn Dowd Hall, *Revolt Against Chivalry: Jessie Daniel Ames and the Women's Campaign Against Lynching* (New York: Columbia Univ. Press, 1979), 68.

21. Ibid., 68.

22. McDowell, *Social Gospel in the South*, 121.

23. Hall, *Revolt Against Chivalry*, 71.

24. Scott, *Natural Allies*, 92.

25. McDowell, *Social Gospel in the South*, 94.

26. "Lynchings in Tennessee, 1882–1900," Reel 3, ASWPL Papers; "Lynchings Committed in 1935," Reel 2, ASWPL Papers.

27. Rosalyn Terborg-Penn, "African-American Women's Networks in the Anti-Lynching Crusade," in *Gender, Class, Race, and Reform in the Progressive Era*, ed. Noralee Frankel and Nancy S. Dye (Lexington: Univ. Press of Kentucky, 1991), 150–51.

28. Scott, *Natural Allies*, 168.

29. Terborg-Penn, "African-American Women's Networks," 157.

30. McDowell, *Social Gospel in the South*, 84–85; Dorothy Schneider and Carl J. Schneider, *American Women in the Progressive Era, 1900–1920* (New York: Facts on File, 1993), 131.

31. Grant, *Anti-Lynching Movement*, 131.

32. Patricia A. Schechter, *Ida B. Wells-Barnett and American Reform, 1880–1930* (Chapel Hill: Univ. of North Carolina Press, 2001), 166.

33. Vandiver, *Lethal Punishment*, 174.

34. Commission on Interracial Cooperation, "Southern Women and Race Cooperation: A Story of the Memphis Conference, October Sixth and Seventh, Nineteen

Hundred and Twenty," 1921, Documenting the American South, http://docsouth.unc.edu/nc/racecoop/racecoop.html/.

35. Ibid.; Hall, *Revolt Against Chivalry,* 90.

36. Commission on Interracial Cooperation, "Southern Women and Race Cooperation," 157.

37. Terborg-Penn, "African-American Women's Networks," 157.

38. McDowell, *Social Gospel in the South,* 91; "Miss Belle Bennett," 4–5, Reel 5, ASWPL Papers.

39. Henry E. Barber, "The Association of Southern Women for the Prevention of Lynching, 1930–1942," *Phylon* 34, no. 4 (1973): 379.

40. Hall, *Revolt Against Chivalry,* 180, 182, 185, 186.

41. Grant, *Anti-Lynching Movement,* 137; McDowell, *Social Gospel in the South,* 95; Scott, *Southern Lady,* 196; Dray, *At the Hands of Persons Unknown,* 329.

42. Scott, *Southern Lady,* 198; Brown, "Eradicating This Evil," 12; Barber, "Association of Southern Women," 382.

43. "Technique for Carrying on the Work," Reel 4, ASWPL Papers; Barber, "Association of Southern Women," 380.

44. Brown, "Eradicating This Evil," 12.

45. Dray, *At the Hands of Persons Unknown,* 330.

46. Grant, *Anti-Lynching Movement,* 137.

47. Ibid., 138.

48. Miss Estelle Haskin to Jessie Daniel Ames, Nov. 11–12, 1931, Reel 1, ASWPL Papers. Haskin's negative comment about the governor refers to Governor Henry Horton, who was under attack for corruption at the time, including for his alleged role in a banking scandal, and in 1931 the Tennessee House came close to impeaching him, in a vote of 58 to 41; see Jeanette Keith, "Henry Horton," *Tennessee Encyclopedia of History and Culture,* http://tennesseeencyclopedia.net/imagegallery.php?EntryID=H072/ (accessed 28 July 2009).

49. "Messages from Governors to ASWPL—November 1931—Letter from Governor Henry H. Horton to Mrs. F. C. Paschal, Chairman, Tennessee Association of Women for the Prevention of Lynching, Nashville, Tennessee," Nov. 16, 1931, Reel 1, ASWPL Papers.

50. *Atlanta Constitution,* Nov. 22, 1931, Reel 1, ASWPL Papers; "Minutes, Central Council," Reel 4, ASWPL Papers; Miss Estelle Haskin to Jessie Daniel Ames, Nov. 11–12, 1931, Reel 1, ASWPL Papers.

51. "Minutes, ASWPL meeting, Monday morning," Jan. 13, 1936, 3, Reel 4, ASWPL Papers; Barber, "Association of Southern Women," 378.

52. Grant, *Anti-Lynching Movement,* 138; Jessie Daniel Ames to "Council Members," July 5, 1934, Reel 1, ASWPL Papers.

53. Dray, *At the Hands of Persons Unknown,* 330; "Plan of Action in a Movement of Southern White Women to Eradicate Lynching in the South," Reel 4, ASWPL Papers.

54. Bessie O'Neal to Jessie Daniel Ames, Feb. 20, 1935, Reel 1, ASWPL Papers; Jessie Daniel Ames, "Southern Women and Lynching," reprint from *Crime Survey* 1 (Apr. 1935): 2.

55. Jessie Daniel Ames to "All Southern Christian Social Relations Chairs," Apr. 14, 1936, Reel 1, ASWPL Papers.

56. Jessie Daniel Ames to Mrs. Helen M. Bourne, Nashville Board of Missions, Methodist Episcopal Church, South, Nashville, July 13, 1936, Reel 1, ASWPL Papers.

57. Mrs. J. W. Mills to "My dear Friends," Jan. 10, 1936, Reel 7, ASWPL Papers.

58. "Plan of Action in a Movement of Southern White Women to Eradicate Lynching"; "Suggested Points in Presenting Purpose of A.S.W.P.L.," Reel 4, ASWPL Papers; "Technique for Carrying on the Work."

59. Ames, "Southern Women and Lynching," 1; Barber, "Association of Southern Women," 380.

60. Jessie Daniel Ames to State Councils, Mar. 16, 1933, Reel 1, ASWPL Papers.

61. "Association of Women of the South for the Prevention of Lynching," July 15, 1931, Reel 4, ASWPL Papers; "Association of SWPL," Jan.–Nov. 15, 1931, 5, Reel 5, ASWPL Papers.

62. Jessie Daniel Ames to: Mrs. R. L. Harris, Knoxville; Mrs. Robert O'Neal, Clarksville; Mrs. Neal Spahr, Knoxville; Miss Louise Young, Nashville; Mrs. P. B. Lowrance, Chattanooga; Mrs. J. R. Wheeler, Nashville; Mrs. Zetta Paro, Paducah, Kentucky; Mrs. Arch Trawick, Nashville; Miss Estelle Haskin, Nashville; Mrs. J. W. Downs, Nashville, Mar. 9, 1933, all in Reel 1, ASWPL Papers.

63. The following women served as Tennessee state representatives to the ASWPL Central Council at various times: Mrs. Robert O'Neal, Clarksville; Mrs. Charles E. Maddry, Nashville; Mrs. P. B. Lowrance, Chattanooga; Mrs. R. L. Harris, Knoxville; Mrs. Neal Spahr, Knoxville; Miss Louise Young, Nashville; Miss Estelle Haskin, Nashville; Mrs. C. V. Biddle, Knoxville; Mrs. K. W. Warden, Memphis; Mrs. Carl McRae, Camden; Mrs. Julia Collier Harris, Chattanooga; Mrs. E. U. Robinson, Old Hickory; Mrs. E. W. Warden, Memphis; Mrs. S. W. Duggan, Knoxville; Mrs. D. W. Proffitt, Maryville; Mrs. Carlisle Smith; Mrs. Arch Trawick, Nashville; and Mrs. Fred Ramsey, Knoxville. "Minutes ASWPL Central Council," Nov. 18–19, 1932, Reel 4, ASWPL Papers; "1934 ASWPL Central Council," Reel 1, ASWPL Papers; "ASWPL Central Council, 1935," Reel 7, ASWPL Papers; "ASWPL Central Council, 1936," Reel 7, ASWPL Papers; "Minutes, ASWPL Meeting, Monday morning," Jan. 13, 1936; Mrs. Neal Spahr to Jessie Daniel Ames, Mar. 6, 1942, Reel 7, ASWPL Papers; Jessie Daniel Ames to Mrs. McClure, Apr. 6, 1937, Reel 7, ASWPL Papers.

64. Jessie Daniel Ames to Mrs. Julia Collier Harris, May 21, 1937, Reel 7, ASWPL Papers.

65. Mrs. K. W. Warden to Jessie Daniel Ames, Oct. 30, 1935, Reel 6, ASWPL Papers.

66. Mrs. Frances Spahr to Ames, Mon., 8 A.M., Reel 3, ASWPL Papers.

67. Mrs. J. R. Wheeler to Ames, Oct. 24, Reel 3, ASWPL Papers.

68. Mrs. K. W. Warden to Ames, May 12, 1936, Reel 7, ASWPL Papers; Kate Trawick to Ames, Oct. 28, 1935, Reel 7, ASWPL Papers.

69. Mrs. K. W. Warden to Ames, May 12, 1936; Kate Trawick to Ames, Oct. 28, 1935; Ames to Mrs. Trawick, Oct. 16, 1935; Mrs. Trawick to Mrs. O'Neal, Feb. 8, 1936, all in Reel 7, ASWPL Papers.

70. Mrs. P. B. Lowrance to Ames, July 2, 1934; Kate Davis to Ames, Aug. 28, 1934; Ames to Mrs. George (Kate) Davis, Oct. 3, 1934; Ames to Mrs. Robert O'Neal, Oct. 8, 1934, all in Reel 7, ASWPL Papers; Frances (Mrs. P. B.) Lowrance to Ames, Dec. 15, 1934, Reel 4, ASWPL Papers.

71. "Minutes, Anti-Lynching Conference of Southern White Women," Nov. 1, 1930, Reel 3, ASWPL Papers.

72. Jessie Daniel Ames to Mrs. George Davis, Mar. 9, 1937, Reel 7, ASWPL Papers; Interview of Louise Young by Jacquelyn Hall, Feb. 14, 1972, Interview #60, G-0066, "Documenting the American South: Oral Histories of the American South, Southern Women," http://docsouth.unc,edu/sohp/women.html/.

73. Mrs. K. W. Warden to Jessie Daniel Ames, Feb. 10, 1935, Reel 7, ASWPL Papers; Mrs. K. W. Warden to Jessie Daniel Ames, Mar. 6, 1935, Reel 7, ASWPL Papers.

74. "1931 Itinerary—Jessie Daniel Ames," Reel 2, ASWPL Papers.

75. "General News: 1938," 3, Reel 5, ASWPL Papers; "Distribution of 'This Business of Lynching,'" Jan. 25, 1935, Reel 1, ASWPL Papers; *"With Quietness They Work": Report of the Activities of Southern Women in Education Against Lynching During 1937* (Atlanta: Association of Southern Women for the Prevention of Lynching, 1938), 12.

76. *"With Quietness They Work,"* 3.

77. "Literature on Race Relations," Reel 1, ASWPL Papers.

78. "Minutes—Association of Southern Women for the Prevention of Lynching—Atlanta, Ga., January 10, 1935," 9, Reel 4, ASWPL Papers.

79. Ibid., 10.

80. Barber, "Association of Southern Women," 382.

81. "ASWPL, Jan.–Nov. 15, 1931," 5, Reel 5, ASWPL Papers; "Association of Southern Women for the Prevention of Lynching, Central Council, Nov. 18–19, 1932," Reel 4, ASWPL Papers.

82. "Report of Director of Woman's Work, April 18,1933," 2, Reel 5, ASWPL Papers; Nettie E. Brogdon, Copperhill, Tenn., to Jessie Daniel Ames, Jan. 15, 1935, Reel 4, ASWPL Papers; "Annual Bulletin," Jan. 1933, Reel 1, ASWPL Papers; "Organizations Committed to a Program of Education for the Prevention of Lynching," 11–13, Reel 2, ASWPL Papers.

83. "Conference Superintendents of Christian Social Relations, M.E. Church, South—1938," Reel 2, ASWPL Papers; Louise Young to Conference Superintendents of Christian Social Relations, Apr. 14, 1934, Reel 7, ASWPL Papers; "Board of Missions,

Methodist Episcopal Church, South," Reel 1, ASWPL Papers; Louise Young to Ames, Sept. 20, 1935, Reel 7, ASWPL Papers; Mrs. K. W. Warden to Ames, Oct. 30, 1935, Reel 6, ASWPL Papers; Interview of Louise Young by Jacquelyn Hall, Feb. 14, 1972; Mrs. K. W. Warden to Ames, Feb. 20, 1936, Reel 7, ASWPL Papers; Mrs. W. A. Newell to Mrs. Rubye Rains, May 1, 1936, Reel 7, ASWPL Papers.

84. Virginia MacKenzie Ritter to Mrs. G. G. McClure, Oct. 5, 1936, Reel 7, ASWPL Papers; "Woman's Missionary Union, S. B. C.," Apr. 14, 1937, Reel 7, ASWPL Papers; *The Knoxville Woman's Club Yearbook of the Sixteenth Session: 1943–1944;* http://library.cn.edu/speccolyAppMSS/15WMUFINDINGINVENTORYFinal.pdf/; *Tennessean,* Mar. 21, 1926; *Missionary Voice* 3 (Jan. 1913): 55, 65; Carole Stanford Bucy, *Women Helping Women: The YWCA of Nashville, 1898–1998* (Nashville: YWCA of Nashville and Middle Tennessee, 1998), 146; http://www.discoveret.org/ossoli/history(a).html/; *Robesonian* (Lumberton, N.C.), Oct. 7, 1955, 15.

85. The pledges that were signed read, "A Declaration and Personal Pledge: I declare lynching is an indefensible crime, destructive of all principles of government, hateful and hostile to every ideal of religion and humanity, debasing and degrading to every person involved. I believe that the creation of a new public opinion through the education of citizens to recognize and abhor the evils out of which lynchings grow is the only sure way to stop lynchings. Therefore, I pledge myself to assist in my community to create this new public opinion, which will not condone for any reason whatever acts of mobs or lynchers." Reel 2, ASWPL Papers.

86. Jessie Daniel Ames to Mrs. Robert O'Neal, Clarksville, Tenn., Oct. 17, 1934, Reel 7, ASWPL Papers.

87. Hall, *Revolt Against Chivalry,* 180; Lewis T. Nordyke, "Ladies and Lynchings," reprinted for *Survey Graphic* for ASWPL, Atlanta, Nov. 1939, 1.

88. Mrs. Neal Spahr to Jessie Daniel Ames, Mar. 6, 1942.

89. "Signature Record as of July 1, 1940," Reel 4, ASWPL Papers.

90. Lists of signatures, Reel 7, ASWPL Papers; Mrs. K. W. Warden to Jessie Ames, Apr. 27, 1935, Reel 7, ASWPL Papers; Mrs. O. C. Hatcher, Spring Hill, Tenn., to Jessie Ames, June 14, 1934, Reel 7, ASWPL Papers.

91. Interview of Louise Young by Jacquelyn Hall, Feb. 14, 1972.

92. *Southern Women Look at Lynching,* 7.

93. Ibid., 8.

94. "These Women and Lynching," 2.

95. Jessie Daniel Ames, *Southern Women and Lynching* (Atlanta: Association of Southern Women for the Prevention of Lynching, 1936), 4.

96. Nordyke, "Ladies and Lynching," 2.

97. "Minutes, ASWPL Meeting, Monday morning," Jan. 13, 1936.

98. ASWPL to Tennessee Governor McAlister, Reel 2, Dec. 18, 1933, ASWPL Papers.

99. "Annual Bulletin," Jan. 1933.

100. Ibid.; "Lynchings by State, 1931," 3, Reel 2, ASWPL Papers; "Lynchings Prevented in Tennessee—1930," Reel 7, ASWPL Papers; "Reported Prevented Lynchings, January 1–November 15, 1931," Reel 4, ASWPL Papers.

101. Dray, *At the Hands of Persons Unknown,* 281; Jessie Daniel Ames to Mrs. J. Morgan Stevens of Mississippi, Apr. 21, 1931, Reel 6, ASWPL Papers; "Association of Women of the South for the Prevention of Lynching, January–April 30, 1931," Reel 4, ASWPL; *Atlanta Constitution,* Apr. 19, 1931; *New York Times,* Nov. 10, 1931; *Nashville Banner,* Oct. 27, 1931; *Tennessean,* Oct. 27, 1931; *Nashville Globe,* Nov. 13, 1931.

102. "Messages from Governors to ASWPL—November 1931."

103. "Some Prevented Lynchings, 1932," Reel 3, ASWPL Papers; Jessie Daniel Ames to Mrs. Robert O'Neal, Sept. 8, 1932, Reel 5, ASWPL Papers.

104. "Lynchings by State—1933," Reel 3, ASWPL Papers.

105. "Prevented Lynchings—1934," Reel 3, ASWPL Papers.

106. "Lynchings by State—1934," Reel 2, ASWPL Papers.

107. "A Responsibility," *Tennessean,* Nov. 21, 1934, Reel 7, ASWPL Papers.

108. Mrs. King to Mrs. Robert O'Neal, Nov. 21, 1934, Reel 7, ASWPL Papers.

109. Ames, "Southern Women and Lynching," 2.

110. Frank Shay, *Judge Lynch: His First Hundred Years* (New York: Biblo-Moser, 1969), 253.

111. Jessie Daniel Ames to Mrs. Robert O'Neal, Dec. 21, 1934, Reel 7, ASWPL Papers; Jessie Daniel Ames to Mrs. J. W. Perry, with copies to Mrs. K. W. Warden, Mrs. J. W. Perry, Miss Estelle Haskin, Miss Louise Young, Mrs. Neal Spahr, Mrs. R. L. Harris, Mrs. P. B. Lowrance, and Mrs. C. V. Biddle, Dec. 21, 1934, Reel 7, ASWPL Papers.

112. Barbara Lewis (Young's secretary) to Jessie Daniel Ames, Dec. 26, 1934, Reel 7, ASWPL Papers; Louise Young to Governor Hill McAlister, Dec. 25, 1934, Reel 7, ASWPL Papers.

113. *Christian Social Relations,* Second Quarter, 1935, 1, Reel 4, ASWPL Papers.

114. "Minutes, ASWPL Meeting, Monday morning," Jan. 13, 1936, 8.

115. Ibid.; "Death by Parties Unknown," *ASWPL Bulletin* 6, Jan. 1936, ASWPL Papers.

116. "Death by Parties Unknown"; "Lynchings by States—1935," Reel 2, ASWPL Papers.

117. "Record of Mob Violence, January–June 1936," ASWPL Papers, 2, Reel 5, ASWPL Papers.

118. "Lynching Is Wholesale Murder," *ASWPL Bulletin* 7, Feb. 1937, 15–16, Reel 4, ASWPL Papers.

119. "Feeling Is Tense," *ASWPL Bulletin* 8, Feb. 1938, 6, 8, 9, 17, ASWPL Papers.

120. "Prevented Lynchings, January–April, 1938," ASWPL Papers, reel 3.

121. "Prevented Lynchings—1939," 2, Reel 3, ASWPL Papers.

122. Jessie Daniel Ames to Mrs. G. G. McClure, July 7, 1939, Reel 2, ASWPL Papers.

123. "Lynchings Committed, 1940," Reel 2, ASWPL; "Reported Lynching at Dyersburg, Tenn.," Reel 2, ASWPL Papers.

124. Terborg-Penn, "African-American Women's Networks," 148; Brown, "Eradicating This Evil," 14.

125. "The Decline in Lynching," *Chattanooga Times,* Jan. 3, 1940, 6.

126. Ibid.

127. *Southern Women Look at Lynching,* 117.

128. "These Women and Lynching," 1–2.

129. Brown, "Eradicating This Evil," 14.

130. Ibid.

131. "Feeling Is Tense," 2.

132. "Minutes, ASWPL Meeting, Monday morning," Jan. 13, 1936.

133. John Shelton Reed, "An Evaluation of an Anti-Lynching Organization," *Social Problems* 16, no. 2 (Autumn 1968): 181.

134. "One Woman and a Mob, July 1932."

Chapter 6

"The Destiny of Our Race Lies Largely in Their Hands": African American Women Teachers' Organizational Efforts in Memphis and Nashville during the Progressive Era

Sonya Ramsey

> *Of the teachers engaged in instructing Colored youth, it is perhaps no exaggeration to say that fully ninety percent are women. Many a heroine, of whom the world will never hear, has thus sacrificed her life to her race, amid surroundings and in the face of privations which only martyrs can tolerate and bear. Indefatigably and conscientiously, in public work of all kinds they engage that they may benefit and elevate their race.*
>
> —Mary Church Terrell, 1898

In September 1897 representatives from black women's charitable clubs across the nation journeyed to Howard Congregational Church in Nashville to hold the first convention of the National Association of Colored Women's Clubs. Hosted by Nashville's Phyllis Wheatley Club, meeting attendees included several prominent former and current Tennessee educators, such as Memphis' Mary Church Terrell and Virginia Broughton. Other representatives were from the Memphis Hooks School Association, Knoxville Woman's Mutual Improvement Club, and the Jackson Woman's Club. Adopting the motto "Lifting as We Climb," these clubwomen vowed to develop service programs, eliminate negative stereotypes, maintain a proper home life, and fight against Jim Crow. These women were often wives of prominent African American professional men and, quite often, teachers.[1]

When historians tell the story of the Progressive Era, they often describe the significant efforts of organized women to solicit governmental support to alleviate poverty, improve the conditions of immigrants and the poor, eliminate vice, and obtain suffrage. Despite these descriptions of progress, progressivism in the South also marks the rise of legal Jim Crow segregation, lynching, and political disenfranchisement for African Americans. Reacting to this onslaught, African American women teachers in Memphis and Nashville reshaped Progressive Era goals to remedy problems within their own segregated communities. If progressivism suggested that women act as moral voices and serve the community, these teachers believed that it was their special duty to uplift the race by improving education for all African Americans and working to better the reputation of African American women. In 1892, teacher and Progressive activist Anna Julia Cooper claimed that "only the black woman can say when and where I enter, in the quiet, undisputed dignity of my womanhood, without violence and without suing or special patronage, then and there the whole Negro race enters with me."[2] Called to go forth and serve by their educational institutions and home communities, urban Tennessee teachers made up most of the leaders in black women's organizations during the Progressive Era. Through the leadership, goals, and efforts of these women, their social service was just another way African American teachers defined themselves as middle-class professionals.

Women who entered the work force relied upon their training and their self-perceptions as professionals to develop strategies to counter discrimination and injustice. At Tennessee institutions such as Fisk University, Howe Institute, LeMoyne (now LeMoyne-Owen) College, and, later, Tennessee Agricultural and Industrial State Normal School, students who were training to become educators in their communities learned that their mission included not only preparing children for upward mobility but also behaving as positive representations of African American womanhood. The charge to improve the image of black women as well as to serve the race attracted women to teaching, a field that offered them dignity and social standing in both black and white society.

As the demand for African American educators increased in the South during Reconstruction, missionary associations developed the first black institutions of higher learning in Nashville and Memphis to prepare teachers for working with African American youth. Fisk founders, Union army veterans and Freedmen's Bureau officers John Ogden, Erastus M. Cravath, and Edward P. Smith requested in 1866 that the American Missionary Association (AMA) open a normal school for blacks. Ogden maintained that spending one hundred thousand dollars of the association's money on training people to teach "would do much more towards educating freedmen of the South than three times that sum spent in supporting northern teachers" to come south for limited periods of teaching duty.[3]

After the opening of public schools for black children in Nashville in 1867, Fisk discontinued an elementary program it had begun the prior year to focus primarily on training teachers in a normal-school, teacher-education program. Renamed Fisk University that same year, it offered basic secondary educational courses as well as classes in botany, geometry, chemistry, algebra, and natural history. The school also provided a small model elementary school for daily hands-on training for its normal students, and in 1871 Fisk enrolled its first students in a three-year college-level program.[4] To augment limited funding from the AMA, the university used its own students as musical performers. The internationally known Fisk Jubilee Singers raised funds for the school by entertaining audiences across the United States and Europe helping to promote the Negro spiritual.[5]

African Americans in Memphis also sought avenues for higher education. The American Missionary Association actually started a school in Memphis some two years earlier than the opening of Fisk. In 1862, after the federal occupation of the city, the AMA sponsored Lincoln Chapel School, first at Camp Shiloh and later, after a year, at Memphis. Tragically the school burned to the ground during the Memphis Race Riots of 1866, but it was rebuilt in 1867. Three years later the struggling school received a donation of twenty thousand dollars from Pennsylvania abolitionist Francis J. LeMoyne for teacher education. In 1888, the American Baptist Association opened Howe Institute, another institution of higher education for blacks. These institutions struggled to continue their missions; they struggled financially, they encountered hostile whites who objected to the idea of higher education for blacks, and when a deadly yellow fever epidemic swept through the city in 1878, it negatively affected students and faculty alike. Although students from Memphis attended the Memphis schools, Fisk University quickly emerged as the most prominent private institution for African Americans in the state.[6]

Graduates of institutions such as Fisk received an elite education compared to their peers, but all of the schools trained their students who would become teachers to instruct students despite the likely substandard conditions of their future classrooms. The nationally known and internationally renowned president of Tuskegee Institute, Booker T. Washington, asserted in 1910, "The Fisk students seem to have but one object in view, that of preparing themselves for service to their race. . . . I find that considerably more than half of them have gone out into different parts of the South as teachers. In my recent trips through southern states, I have met, and almost without exception, I have found that they are leading useful and honorable lives."[7]

Numerous individual examples demonstrate the influence of Fisk on black women teachers and the influence these teachers had on their students. Born in 1860 in Nashville, Minnie Lou Scott graduated from Fisk University's normal school in 1877. She became the first black teacher in the Nashville public schools in 1879. She then married the Knowles Elementary School principal Scott Washington Crosthwaite, who was also a physician. Minnie Lou Crosthwaite later became an administrator at Fisk University and worked as an avid clubwoman and suffrage activist. Later she served as Fisk's first female registrar and as a trustee during the 1930s. Throughout her career, Crosthwaite was a professional role model for women who aspired to middle-class status by becoming teachers.[8]

Virginia E. Walker Broughton, born in 1856, entered Fisk and was a member of its first graduating class in 1875. After receiving an honorary master's degree from Fisk in 1878, she started teaching in the Memphis schools. She served as principal of North Memphis Grammar School and later taught at the prominent Kortrecht Grammar School, which offered one year of high school instruction. She successfully challenged the school

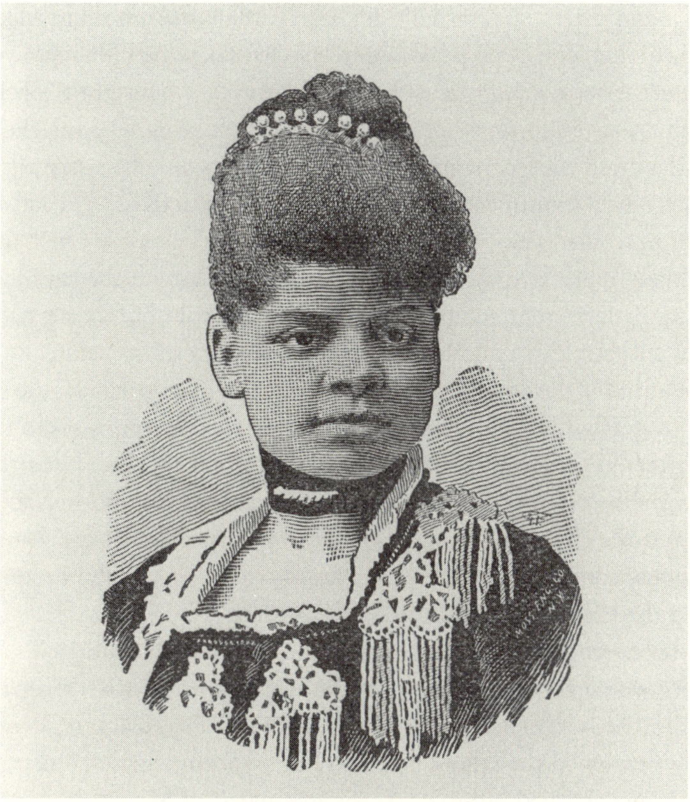

In honor of her achievements as an educator, journalist, and civil rights activist, the United States Postal Service issued a commemorative Ida B. Wells postal stamp in 1990. *From I. Garland Penn, The Afro-American Press and Its Editors*, 1891. Library of Congress.

board when it offered the position of head teacher or assistant principal to a lesser-qualified male teacher and subsequently received the post.[9]

Ida B. Wells, the nationally known antilynching activist, also went to Fisk. Born during slavery in 1862, in Holly Springs, Mississippi, she attended local freedmen schools after emancipation. Wells faced tragedy at age sixteen when the yellow fever epidemic swept through her town, killing her parents and a younger sibling. Responsible for supporting five brothers and sisters, she started teaching. In 1883, she moved to Memphis to live with her aunt, who promised to help her take care of her two youngest sisters. After teaching outside of Memphis, she later got a job in the Memphis City Schools, where she taught for six years. During thc summers, she often took courses at Fisk and other local colleges. Wells went on to become a prominent suffragist, antilynching activist, and active participant in women's clubs.[10]

Although black women from Memphis and Nashville began to graduate from college, segregation often kept them from obtaining teaching jobs. While African American parents and community leaders in both cities fought for the employment of African American teachers, the school board in Nashville refused to employ black teachers even some several years after they were hired in Memphis. Counter to Nashville's reputation as the so-called Athens of the South, city leaders did not act early to expand the city's educational quality to incorporate African American educational concerns. Nevertheless, black Nashvillians established and developed their own centers of academic excellence.

After northern white teachers left the South in the late 1870s, white southern women with low scores on the teaching exam often received positions in black schools. In Nashville and Memphis, black residents frequently petitioned the school board to hire African American instructors. In 1873, a concerned group of "Colored citizens of Memphis" circulated a petition maintaining that "in view of the fact that we are proscribed by law to separate schools for our children, upon the presumption of 'inferiority' we respectfully ask that we may have the benefit in full and that every teacher, from principal down, be elected from the proscribed class." Since the late 1860s black Nashvillians had been asking the city's school board to employ black teachers, and in 1878 James C. Napier, a prominent black attorney and businessman, successfully won election to the Nashville City Council by promising his black constituents that he would fight for the employment of black teachers. He contended that they offered an "incentive to Colored pupils" and that southern white teachers cared more for their salaries than for helping black children. Memphis began hiring black teachers in the mid-1870s, but the Nashville School Board did not start employing African Americans until the late 1870s, professing that it had to wait until it could hire entire black faculties for black schools, to prevent the "embarrassment" of white teachers.[11]

When the Tennessee General Assembly passed several segregation acts in 1901, including one barring teachers from instructing students of another race, neither the Memphis nor Nashville African American community objected to this particular ruling. The new state educational law reinforced African Americans' desire for black teachers in black schools and supported the demand for increased professional opportunities for black teachers.[12]

Activists and clubwomen, such as Memphis' Virginia Broughton and Nashville's Minnie L. Crosthwaite, were some of the first black teachers in the public schools.[13] Black parents and community leaders expected these women to serve as role models in and out the classroom. Working against overwhelming circumstances, teachers sometimes fell short of their mandate to uplift the race through education, but their efforts offered the black community the comfort of knowing that their children had caring instructors who were accountable. In 1884, Nashville's public schools spent $12.77 per year to educate a white student but allocated only $8.55 for each black student. Moreover, schools for African Americans tended to be poor structures, and some, including Nashville's Vandaville Elementary School, proved uninhabitable.[14] By 1889, there were 51 black teachers and 187 white teachers employed in the Nashville public schools. In 1900, blacks made up 23.2 percent of the population in Nashville and a sizable 48.8 percent in Memphis. By 1910, there were 196 African American women teaching in Memphis' public schools.[15]

While Fisk and the state's other private colleges continued to produce classically educated graduates to work in the public schools, there remained a shortage of teachers in rural areas. Many blacks wanted a state-funded, lower-cost institution of higher learning where they could train as educators. After Tennessee received federal funds from the Morrill Act to open public normal schools in 1909, the Tennessee General Assembly passed a general education bill allocating funding for four teacher-training schools in the state, three for whites and one for African Americans.[16] In an attempt to alleviate whites' concerns that a classically educated black teacher would preach social equality, attorney James C. Napier, then the registrar of the U.S. Treasury, along with other Tennessee black leaders, maintained that the black normal school could offer industrial classes to future teachers. The African American leaders failed to mention, however, that the new school's other mission included training students to teach rigorous academic material in Tennessee schools.[17] Proposing to "educate and train teachers for the public schools of the state," Tennessee Agricultural and Industrial State Normal School for Negroes (A&I) opened in 1912 with a predominately black faculty of 10 and with 247 students; a summer session for teachers began on June 19, having more than 250 teachers in attendance. Fall classes began on September 16.[18]

A&I and other black schools indeed offered classical subjects as well as domestic courses to their students. Universities such as Fisk endeavored to prove the competency of black teachers by displaying their intellectual acumen in and out the classroom. Linda Perkins claimed that while "rural areas of the South attracted the least-prepared teachers, the opposite was true of urban areas." While some districts hired grammar school graduates or refused to hire competent teachers, Nashville's and Memphis' black urban professional instructors were exceptions to that practice.[19]

In addition to their academic subjects, the domestic courses schools offered not only provided students with skills but also ensured that they would be good housekeepers, something essential to achieving middle-class respectability. Female students learned how to maintain a proper home and put on teas and galas. Given their low salaries, black teachers were rarely able to afford domestic help and thus took care of their own homes in addition to their responsibilities as educators. Many of the teachers who would share their programs for racial uplift during the Progressive Era were in normal school or college when they formed their perceptions about middle-class respectability and the appropriate roles for professionals. There they received instruction to serve by precept and example, believing that women should be feminine and genteel outside the classroom. Yet as teachers they defied stereotypes regarding women's work, intelligence, and strength.[20]

The African American community demanded that its teachers portray themselves as leaders, which included dressing as though they received adequate pay and worked in comfortable surroundings. Whether they sewed their own clothes or wore a few key pieces, these women considered conservative attire and good manners critical to garnering respect and assistance from their communities and possibly from the white power structure. Wages were low, but dressing well reinforced their identities as middle class and professional. Working-class women, by comparison, often looked forward to dressing stylishly for church or social functions as a way of reclaiming an identity apart from their jobs. For them, what they wore for work did not embody who they were. In contrast, black women teachers longed to be recognized by their work apparel. Indeed, professional dress served as the urban teacher's uniform.[21] By maintaining an image of piety and respectability, they could also inspire their students to become professionals. Community approval of their moral character helped teachers withstand discrimination from white members of their profession.[22]

One of the primary duties of the professional teacher during the Progressive Era was public service. "Teachers," as Sharon Harley suggested, "thought that they had a special responsibility to serve the community that only they as educated, unmarried women could fulfill."[23] As the nation embarked upon a new century, the hard-fought freedoms African Americans had acquired during Reconstruction were evaporating as legal segregation took hold in the South. Along with the rise of restrictive laws limiting the freedoms of African Americans, lynching and race riots became the preferred way to reinforce white control and supremacy. Teachers attempted to redress these mounting problems of discrimination and poverty by serving as community leaders. They established clubs and organizations and worked with religious groups to help better the race. The call to service was very much at the forefront of teachers' efforts throughout the Jim Crow era, although free African American women had participated in cultural clubs and service organizations since the early 1800s.[24]

While individual black women's organizations worked to address their respective communities' charitable and cultural needs, Memphis former teacher Ida B. Wells's outspoken activism helped to spark the formation of a national black women's organization in the late 1890s. She challenged Jim Crow as a young teacher when she won a suit against the Chesapeake and Ohio Railroad Company in 1884 after being physically forced out the ladies' car because of her race, despite possessing a first-class ticket.

Her victory did not last, however, when the Tennessee Supreme Court reversed the verdict in 1887. Outraged by this injustice, Wells wrote an article about the incident. It was so well received that she decided to work as a journalist. Assuming the pen name "Iola," her articles started to appear in black newspapers across the nation. In 1889, a local minister asked her to serve as the editor of the *Memphis Free Speech and Headlight.* She lost her teaching position in 1891 after she wrote an editorial describing the deplorable conditions of the segregated schools. Undeterred, Wells wrote a scathing editorial a year later calling for blacks to leave the city after envious whites lynched three of her friends because they opened a successful grocery store that competed with white businesses. Faced with retaliation and riots, some six thousand blacks heeded her advice and fled the city.[25]

As teacher-turned-activist, Wells then decided to systematically study lynching and published her findings in *Southern Horrors: Lynch Law in All Its Phases.* In this pamphlet, she declared, "Nobody in this section of the community believes that old threadbare lie that Negro men rape white women. If Southern men are not careful, a conclusion might be reached which will be very damaging to the moral reputation of their women." An enraged white press wrote livid responses, calling for her punishment, and a mob burned down her newspaper and vowed to kill her. Although the threats upon her life caused Wells to make a new life in Chicago, her mission remained. She dedicated her life to activism by continuing her antilynching activities, working for suffrage, and participating in the club movement. Using a tactic similar to that employed during the abolitionist movement, Wells made her cause an international one, taking her message overseas. When she traveled to England to speak about the horrors of lynching and promote antilynching activities as part of a tour, Missouri reporter James W. Jacks and other white journalists called for the dismissal of Wells's claims by saying that she and black women were just prostitutes and should not be trusted.[26]

In reacting to Jacks's outrageous attack upon Wells, now Wells-Barnett after marrying newspaper editor and activist Ferdinand Barnett in 1895, club representatives from across the nation decided to meet in Washington, D.C., in July 1896. At that historic meeting, they determined to combine the National Federation of Afro-American Women, which had 85

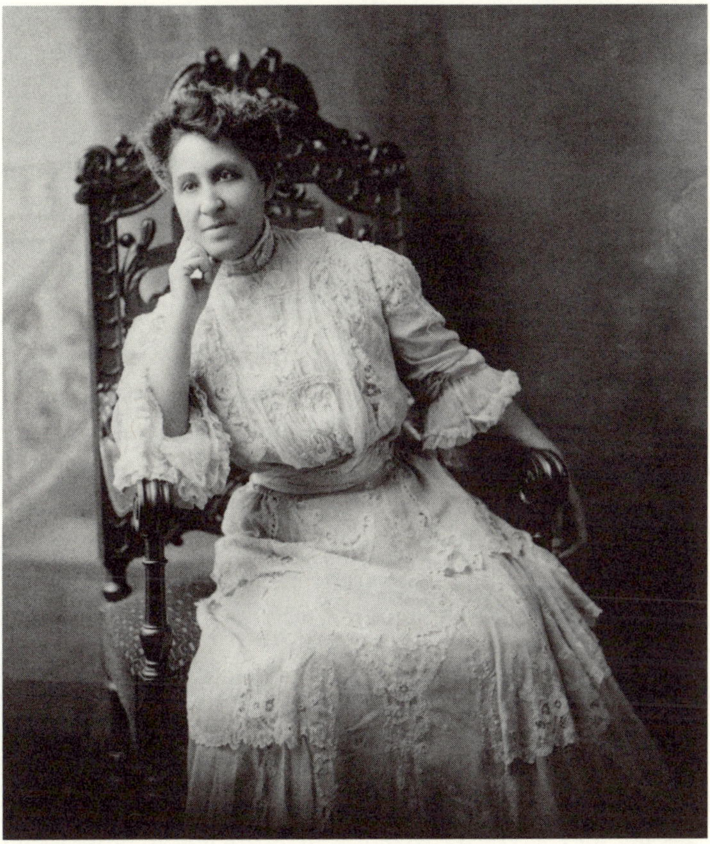

As a tireless activist against social injustice, in 1950 Mary Church Terrell led a protest against a segregated cafeteria when she was in her late 80s. Library of Congress.

clubs, and the Colored Women's League, with 115 groups, to form the National Association of Colored Women (NACW). While Jacks's statement may have led these powerful clubwomen to organize nationally, the NACW was a natural expansion of the activities black women were already doing in regional and local organizations.[27]

Several Tennessee women played active leadership roles in the NACW. Born in Memphis, Mary Church graduated from Oberlin College and became a well-known teacher in Washington, D.C. After marrying educator and attorney Robert Terrell, she dedicated herself to public service. Active in club work in her city, Terrell became the first president of the NACW. Teachers served in the forefront as leaders in several NACW clubs in Tennessee. Many officers of the NACW, such as Fisk graduate Margaret Murray Washington, once worked as teachers. Moreover, Tennessee members also included Nashville's Belle View Elementary School teacher Frankie J. Pierce, a member of the NACW-affiliated Phyllis Wheatley Club, and Memphis clubwomen Virginia Broughton and Julia A. B. Hooks, who both also taught in the public schools.[28]

Historians of the black clubwomen's movement contend that it adopted some of the stereotypical attitudes of the larger society when it suggested that African American women assume the responsibility of eliminating white prejudice and disrespect by improving their own morals and behavior. Scholars call this strategy the politics of respectability.[29] Critics also claim that such efforts to correct the behavior of the poor aggravated class tensions. While these arguments have merit, historians also acknowledge the detrimental impact of racism and white American middle-class culture on black women's views.[30] As members of a larger, white-dominated society, black women could not avoid internalizing some of the stereotypical representations thrust upon them. Nevertheless, they considered self-improvement to be the best way toward progress when political and legal remedies proved ineffectual. They often adopted middle-class attitudes, but they accepted these ideas in an attempt to prove themselves worthy to whites. As "self-respecting" women, they stressed adhering to a strict moral code as a way of dispelling negative stereotypes. Terrell maintained, "It is unfortunate, but it is true, that the dominant race in this country insists upon gauging the Negro's worth by his most illiterate and vicious representatives rather than by the more intelligent and worthy classes."[31]

Clubwomen focused a great deal of their energy on encouraging mothers to impart moral values to their children. The clubs also emphasized good housekeeping as a sign of proper upbringing and virtue. Teachers, as surrogate mothers, shared the responsibility of instilling these ideals in their pupils.[32] They expanded their motherly role when helping to educate parents about domestic issues. In a 1913 meeting of the NACW in Nashville, former teacher Margaret Murray Washington, wife of Booker T. Washington, called for educators to form mothers' clubs: "Schoolteachers should come in contact with the children's parents, and if there is not a mothers' meeting organized in the community where they teach, they should call the mothers together and organize them. The subject: 'At what age shall I allow my daughter to receive company?'—Subjects like this and similar subjects, as, what our children should wear, what they should eat, and where they should go are discussed in this department. This helps to improve our homes."[33] Nashville's teachers responded enthusiastically to aid parents in forming associations that raised funds and supported activities at their children's schools.

Teachers joined with the wives of dentists and business leaders to compose the majority of Nashville's Phyllis Wheatley Club, named in honor of the famous eighteenth-century African American poet. From its founding in 1895 to its disbanding in 1920, the club supported a day-care center, raised money for the sick and needy, and campaigned for equipment for Pearl Senior High School.[34] Teachers also participated in many other women's clubs in Nashville, among them the Ladies Christian Aid Society, the Homemaker's Club, the Woman's Supply Club, the Busy Bee Club, the Progressive Sewing Circle, and the Women's Day Home Club, which provided day-care services for children of working parents. The teaching philosophies of most women easily meshed with the principles of these clubs—for both teachers' roles, inside and outside of the classroom—and the clubs' purposes emphasized moral responsibility, middle-class respectability, and the vital importance of obtaining an education for social and economic uplift.[35]

Memphis teachers also worked to uplift the race through community service. Born in 1862, Julia Britton Hooks was a classically trained musician who taught and served as a principal in the Memphis public schools and later opened her own private kindergarten. In 1891, she and Daisy Harvey founded the Colored Old Folks Home (later Hooks-Edward Rest Home) and the Orphan Home Club. Hooks and her husband Charles also established and supervised a juvenile detention home in 1907. She started the Phillis Wheatley Union in the 1890s to help "improve the conditions of women, morally, intellectually, financially and civilly, and to assist in the elevation of youths in the land." Other important clubs included the Memphis Orphans and Old Folks Club, which also operated a home for orphans and the elderly.[36]

While these women knew that their positions called for them to help the less fortunate, some African American teachers balanced their responsibility as community leaders with their desire to enjoy the social pleasures of middle-class life and escape the daily responsibilities of being a role model. In an effort to build character and expose women to prominent speakers, Memphis teachers, among them Florence P. Cooper, Daisy Harvey, and Virginia Broughton, also joined cultural enrichment clubs, such as the Coterie Migratory Assembly, the Liszt Musical Club, and various literary and social clubs.[37]

During the Progressive Era, elementary school teacher Frankie J. Pierce helped organize the Nashville Federation of Colored Women's Clubs under the auspices of the NACW. In a 1910 article describing the

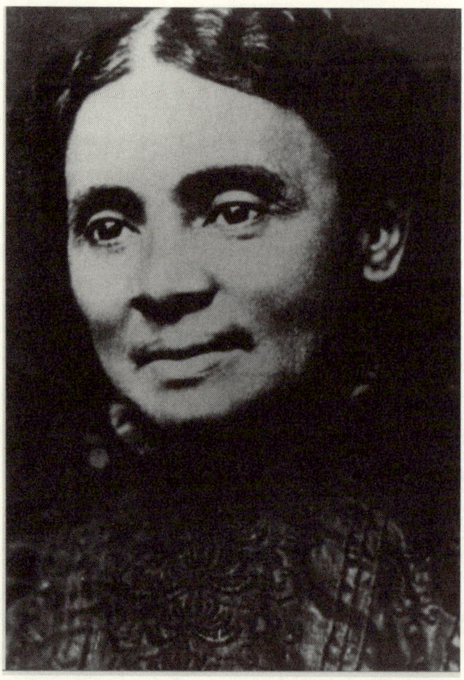

Known as the "Angel of Beale Street" because of her philanthropic efforts, Julia Britton Hooks was also the grandmother of late civil rights activist and National Association for the Advancement of Colored People executive director Benjamin Hooks. Courtesy of Special Collections and Archives, Berea College.

Nashville meeting of the Tennessee Federation, the *Nashville Globe* newspaper reported, "Wholesome enthusiasm pervaded every session, such as is usually characteristic of earnest determined women who are engaged with strength of soul and body in furtherance of some cherished cause. These women have shown by their words of hope and cheer and encouragement and determination their optimism in the possibilities of the race and their belief in themselves as a power to help bring them to pass as useful, uplifting realities."[38] Working collectively with the Tennessee Federation of Colored Women's Clubs, the Nashville Federation raised money to open a home for orphaned children in 1925.[39]

While many of the tenets of the NACW called for women to adhere to Christian principals of morality, teachers such as Virginia Broughton also believed that racial uplift involved improving the spiritual life of African Americans. An active member of several women's clubs in the city, Broughton published a groundbreaking article in the *Memphis Commercial Appeal,* the city's white newspaper, in which she praised the efforts of clubwomen and extolled the virtues of black womanhood in 1895. Active in the temperance movement, Broughton served as president of the Tennessee Colored Department of the Women's Christian Temperance Union. Broughton, Julia Hooks, and other black Progressive teachers stressed the need for temperance for religious and moral reasons, and they thought that the prohibition of alcohol would prevent abuse from men, provide more family income, and help to better the overall reputation of African Americans.[40]

As Progressives stressed the need to eliminate vice and uplift the moral fabric of society, Broughton and other black teachers and clubwomen adopted this stance against the "ills of society" as a method of racial uplift. Broughton suggested, "The women now realize their responsibilities as never before, and from the weight of this realization they are organizing their forces to better prepare themselves to perform, in the best manner, every duty incumbent upon them, from the cellar to the garret; in the home; or their lot in the church and other religious organizations, and in the world."[41] Mary Church Terrell added that "by coming into close touch with the masses of our women it is possible to correct many of the evils, which militate so seriously against us and inaugurate the reforms,

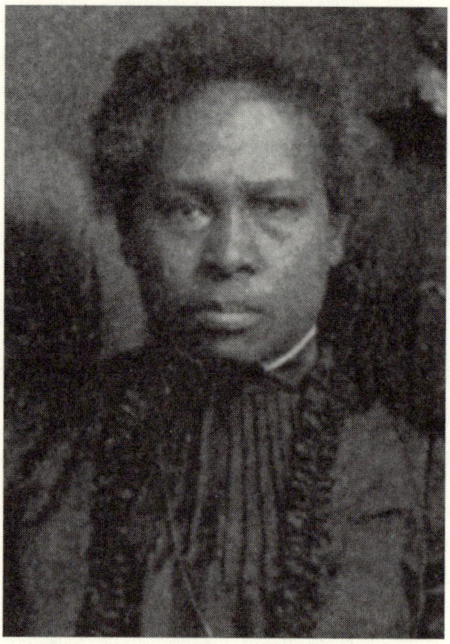

In 1907, Virginia Broughton published her autobiography, *Twenty Years a Missionary*, which chronicled her experiences as a traveling Christian missionary and women's rights advocate in the Baptist church. From Joanna P. Moore, *"In Christ's Stead": Autobiographical Sketches*, 1902.

without which, as a race, we cannot hope to succeed."[42] To protect rural black women from the lures of prostitution, clubwomen sponsored the Memphis office of the National League for the Protection of Colored Women in 1909. Nashville teacher Frankie J. Pierce also ran the Negro Women's Reconstruction League, which worked to establish a school for delinquent black girls.[43]

Teachers also participated in missionary societies and clubs within their respective churches. In these organizations, educators worked alongside working-class women to help serve the community and support the church. During the 1890s, black women worked as assistant teachers in the Nashville chapter of the Women's Baptist Home Mission Society. This national organization worked with black churches to sponsor mothers' groups and provided religious-themed educational materials for black children.[44] Broughton eventually became a Baptist missionary who traveled throughout the state. In later years, she became a feminist within the Baptist faith, organizing the first Tennessee Women's Convention as part of the National Baptist Convention and serving as a speaker and writer on women's causes in the church.[45]

Other black religious Progressive educators worked with white religious organizations to help their communities. Fisk graduate and former teacher Sallie Hill Sawyer asked Estelle Haskin, director of community service programs for the Methodist Episcopal Church, South, to open a settlement house for black children in Nashville.[46] Sawyer described the appalling conditions of the poor girls and boys left to wander the streets while their parents worked. She often took care of children while their mothers worked as domestics. Haskin, a leader in the Social Gospel movement, then asked the Methodist Episcopal District for help. In 1913, the district provided funds to open the Bethlehem House, later renamed Bethlehem Center, in the basement of St. Andrews Presbyterian Church, and Sawyer became its housemother. The Department of Social Science at Fisk worked closely with the Bethlehem House from its inception, requiring sociology students to be there four hours per week. In addition to providing a kindergarten, the Bethlehem House served more than three hundred families during its first years by hosting two boys' clubs, a Sunday children's hour, and a mothers' club, and by offering courses in sewing and domestic science. Looking back at the success of the Bethlehem House, Haskin remembered, "It was nearly twelve years ago that [Sawyer] came to my office door in the Mission Training School to ask for help to do the things for blacks being done in the Wesley house in South Nashville for the whites. She wanted a sewing school in the Capers Chapel for the children. And we responded gladly."[47]

While most rural southern African Americans became disenfranchised by the turn of the century, black men could still vote in Nashville and Memphis. However, even if they did exercise the franchise, the passage of an 1883 Progressive Era law created citywide voting, instead of ward or block voting, which severely hindered black political power. African Americans in Memphis faced similar restrictions when the city enacted a poll tax in 1890 limiting voter participation.[48] Although black women could not vote, they viewed, as Elsa Barkley Brown maintained, the political process as a communal effort and assumed the right to offer opinions and participate. Some teachers worked for suffrage because if black voter turnout increased, they could obtain more economic and medical resources and change negative laws affecting the educational system.[49]

A number of black teachers in Nashville joined in the fight for the franchise. Nashville's black suffrage leaders, Frankie J. Pierce and Minnie Lou Crosthwaite, spoke at citywide debates, as well as to students and other interested persons, about the necessity for female suffrage. They wanted to vote to address issues such as juvenile delinquency and the establishment of schools for wayward children. After the Tennessee legislature ratified the Nineteenth Amendment by one vote, black women's organizations continued to work with white groups to encourage women at the polls. African American physician Mattie Coleman and a white suffragist sponsored an August workshop in 1919 to teach about voting.[50] In that year, 1,300 of 6,007 registered women voters were black.[51] Pierce asked fellow suffrage activists in a state convention, "What will the Negro woman do with the vote? We are asking only one thing–a square deal." She reminded the suffragists of the needs of African American women. "We want recognition in all forms of this government. We want a state vocational school and a child welfare department of the state, and more room in state schools." In 1920, more than twenty-five hundred black women had registered to vote in Nashville.[52] As strong advocates for suffrage, Nashville's black women leaders, like Crosthwaite, even challenged antisuffrage Booker T. Washington supporters. "I cannot agree with them on this question," Crosthwaite declared, "because I am so sick and tired of dodging and parleying over things I know to be right."[53]

Surprisingly Nashville's black and white suffragists worked together to push for suffrage to address each group's individual goals, an end to machine politics in Nashville, and a vocational school for delinquent girls. Black women in Memphis, however, did not form strong alliances with white suffrage activists. In fact, black women faced voter intimidation and white women pushed for the election of a reform candidate who campaigned on a segregationist platform. Nevertheless, 1,197 black women did register to vote in Memphis, accounting for 22 percent of all female registered voters.[54]

While black teachers worked with whites to fight for suffrage, other reformers attempted to form alliances with white women's service organizations. Although these white organizations, such as the Nashville and Memphis chapters of the General Federation of Women's Clubs, re-

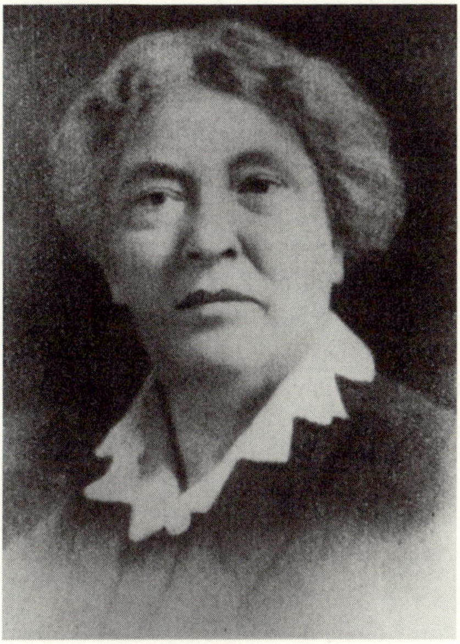

After serving as an educator, administrator, and its first female alumna trustee, in 1963 Fisk University named its new women's dormitory Crosthwaite Hall to honor Minnie Lou Crosthwaite's contributions to the university. Courtesy of Special Collections and Archives, Fisk University.

mained segregated, some black teachers were willing to work within these constraints in order to better their race, insofar as women were a driving force behind so much progressivism in the South. The General Federation of Women's Clubs, for example, worked in several areas in which African American teachers were seeking improvement and intervention, including juvenile delinquency, settlement house work, and public health instruction.[55]

Notwithstanding their focus on improving black home life and their efforts to form coalitions with whites, African American teachers as women leaders in their communities assumed a primary responsibility in supporting their communities—as did blacks in general due to the disregard of white society. During this so-called Progressive Era, black women in the South watched as the charitable and religious groups of their white counterparts successfully petitioned local and state governments for programs and laws to protect children, the sick, and the poor. Few of the laws, however, applied to African Americans. Glenda Gilmore contended that despite the obstacles they faced, black women sought to institute similar types of reforms but did not benefit as much as did white women, who had the financial support, the mainstream publicity, and the political protection of their husbands.[56]

Black teachers in Memphis and Nashville faced similar problems in both cities of child poverty and overcrowding in their schools, and these teachers also worked in cities where the specter of racial violence remained ever present. Recognizing that they, personally, with their middle-class status, possessed more advantages than their less privileged black counterparts, educated black women Progressives strived to create social and cultural spaces where all blacks could flourish without the stings of racism. Although living in different cities, black teachers of Memphis and Nashville often found themselves working together in state educational and women's associations to address problems of shared concern, and they socially interacted as members of the small black middle class.

Although much looked bleak for black women teachers during the Progressive Era, they, their schools, and their communities had come a long way since the years immediately following the Civil War. When black leaders first petitioned school boards to hire black teachers, those instructors bore the enormous responsibility of ensuring the mental wellbeing of their students and helping them to learn in a society that offered them little financial or cultural support. The black teachers of Nashville and Memphis entered into an unwritten contract with the black community. The educators promised to serve the city's children, and the community assured the teachers they would receive professional status in return. Placed within the larger burden of educating students in a system designed to circumscribe their intelligence, black women knew that their duties continued well after school as they worked in organizations to help their community. Black teachers in Nashville and Memphis were in the vanguard of the movement for racial uplift during the Progressive Era.

NOTES

Portions of this essay have been taken from the first chapter of my book, *Reading, Writing, and Segregation: A Century of Black Women Teachers in Nashville* (Urbana: Univ. of Illinois Press, 2008). The title quote is from an editorial, "School Teachers," in the *Nashville Globe,* Mar. 28, 1913, 4. The opening epigraph refers to Mary Church Terrell, "The Progress of Colored Women Clubs" (speech given at the National American Women's Suffrage Association, Feb. 18, 1898), cited Gifts of Speech, http://gos.sbc.edu/t/terrellmary.html/ (accessed July 3, 2007).

1. Minutes of the National Convention of the National Association of Colored Women, Nashville, Tenn., Sept. 15–18, 1897 (Washington, D.C.: Smith Brothers, 1901), in Records of the National Association of Colored Women, 1895–1992, pt. 1, Minutes of National Conventions, Publications, and President's Office Correspondence, Reel 2, University Publications of America, Bethesda, Md., 1993.

2. Anna Julia Cooper, *A Voice from the South* (Xenia, Ohio: Aldine Printing House, 1892), in Documenting the American South, North Carolina Collection, Louis Round Wilson Library, University of North Carolina at Chapel Hill, 31, http://docsouth.unc/church/ cooper/cooper.html/ (accessed July 3, 2007).

3. John Ogden, circular letter, Oct. 3, 1865, in Selected Records of the Tennessee Field Office Bureau of Refugees, Freedmen, and Abandoned Lands, 1865–1872, National Archives, quoted in Paul David Phillips, "Education of Blacks in Tennessee During Reconstruction, 1865–1870," in *Trial and Triumph: Essays in Tennessee's African American History,* ed. Carroll Van West (Knoxville: Univ. of Tennessee Press, 2002), 155.

4. Joe M. Richardson, *A History of Fisk University, 1865–1946* (Tuscaloosa: Univ. of Alabama Press, 1980), 15. Nashville's first public schools for whites opened in 1855. The schools closed during the Civil War and reopened shortly after the war.

5. See Andrew Ward, *Dark Midnight When I Rise: The Story of the Fisk Jubilee Singers Who Introduced the World to the Music of Black America* (New York: Farrar, Straus, Giroux, 2000); Cynthia Fleming, "A Survey of the Beginnings of Tennessee's Black Colleges and Universities, 1865–1920," *Tennessee Historical Quarterly* 39 (Summer 1980): 198–99; Richardson, *History of Fisk University,* 14.

6. Juan Williams and Dwayne Ashley with Shawn Rhea, *I'll Find a Way or Make One: A Tribute to Historically Black Colleges and Universities* (New York: Amistad Press, 2004), 365.

7. Booker T. Washington, "An Article in the Independent," Mar. 24, 1910, 613–18, in *Booker T. Washington Papers,* vol. 10 (Urbana: Univ. of Illinois Press, 1981, 2000), 288.

8. "Minnie Lou Crosthwaite," in *Notable Black American Women,* bk. 2, ed. Jessie Carney Smith (New York: Gale, 1996), 156–57. For more information regarding African American female teachers in Nashville, see Sonya Ramsey, *Reading, Writing, and Segregation: A Century of African American Teachers in Nashville* (Urbana: Univ. of Illinois Press, 2008).

Sonya Ramsey

9. "Virginia E. Walker Broughton," in *Notable Black American Women,* bk. 2, ed. Jessie Carney Smith (New York: Gale, 1996), 57. For more information regarding the writings of Virginia Boughton, see Sonya Ramsey, "Of Culture and Conviciton: African American Women Nonfiction Writers and the Gendered Definitions of Class," in *The Southern Middle Class in the Long Nineteenth Century,* ed. Jonathan Wells and Jennifer Green (Baton Rouge: Louisiana State Univ., 2011), 263–84.

10. Ida B. Wells-Barnett, *Crusade for Justice: The Autobiography of Ida B. Wells,* ed. Alfreda M. Duster (Chicago: Univ. of Chicago Press, 1970), 12; Dorothy Sterling, *Black Foremothers: Three Lives* (New York: Feminist Press, 1979), 66, 67.

11. Christopher Caplinger, "Conflict and Community: Racial Segregation in a New South City, 1860–1914" (PhD diss., Vanderbilt Univ., 2003), 183; Joseph H. Cartwright, *The Triumph of Jim Crow: Tennessee Race Relations in the 1880s* (Knoxville: Univ. of Tennessee Press, 1976), 29; Herbert Leon Clark, "The Public Career of James Carroll Napier, Businessman, Politician, and Crusader for Racial Justice, 1845–1940" (PhD diss., Middle Tennessee State Univ., 1980), 26. See Papers of James Carroll Napier, Special Collection, John Hope and Aurelia E. Franklin Library, Fisk University, Nashville.

12. Public Acts of the State of Tennessee, Tennessee General Assembly, chapter 108, Senate Bill 108, Mar. 18, 1901; James D. Anderson, *The Education of Blacks in the South, 1860–1935* (Chapel Hill: Univ. of North Carolina Press, 1988), 104.

13. Minutes, Nashville City Board of Education, Nov. 5, 1878, Office of the Board of Education, Metropolitan Nashville Public Schools, Nashville, Tenn.; Caplinger, "Conflict and Community," 185; see Smith, *Notable Black American Women,* Crosthwaite and Broughton entries.

14. Annual reports, Board of Education, Nashville City Schools, 1884, 1886, Office of the Board of Education, Metropolitan Nashville Public Schools, Nashville, Tenn.

15. Harold Rabinowitz, "Half a Loaf: The Shift from White to Black Teachers in the Negro Schools of the Urban South, 1865–1890," *Journal of Southern History* 40 (Nov. 1974): 579; Bobby Lovett, *The African American History of Nashville, Tennessee, 1780–1930: Elites and Dilemmas* (Fayetteville: Univ. of Arkansas, 1999), 138; Beverly Bond, "'Till Fair Aurora Rise': African American Women in Memphis, Tennessee 1840–1915" (PhD diss., Univ. of Memphis, 1996), 162.

16. Public Acts of the State of Tennessee, Tennessee General Assembly, "General Education Bill," House Bill 242, 1909; Fleming, "Survey of the Beginnings," 202.

17. Clark, "Public Career of James Carroll Napier," 116.

18. Ibid., 117; "Tennessee Agricultural and Industrial State Normal School," *Tennessee Agricultural and Industrial State Normal School Bulletin* 3, no. 8 (1914–15): 3, on file, Special Collections and Archives, Tennessee State University Library, Nashville.

19. Linda M. Perkins, "The History of Black Teaching: Growth and Decline within the Profession," in *American Teachers: Histories of a Profession at Work,* ed. Donald

Warren, American Education Research Association (New York: McMillan, 1989), 389; Lovett, *African American History of Nashville,* 169.

20. Stephanie Shaw, *What a Woman Ought to Be and to Do: Black Professional Workers in the Jim Crow Era* (Chicago: Univ. of Chicago Press, 1996), 90–91.

21. See Sharon Harley, "For the Good of the Family and Race: Gender, Work, and Domestic Roles in the Black Community, 1880–1930," *Signs* 15 (1990): 336–49; Shaw, *What a Woman Ought to Be,* 89–90; Shane White and Graham White, *Stylin': African American Expressive Culture from Its Beginnings to the Zoot Suit* (Ithaca: Cornell Univ. Press, 1998), 164.

22. Shaw, *What a Woman Ought to Be,* 81; Michael Fultz, "African American Teachers in the South: Powerless and the Expectations of Protest," *History of Education Quarterly* 35, no. 4 (Winter 1995): 408.

23. Sharon Harley, "Beyond the Classroom: The Organizational Lives of Black Female Educators in the District of Columbia, 1880–1930," *Journal of Negro Education* 51, no. 3 (Summer 1982): 256.

24. Stephanie J. Shaw, "Black Club Women and the Creation of the National Association of Club Women," *Journal of Women's History* 3 (Fall 1991): 19.

25. Wells-Barnett, *Crusade for Justice,* 18, 37.

26. Ibid.; Sterling, *Black Foremothers,* 75; see Ida B. Wells, *Southern Horrors: Lynch Law in All Its Phases (*Memphis: Self-published, 1892); Gail Bedderman, "Civilization, the Decline of Middle-Class Manliness, and Ida B. Wells' Anti-lynching Campaign (1892–94)," in *We Specialize in the Wholly Impossible: A Reader in Black Women's History,* ed. Darlene Clark Hine, Wilma King, and Linda Reed (New York: Carlson Publishing, 1995), 407, 414.

27. For more information, see Shaw, "Black Club Women," 19; Deborah Gray White, *Too Heavy a Load: Black Women in Defense of Themselves, 1894–1935* (New York: W. W. Norton, 1999); Minutes of the National Convention of the National Association of Colored Women, Nashville, Tenn., Sept. 15–18, 1897.

28. The Revolutionary-era poet spelled her name "Phillis."

29. For a discussion of the politics of respectability, see Evelyn Brooks Higginbotham, *Righteous Discontent: The Women's Movement in the Black Baptist Church, 1880–*1920 (Cambridge: Harvard Univ. Press, 1993), 185–229; and Gray White, *Too Heavy a Load,* 70. And for more information, see Kevin Gaines, *Uplifting the Race: Black Leadership, Politics, and Culture in the Twentieth Century* (Chapel Hill: Univ. of North Carolina, 1996); and E. Franklin Frazier, *The Black Bourgeoisie: The Rise of a New Middle Class in the United States* (New York: Free Press, 1957; Collier Books, 1975).

30. Gray White, *Too Heavy a Load,* 71.

31. Ibid., 77; Mary Church Terrell, "What Role Is the Educated Negro Woman to Play in the Uplift of Her Race?" in *Twentieth Century Negro Literature,* ed. D. W. Culp (Naperville, Ill.: J. L. Nichols, 1902), 172.

32. Harley, "For the Good of Family and Race," 348–49, cited in Shaw, "Black Club Women," 27.

33. "Mrs. Washington to Women's Clubs," *Nashville Globe,* June 20, 1913, 1.

34. Lester C. Lamon, *Black Tennesseans, 1900–1930* (Knoxville: Univ. of Tennessee Press, 1976), 213.

35. Yollette Trigg Jones, "The Black Community, Politics, and Race Relations in the 'Iris City' Nashville, Tennessee, 1870–1954" (PhD diss., Duke Univ., 1985)," 153; Cynthia Fleming, "The Development of Black Education in Tennessee, 1965–1920" (PhD diss., Duke Univ., 1977), 29.

36. Nannie E. Whiteman served as the president of the Memphis or City Federation of Colored Women's Clubs, which organized in 1905. Bond, "Till Fair Aurora Rise," 192, 199.

37. One such club was the Phyllis Wheatley Literary and Social Club, which differed in goals from Hooks's 1895 club, but during the late nineteenth century, several organizations across the country titled themselves after Phillis Wheatley. Bond, "Till Fair Aurora Rise," 193, 198.

38. "Negro Women, Tell to the World Their Purposes," *Nashville Globe,* June 24, 1910, 1.

39. Trigg Jones, "Black Community," 153.

40. Smith, "Virginia E. Walker Broughton," 58; Bond, "Till Fair Aurora Rise," 195.

41. Virginia Walker Broughton, "Editorial—No Author Given," *Memphis Commercial Appeal,* Feb. 14, 1895, quoted in Bond, "Till Fair Aurora Rise," 166.

42. Terrell, "What Role,"172.

43. Anita Shafer Goodstein, "A Rare Alliance: African American and White Women in the Tennessee Elections of 1919 and 1920," *Journal of Southern History* 2 (May 1998): 228.

44. Joanna P. Moore, *In Christ's Stead: Autobiographical Sketches* (Chicago: Women's Baptist Home Mission Society, 1902), 204–5, reprinted from Documenting the American South Collection, Special Collections, Louis Round Wilson Library, University of North Carolina at Chapel Hill.

45. Bond, "Till Fair Aurora Rise," 168; and Virginia Broughton, *Twenty Year's Experience of a Missionary* (Chicago: Pony Press, 1907), 7–10.

46. See Janice M. Leone's chapter, this volume; Ramsey, *Reading, Writing, and Segregation,* 30.

47. "Report of the Director from September 22 to October 20, 1913 to the National League on Urban Conditions Among Negroes" and Haynes to Mr. L. Hollingsworth Wood, Oct. 23, 1915, both in the George Haynes Papers, Special Collections, John Hope and Aurelia E. Franklin Library, Fisk University, Nashville; Richardson, *History of Fisk University,* 64; Lynda Wynn, "Bethlehem Centers of Nashville," Tennessee State University Libraries and Media Centers, http:/www.tnstate.edu/library/digital//beth.

htm/; Floris Barnett Cash, *African American Women and Social Action: The Club Women and Volunteerism for Jim Crow to the New Deal, 1896–1936* (New York: Greenwood Press, 2001), 83. Estelle Haskin is also referred to as Estelle Haskins in other references.

48. Shelia Wisner, "Whites Found Ways to Silence Black Vote for Nearly 40 Years," *Tennessean,* Feb. 9, 1992, 1B, Views and News Second Impressions from the Press Clippings File, fl. 27, Box 4, Metropolitan Government Archives, Nashville (hereafter cited as Metro Archives).

49. Elsa Barkley Brown, "Negotiating and Transforming the Public Sphere: African American Political Life in the Transition from Slavery to Freedom," *Public Culture* 7 (Fall 1994): 134; Rosalyn Terborg-Penn, *African American Women in the Struggle for the Vote, 1850–1920* (Bloomington: Indiana Univ. Press, 1998).

50. "Negro Women Prepare to Vote," *Nashville Banner,* Aug. 5, 1919, Reel 10, Tuskegee Institute Newspaper Clipping Files, Special Collections, Tuskegee University, Tuskegee, Ala.

51. Goodstein, "Rare Alliance," 227, 228.

52. Adele Logan Alexander, "Adella Hunt Logan, The Tuskegee Woman's Club, and African Americans in the Suffrage Movement," in *Votes for Women: The Woman Suffrage Movement in Tennessee, the South, and the Nation,* ed. Marjorie Spruill Wheeler (Knoxville: Univ. of Tennessee Press, 1995), 95.

53. Minnie L. Crosthwaite to Charlotte Hawkins Brown, July 16, 1921, File July–Dec. 1921, Reel 3, No. 41, Brown Collection, Arthur and Elizabeth Schlesinger Library on the History of Women in America, Radcliffe College, Cambridge, Mass., quoted in Glenda Gilmore, *Women and the Politics of White Supremacy in North Carolina, 1896–1920* (Chapel Hill: Univ. of North Carolina Press, 1996), 202.

54. Goldstein, "Rare Alliance," 242.

55. For more information about white clubwomen's work in Nashville, see Tennessee State Federation of Women's Clubs, *Woman's Work in Tennessee* (Memphis: Jones-Briggs, 1916).

56. Gilmore, *Women and the Politics of White Supremacy,* 174.

Chapter 7

"Dangerous" Women's Work: Expanding Acceptable Women's Roles and Developing Primary Education in Tennessee in the Early Twentieth Century

Mary A. Evins

"It is our qualities as women, lifted by conscious education to a point of a clear directing purpose in life, that . . . make women's contributions significant for the home, the state, the nation, and the world."

—Lucy Gage, 1933

A woman who served Davidson County, Tennessee, as its first supervisor of schools in the early 1900s said of her educational administrative work in the public elementary system that her supervisory job was "dangerous," she experienced acute "opposition from officials," and "all the principals were hostile."[1] Perhaps her observations overreached. Certainly women taught school and worked as educators in many and varying capacities through the nineteenth century. Among Tennessee's ninety-six counties, in rural Campbell County a woman even functioned as a school superintendent as early as 1893.[2] Yet at the turn of the last century, women administrators of any sort were few, and we must not dismiss the concerns of those who attained positions of authority and wrote candidly of their professional difficulties. Women strived for and achieved professional successes in the early twentieth century, but gendered realities limited options in the working world of one hundred years ago, even in the field of elementary education, which by the early twentieth century had become a female profession.

In the largely gender-neutral work environments of today, women can continue to feel workplace resistance. The appointment of southern women's historian Drew Gilpin Faust to the presidency of Harvard University in 2007 placed a woman for the first time ever as that institution's head, in one of the most visible positions for a woman in educational administration in the present day. However, only a few months earlier, her male predecessor, in a comment questioning women's "innate ability" in math and science, generated considerable fallout for his public reassertion of stereotypes that have circumscribed women's advancement.[3] When institutional culture and prominent opinion still openly verbalize biased attitudes that diminish women, how much more thoroughgoing, internalized, and unquestioned were circumscribed perceptions of women at the turn of the last century?

Two Nashville women educators whose careers pushed against those prejudices in the early twentieth century, who had visions of enlarged roles for women in society, and who themselves achieved measures of professional success locally and nationally despite limitations to advancement were Lucy Gage of Peabody College and Julia Green of Davidson County Public Schools. Both women worked in the field of primary education and became preeminent names in their specialization. They improved early elementary education within Tennessee, and the effects of those improvements were felt beyond the state. Gage was a professor of elementary education at Peabody. Green was an administrator who oversaw elementary classroom teachers in her public school district surrounding Nashville. Each began her career as a classroom teacher, but each through her own determination became a teacher of teachers and an innovator in her profession.

Early childhood education was an acceptable, proper professional endeavor in which women could engage in their era, but even in primary education the visibility of women in the public sphere challenged gender roles and placed women in caustic work environments. The perseverance and accomplishments of Gage and Green in their chosen areas highlight them as Progressive women who maximized opportunities within male-structured and male-controlled employment hierarchies. Each earned significant professional stature in her work during her lifetime and each was

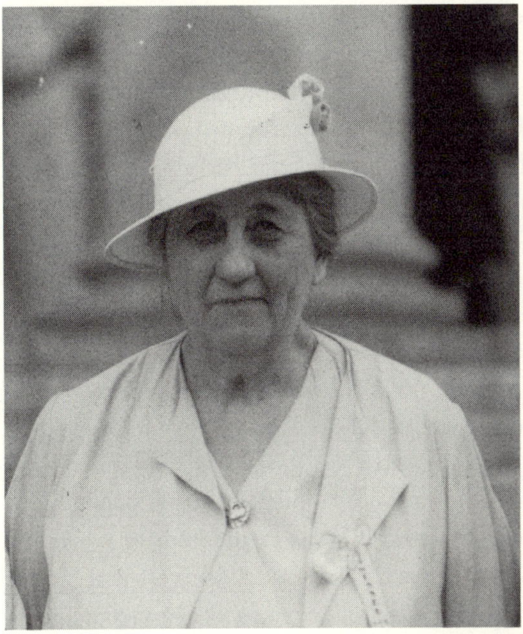

Lucy Elizabeth Gage. Courtesy of the Peabody Photograph Collection, Vanderbilt University Special Collections and University Archives.

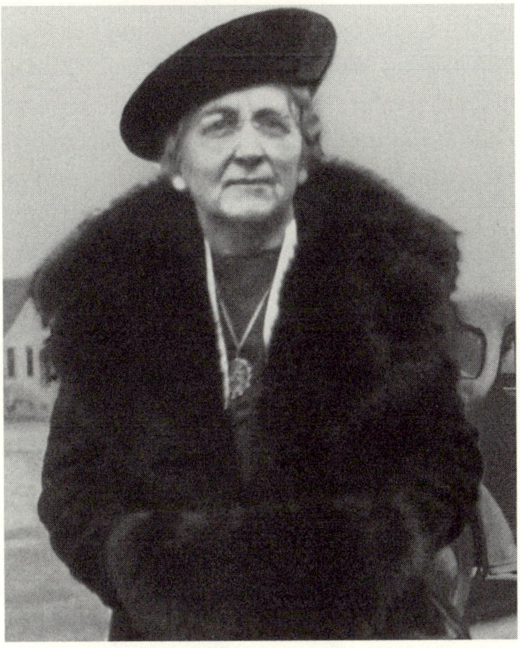

Julia McClung Green. Courtesy of the Waters-Weiland-Green family collection.

lauded for her substantial career achievements. Yet Gage and Green may personally have realized their finest successes in the parallel worlds of their professional associations, where, perhaps even more so than in the male institutions through which they were employed and paid, their contributions were richly valued by women professional peers who gave them respect and professional networks as well as needed emotional support toward their advancement in the male world of work.

The South lagged behind the rest of the nation in its advocacy of public education. Public attitudes, no definition of need by the ruling classes, and inadequate state structures for schools were key reasons for educational deficiencies, and the Civil War's destruction of southern economies undermined any standing public school systems that had operated effectively. In Tennessee even in the early 1800s, the state had taken steps to outline a program for common schools modeled on the pedagogical ideas of Horace Mann's New England schools as adapted for rustic life in the trans-Appalachian West, but resistance by landowners and lack of demand from an uneducated populace stalled progress toward publicly funded education in Tennessee.[4] In the postwar years the state again took stock of its educational situation and began systematic improvements. An 1873 survey reported that not even a third of Tennessee counties levied taxes to pay for public schooling and a significant proportion of Tennessee children received no educational instruction whatsoever.[5] With no regularized public school system, opposition to public education by the most affluent and influential, and indifference for it among the farming and working classes, few school systems existed and many that did were in session three or fewer months a year.[6]

Landmark 1873 legislation in Tennessee undertook substantial changes. The state assembly established a formal structure for public education by legally mandating that every county elect a school board and school superintendent, levy taxes sufficient to build and operate schools at least five months a year, and submit a detailed annual report to the state. A system of record keeping commenced that tracked the development of public education across Tennessee from the late 1800s.[7] No two years of reporting were the same, comparability of information between counties was rare, and some counties failed to comply, but annual tabulations documented educational progress and provided numbers of school-aged children from ages six to twenty-one, white and black, who were in need of instruction and could be served by public schooling.[8]

Part of new tax monies collected for public schooling was applied to improvements in educational infrastructure in each county. Annual reports tabulated globes, chalkboards, and maps per school and in what kinds of buildings instruction took place, because state educational leaders considered the quality of the classroom setting vital to appropriate learning and to modeling middle-class standards. Constructing modern school buildings of stone, brick, or clapboard, toward abandoning old pioneer log cabins as school houses, was an explicit objective, as was schoolyard beautification.[9]

Through the course of the late 1800s, publicly supported education gained popular acceptance in Tennessee, growing with the numbers of small farmers and small businessmen. As more modest-sized farms supplanted older, larger landholdings, and as small-farmers' associations superseded political dominance by an earlier agricultural elite, the state elected populist governors, democratic power gave rise to new expectations of government by the twentieth century, and publicly financed education for children gained force in state and county political agendas.[10] Years of implementing and meeting the first rudimentary requirements paid off, readying Tennessee counties for even greater educational changes to come. By the turn of the century a campaign called for new legislation to revamp the old system and strengthen education mandates. A new bill in 1903 fashioned a twentieth-century vision for public education in Tennessee and reflected a growing progressivism across the state, as well as nationally.[11]

Through all the educational shifts, the state remained consistently concerned to provide for proper instruction, examination, and certification of the state's teachers, many of whom were themselves only nominally educated, most having had no form of professional training whatsoever.[12] Toward that end, the state superintendent's office held teacher institutes throughout the state, lasting from a few days to a few weeks, to upgrade teacher quality and to examine the teachers for competence. Begun in the late 1800s, the institutes continued aggressively into the twentieth century. Annual reports from the counties informed the state superintendent how many training courses had been held each year, how many county teachers had participated in the trainings, how many teachers had applied to be examined, and how many had earned licensure through the institutes or through enrollment in higher education.[13]

For the purpose of training teachers better for elementary classrooms, George Peabody College brought Lucy Elizabeth Gage to Nashville, Tennessee, to develop Peabody's elementary education program for classroom primary teachers. A kindergarten teacher, Gage came to Peabody in 1920, where she taught until her retirement in 1942, and she lived out the remainder of her life in Tennessee.[14] When she arrived, she was in the middle of a career developed from the innovative, scientific, and diverse child development theories that had swept the world of early elementary pedagogy in the late nineteenth century into the twentieth century. Advocates for children demanded a unified program of childhood education, professional respect for the study of children's development, and legitimate academic research into the growth of the young mind, exciting ideas to which she had been exposed during schooling at the Free Kindergarten Collegiate Institute in Chicago and Teachers College at Columbia University in New York.[15] Gage's leadership roles in the International Kindergarten Union (IKU) and National Council of Primary Education (NCPE, or Primary Council), and the force of her potent personality, projected her into national visibility, which attracted Peabody to her. Yet in 1920 she had not even completed a college diploma and her appointment was contingent on finalization of her bachelor's degree in elementary supervision from Teachers College, which she did in 1922.[16] Having only an undergraduate degree herself, during her twenty-two years at Peabody she especially taught undergraduates preparing for their own careers in the classroom. Graduate students were permitted to take a percentage of upper-division undergraduate classes, so Gage also worked closely with grad students and served as major professor on many theses on kindergarten and primary education research.[17]

Born in southern Ohio in 1876 (died in Nashville in 1945), Gage grew up in Ohio and as a teenager moved with her parents to the timber forests of northern Wisconsin, where her father was a lumber man. In Wisconsin she completed high school and began assisting in a local kindergarten, an experience that informed her decision in 1894 to attend Chicago's Free Kindergarten Collegiate Institute. For two years she studied classic Froebel under leaders of free kindergartens, implemented in Chicago missions and settlements of the time. Her exposure also included the newer ideas of G. Stanley Hall on the child as a biological organism and the laboratory school models of John Dewey, who during his University of Chicago years also taught educational philosophy at the institute. The powerful, culture-changing concepts of early childhood education in the teaming urban setting of Chicago were for Gage intellectually heady and empowering, "very strong medicine" for a young lady opening her mind to both social consciousness and human development at the dawn of a new century.[18]

After earning her institute diploma in 1896 at age twenty, for the next five years Gage was director of a kindergarten in Chicago and taught in Wisconsin when at home with her family. In 1901, accompanying her parents who decided to uproot the family again, Gage moved to the Territory of Oklahoma (which did not become a state until 1907). The experience of living initially in a tent encampment on recently opened land and interacting with Native Americans and itinerant cowboys challenged Gage with new perspectives and was the next stage in her personal education. Within a few months of the family's arrival, she secured an elementary teaching position overseeing school children at Fort Cobb. The outback fort conditions were difficult and untenable, and when the school term ended, Gage left for Oklahoma City, itself a rough and muddy frontier town, determined to start a kindergarten program with herself as teacher. Lucy Gage had a broad vision. She set about to orchestrate politically the establishment of kindergartens in the public school system through the territory and to convince the territorial legislature that commencing a kindergarten program would identify Oklahoma as forward thinking and would reflect well in its application for statehood. In order to model what a proper kindergarten should entail, she solicited the support of clubwomen, businessmen, civic leaders, and clergy in Oklahoma City to underwrite the first kindergarten in the territory. Together the group founded the Oklahoma Kindergarten Association and funded an initial school year. Gage sought out families to send their children, taught the students, ran the school, and often dusted the building and stoked the wood stove.[19]

The demonstration kindergarten proved highly successful; Gage won converts. The first endeavor, however, was privately funded and open to only select children. Gage was committed to free kindergartens for all children, a system paid for by public funding and available throughout the territory. She knew that a territorial law would be required to achieve her objective. So she herself wrote a legislative bill for the public education of children under six years of age and for the establishment of training programs for kindergarten teachers in every normal school in the territory. By trudging the muddy streets and wooden sidewalks of Oklahoma City and Guthrie, the first capital, and actively working the local personalities and tumultuous territory politics, she succeeded in securing passage of the kindergarten bill through the territorial legislature in 1903. She even sat on the floor of the territorial senate during the middle-of-the-night vote on the bill, her presence emphasizing the imperative of its passage. She was twenty-six years old and already taken seriously as a respected educator and leader in the field of early learning.[20]

In the years following the Oklahoma law for public kindergartens and commensurate teacher training, Lucy Gage was a prime mover in their development. She worked to open schools, taught in them, supervised them, developed kindergarten training programs, advocated widely across the territory, promoted the progressivism of Oklahoma back East, gave academic papers at national meetings, and in the process advanced her own name professionally.[21] In the territory there were already a few state normal schools that had been established following white settlement.[22] No normal school, however, had yet been located in Oklahoma City, where Gage lived and the town she considered the "metropolis of the territory."[23] Fortuitously for Gage and for her kindergarten work, Epworth University was under construction in 1903 and opened in the fall of 1904 to educate the city's first college students. From the school's inception, Gage began developing Epworth's kindergarten program. She was professor of kindergarten training in the College of Arts and Sciences in the first college in Oklahoma City.[24] Epworth was a joint venture of the Methodist Episcopal Church and the Methodist Episcopal Church, South, an intriguing pairing in the West since the two churches still remained divided nationally. Gage herself was Presbyterian, but Epworth's ecumenism, apparent from its charter that brought together the two Methodisms, extended liberally across denominational lines. Ministers and members of different faiths, including the local Presbyterian church, participated in Epworth's opening ceremonies, warmly welcoming the new university to the city and lauding the benefits and respect to be accrued by everyone because of the new collegiate enterprise.[25]

Gage's years of successful politicking, building a public kindergarten program from scratch, accelerating rapidly within a higher-educational academic structure, and presenting Oklahoma and Epworth's innovations to a national audience positioned her for further advancement. She was an acknowledged program starter, someone who could formulate and implement from no preexisting infrastructure. The president of Western State Normal College in Kalamazoo, Michigan, invited her to develop a primary training program at his school, which itself was only founded in 1903. Gage accepted another challenge. She moved to Michigan in 1907 and determined at the same time to upgrade her own education. While developing the curriculum at Western State Normal (now Western Michigan University), she enrolled in Teachers College at Columbia University, taking classes periodically as she could in New York over the next years and exposing herself to the newest research and best practices in the field.[26] The pedagogical focus at Teachers College emphasized integration of kindergarten and the early school grades; early elementary education as the unification of all aspects of childhood development remained the unfulfilled agenda of primary educators for years. Toward that objective, one of the challenges within the field was unified training of primary educators within universities, versus separate programs for kindergarten teachers such as the institute that Gage herself had attended. Gage was inspired by the Columbia coursework on unification and contemporary ideas on human growth. Back at Kalamazoo, where her kindergarten training classes were included within the collegiate curriculum, she developed classes suitable for teachers of kindergarteners and grades one and two and exposed her Michigan students to broad, divergent educational theories.[27]

During the Michigan years, Gage grew more prominent in the International Kindergarten Union, founded in the United States in 1892. She had been introduced to IKU in Chicago and had presented papers at its conferences when at Epworth. As a professor at Western State Normal College she served on various IKU committees and became its national vice president by 1918.[28] At the same time she was a charter member of the National Council of Primary Education, founded in 1915 as the logical counterpart to the singularly focused International Kindergarten Union. She joined the NCPE as an educator in both disciplines, taking a personal stance in support of the fusion movement.[29] Teachers in the Midwest had formulated the idea for the NCPE and presented their proposal for the new national professional association "to a group of southern teachers at Peabody College in Nashville" for its early consideration.[30] Gage began teaching at Peabody in the summer of 1919 and relocated permanently to Nashville the following year when Peabody recruited her to join the faculty full time in 1920.[31]

The Peabody College to which Gage moved for the core twenty-two years of her professional life was the epicenter of teacher training in the South. Among the many normal schools founded for teacher training in the late nineteenth century, Peabody Normal College of the University of Nashville was an institution that grew in tandem with the processes of educational development across the South and within Tennessee. After the Civil War, hundreds of northern aid societies, missionary groups, education foundations, and wealthy donors funneled millions of dollars of financial support into war-torn southern states over decades, specifically toward the development of southern education.[32] In an ongoing endeavor to uplift and to lay the foundation of a New South, northern philanthropy attempted to fight rampant illiteracy in both the white and black populations, establish a rash of new schools and new programs, support state and local governments in the creation of their own school systems, and train teachers how to teach. No single effort was more broadly influential than the Peabody Education Fund, and no single institution emerged more pivotal to the work in the South than Peabody Normal College in Nashville, the George Peabody College for Teachers by the time Lucy Gage arrived (present-day Peabody College of Education and Human Development of Vanderbilt University).[33]

In 1903 the state of Tennessee had passed a new, restructured, twentieth-century package of educational legislation to upgrade Tennessee public schools. In that very year the Peabody Education Fund, an endowment for southern education begun by nineteenth-century businessman and philanthropist George Peabody after the Civil War, made the commitment to distribute its fund's remaining principal left over from postwar educational efforts. The trustees chose to allocate the fund's considerable remaining assets to endow permanently the George Peabody College, a decision for which the Tennessee General Assembly had actively lobbied.[34] The college determined to use the assets of the Peabody Education Fund to create in Nashville the premier teacher training institution of the South, comparable only to the School of Education at the University of Chicago and Teachers College at Columbia University. Since there had been a vacuum of educational authority in the South, public and private, Peabody's stated purpose was to provide leadership for all of southern education, across all southern states. The college set out to spearhead education reform in the Southeast and achieve national academic preeminence through rigorous standards of admission, innovative curricula, and world-class faculty. Its quality would be superior by far to every other southern normal school and it would rank among the most elite educational programs in the nation. The new Peabody opened its doors in 1914.[35]

A dynamic nucleus for ideas, scholarship, and educational reforms indeed centered at Peabody College, nourished by a broad student body and nationally recognized faculty. Peabody served the South as an educational think tank, a gathering place for Progressive innovators and their stimulating perspectives, the gateway through which cutting-edge tenets of pedagogy spread into southern schools. It offered a testing ground for new hypotheses and was a catalyst for educational and social change. Excitement was generated there. Not only did Peabody feed into and improve public and private education in Tennessee, but its graduates fanned out across the country and carried the reputation of Peabody with them.[36]

Most recountings of the accomplishments that emanated from Peabody focus on the men who built the school and on the achievements of its male graduates.[37] The pattern at Peabody that emphasized male leadership and scholarship was a means to counter the embarrassment that the field of education had become feminized. Through the course of the nineteenth century, the growing numbers of women in education meant that the stature and esteem men had previously enjoyed as school masters diminished over time, along with the respect and value of schools of education, as teaching became more emasculated in comparison to the standing men enjoyed in other occupations.[38] To counteract this feminization, male and female pathways in education began to follow distinctly different trajectories—women into the lesser areas of elementary education and female arts such as home economics, men into programs of preeminence, upper-level teaching, administration, and positions requiring higher degrees. Balkanization emerged in academic systems, as normal colleges and schools for teachers strived to secure and maintain academic prestige through the numerical dominance of male faculty, as did Peabody.[39] A positive byproduct of the separation was that the women's world, although lacking institutional power, could operate relatively autonomously, as with benign neglect, unhampered by larger administrative concerns about more weighty issues.

The feminization of school teaching in the United States was a process that took place across the country through the 1800s, supported by the emergence of the middle class and the greater access of women to education. Catharine Beecher had termed teaching "woman's express business" in 1829, advocating that women were already teachers in the home and needed but to gain further education for themselves in order to be prepared to properly transmit knowledge in formal settings to the next generations.[40] Her ideas proved prophetic as more and more women, through the nineteenth and into the twentieth centuries, not only took tutoring jobs in private homes but also increasingly taught in schools and classrooms, private and public, beyond the domestic sphere.

That same transition took place in Tennessee. The state's annual public school reports illustrate the steady growth through the 1800s in the number of women teachers. Even as late as the late 1880s, more than two-thirds of all teachers in Tennessee public schools were still men, fewer than a third women.[41] At the turn of the century, between 1901 and 1903 in Tennessee, the tipping point occurred and women numerically superseded men, effectively sealing the fate of the classroom teaching profession as a job of diminished respect and assuring that men would tightly secure control of the leadership positions in education as upper-level teachers, principals, administrators, and superintendents. Further articulating the gender disparity materializing at the turn of the century was that the number of public high schools in Tennessee was small in comparison to elementary schools. In the Davidson County system, for example, in the rural county districts outside of Nashville, there was no high school at all in 1912; students who aspired to high school were sent to Nashville, where high school was actually an option.[42] With teaching young children identified as the appropriate field for women, such positions quantitatively more numerous, and men stepping away from classrooms with younger pupils, gender balance and perception shifted. Men's jobs in education were fewer and more highly prized; teaching small children was the distaff side of education.

In response to the emerging market for the preparation of new women elementary teachers qualified to meet and surpass state educational benchmarks, Peabody College brought Lucy Gage to Tennessee. If educational development in the South and in Tennessee was slow, kindergarten progress was slower, and in Tennessee, it was among the very slowest.[43] Most kindergartens were either established as private preschools for the children of educated parents who sought special exposure for their children or, on other end of the spectrum, founded as means of social reform, to uplift the children of the poor, provided by missionary societies, settlement houses, churches, and philanthropic organizations. Both types of kindergartens advanced in urban areas before extending into rural counties. The same was true for publicly supported kindergartens, which a handful of Progressive city schools undertook long before rural systems did. Incremental improvements across Tennessee proceeded system by system during the course of the twentieth century.[44] Gage aggressively advocated the pressing need for better education for children through her entire professional life, to improve the quality of childhood education and to broaden its scope so that children under age six could also be publicly taught. She witnessed great progress during her lifetime, toward much of which she was a direct social force, but even near the end of her career she lamented that despite significant advancements, the "southern part of the United States trails in this respect. . . . The south is still paying the price of a one-time leisurely plantation life that was secured through the sacrifice of mass education. Naturally public education is young in the south, younger than many Americans realize, and . . . younger children are provided for last."[45]

The program Gage helped develop at Peabody was the early elementary education curriculum, responding to the realities of education in Tennessee and the South while bringing to the discipline the overarching fusion framework for the whole development of the young child, preschool to grade school.[46] The corpus of her own writings, and subsequent analyses of them, showcase Gage's professional philosophies, coursework, teaching styles, and extensive research with elementary school children through her hands-on "Green house" teaching laboratory for her preservice teachers and through the lower school of Peabody Demonstration School.[47] A national leader and one of the preeminent scholars in her field, Gage was termed "the voice of early childhood education."[48] A consistent focus throughout her years of teaching, from Oklahoma to Tennessee, was the "intelligent" teaching of children; she used "intelligent" and "intelligence" consistently in almost every paper or publication she ever wrote in her insistence on educated rather than "sentimental" treatment of children. She insisted concurrently on intelligent parenting and dedicated a significant portion of her professional energy toward educating parents in the work of benefiting their children's best outcomes.[49] Her studies of children's physical development informed her focus on active children, on their need for pure movement, and on motor activities and hands-on learning, which she emphasized was not about the activity itself but the processes of skill building and knowledge acquisition that physical work engenders. Being herself a child of the backwoods and the frontier, she emphasized vigorous outdoor exercise and working with natural, earthy materials. She eschewed academic formalism and promoted fresh research into the growth of children. Gage's students used an empty building on campus, her Green house, in which every term they developed new, innovative environments and materials to engage children.

Without question Lucy Gage was a beloved professor. She was warm and giving of herself, while high minded with high standards. She inspired and motivated cohort after cohort of early elementary teachers. She welcomed students to her rustic mountain home in Beersheba Springs in the Tennessee upper Cumberlands. She never married and never had children of her own, so surely her students were the lives she touched personally, in addition to elevating their classroom skills and elevating the profession. Both at the time of her retirement and her death, the laudatory letters and commemorations poured in, from former students and colleagues alike, from all over the country. Comments demonstrated the admiration others felt for her and reflected on her sweetness, which must have been one aspect of her personality.[50]

What is more striking, however, when reading of Lucy Gage was her personal force, which she used to her advantage to advance her pedagogical ideas and accomplish her objectives for childhood education. Her personal strength must have been a critical factor in her ability to move upward in the male world of higher education. In its benign manifestation, her personality included "her power, her determination, her uncompromising attitude wherever the welfare of children was at stake." She was clear and "so direct, so concrete in her thinking" that she never failed to make her points explicitly understood by her students.[51] Students considered Gage exacting and fiercely committed to quality. Yet her manner was sometimes frankly harsh by today's standards. Her methods included rants and smashing apart those college students' projects that she deemed inadequate. She railed against "genteel, unmarried women" in the classroom, their "sugar-coated methods," and their "vicarious, sentimental motherhood." Her indictment of "sentimentality" in the classroom extended to what she considered inappropriate compliments of elementary students' work as adequate, when teachers might say, "'Oh, it is lovely,' when it was really rotten," applying perhaps present-day "tiger mother" principles to the evaluation of young children's work.[52] Gage was respected, revered, and endeared to many, but she was simultaneously quite controversial, argumentative, and not a woman to be taken lightly. In an educational arena that held conservatively to a narrow range of appropriate women's behaviors, she did not conform.

Gage rose from assistant professor in 1920 at Peabody College to full professor by 1930, a stellar accomplishment because never in the history of Peabody did more than five women hold the title of full professor at any one time until the 1970s, and the five simultaneous professorships for women were only attained during two single years throughout the entire period of the early to mid-twentieth century.[53] At Peabody, most women had positions with support titles, and many held no title at all. Gage broke through the promotion barriers for a variety of reasons, which likely included the assertive, even abrasive, personality that set her apart. Her nontraditional background in the West and Midwest distinguished her from the southern ladies of the culture within which she worked. She did not adhere to the roles of self-effacement and femininity, nor to southern women's place and comportment on campus. Because of the college's environment of intimidation and limitations to women, most women faculty did not open their mouths or engage in dialogues at faculty meetings, but Lucy Gage did.[54] She held sizable power among her male colleagues,[55] which she likely acquired by positioning herself among her male peers with her intellect and biting commentary. She countered hostility with hostility, she herself used fear and intimidation in her working world, and she had no hesitancy whatsoever verbally tearing into people.[56] In the business world of win-lose, Gage liked to win. When she took a position she believed in, she dug in her heels and would not recant or retract. One of her male colleagues wrote that "Lucy Gage does not . . . project herself like a woman; she hits like Joe Louis."[57] Over and above her larger-than-life professional behaviors, Gage was physically quite a large woman; her corporal presence carried weight that she also maximized to personal advantage.

Lucy Gage was no shrinking violet, and it served her well. Peabody brought her to the college with no doctoral degree, no master's degree; in 1920 she did not even have an undergraduate diploma. Her tangible accomplishments in the development of kindergartens and kindergarten education programs were her admission ticket. Perhaps the Peabody administration, in its desire to differentiate women's lesser educational standing from men's higher specialties, preferred her paperless credentials.[58] In such an occupational setting, despite the framework that inherently diminished her work, Gage made her mark. She operated from within the existent system to create programs and personnel for childhood education, and she developed the field. She generated a cadre of followers and admirers around her who advanced her stature. She used her networks and personality to break down barriers and limitations within academia to her personal advantage. She was one of those women who pushed from within. Through her own professional development she helped define pedagogy, establish methodologies, and provide models and opportunities for those to follow. She did it despite all odds, in an era, as she said herself, when "the community was very largely hostile to the idea of higher education for women."[59]

A counterpart in Nashville to Lucy Gage's professorial role in training primary teachers in college was Julia Green's role in overseeing primary teachers in their classrooms. Julia McClung Green was the supervisor of elementary education for Davidson County, Tennessee, from 1911 to 1944. In those days, county government and county schools were separate from the City of Nashville government and Nashville schools. Julia Green and Lucy Gage were contemporaries. They were born in the same decade and retired in the same decade, but Green (1873–1961) lived somewhat longer than Gage.[60] "Miss Julia" was born and reared in privilege in Middle Tennessee and, very unlike Gage, was a consummate southern lady at all times, retaining the trappings of the "true womanhood" of her place and era; she actually taught etiquette and manners and humbly minimized her work. Physically she was a diminutive woman, under five feet tall, petite and unthreatening, master of the genteel grace of self-deprecation that allowed her to be the little woman behind great men within the Davidson County Board of Education. Julia Green was as politically savvy as Gage, but in a very different way: Green never took credit for the successes achieved in her work but instead always publicly deferred to, acknowledged, and praised the powerful men under whom she served, from whom she derived and sustained her authority to act and who were "booster[s] in all our pioneering."[61] And yet it was she, writing in the later years of her life, who remembered her early work as having been, in fact, dangerous, difficult to navigate, and fraught with opposition from hostile male officials.[62] Deference, however, not counterhostility, was her coping mechanism.

Green was the first ever supervisor of elementary education and the first supervisor of any level of teaching in Davidson County and, in fact, the entire state of Tennessee.[63] She actually developed the job description herself in 1911 and confidently persuaded the county school superintendent of the need for someone to oversee teachers directly in their classrooms and convinced him to hire her to do it.[64] At the time, Julia Green had been a teacher for eight years, having taken her first classroom in 1903, teaching first and second grades in an elementary school in rural Davidson County. When she started teaching in 1903, she was one of the entering women primary teachers who helped tip the scales of the teaching profession in Tennessee such that it became a female-dominated occupation. She was about thirty years old when she commenced her career, a decade older than Lucy Gage had been when she began. Green was a well-read and well-educated child of privilege who had grown up in a grand Italianate mansion on an estate outside of Nashville, instructed through her youth by private tutors hired by her parents.[65] At various points she attended county teaching institutes and took classes at Peabody College, the University of Tennessee in Knoxville, and Teachers College in New York;[66] most if not all of her collegiate work was likely taken during her years as a teacher and supervisor. As was true for Lucy Gage, Julia Green's professional accomplishments were achieved without strong academic credentials.

While in the classroom as an elementary teacher, Green became aware of a need within the developing county educational structure; she saw the distance between male principals and the women teachers in their schools, who were left to fend for themselves without any personal guidance. Green's fellow teachers often came to her to ask for teaching help, not wanting to bother the principal or interfere with his lofty duties. Green gave assistance as she could and in the process came to realize that a supervisor to offer regular direct support to primary teachers ought to be provided by the county board of education. She saw a professional advancement opportunity for herself, and through the force of her own personality she proposed to the county superintendent that he create such a position and hire her for it. He did,[67] and she served as primary supervisor for the next thirty-two years. As had Gage, Green comprehended the political steps required to engineer the goal she wanted to accomplish, which would change the status quo and better her own position, and she had no reticence whatsoever in undertaking them.

Julia Green stayed within the Davidson County school system her entire professional life. Although she lived in Nashville as an adult, neither her teaching nor her supervisory oversight was in the city itself; she operated in often hard-to-get-to schools, weaving together classrooms across a geographically spread-out school system dispersed over 510 square miles of Davidson County.[68] She oversaw all of the elementary schools in the county, white and black alike, getting to each school once a month, working with the primary teachers to improve their curricula and classroom techniques and elevate their standards. Every day was different from the next. She intrepidly traversed the county in buggy, by rail when tracks ran to the sectors of the county she needed to access, and eventually by Model T Ford, being perhaps the first woman in Nashville with a driver's license.[69] In making her rounds in the early years, she was subject to runaway horses, being mired in mud and stuck in creeks in districts with no paved roads, and bewilderment by country people who had never seen an automobile, much less a woman driver. "In those days there was no such thing as the 40-hour week," she wrote. "I would go out at 7:30 A.M., ride a street car to Union Station, catch a train to Goodlettsville [for example], hire a horse and buggy there to take me to the school house, visit, guest-teach, confer with the teacher on special problems, reverse my transportation procedure and get home about 9:30 p.m. . . . I was even more of a curiosity in my flivver which I cranked in every corner of Davidson County."[70]

Julia Green was a lifelong, activist Methodist, no doubt inspired by and directly involved in the work of the Methodist mission societies of her era in Nashville. The Methodist Church played a foundational role in her life from her earliest years through her lifetime mission as an educator. She was the granddaughter of circuit-riding Methodist minister Alexander Little Page Green, one of the principle founders of Vanderbilt University (although that detail is not typically recorded in most histories of

Vanderbilt),[71] which had been originally established to train Methodist ministers, as had Epworth later in the West. Julia Green began contributing to her community beyond the home by playing the organ at church as a little girl and teaching Sunday School to adults when she was a teenager. She described herself pointedly as a Progressive her whole life and as someone who daily lived the tenets of her faith.[72] She was expressly socially conscious; she sought to bring change to society and to women, and to be the change herself.

During her tenure as teacher and supervisor in Davidson County, Tennessee—from near the turn of the century to almost the end of World War II—the county's schools underwent marked transformations and systemically experienced twentieth-century progress. Julia Green was "directly responsible for much of it"—"material facilities and equipment," "wage scales," the "application of standard qualifications for its personnel," "the enrollment of pupils," and bringing to the county "the benefits of a modern educational system."[73] She is credited as a force behind forward advancements for schools, children, and teachers over four decades in her school district. Among her areas of accomplishment were her primary-school pedagogical curriculum objectives, the creation of county-wide school hot lunch programs, public health initiatives in the school system, and bringing to Nashville numerous national education organizations.[74] What she facilitated and instigated for Davidson County, in the state capital, were models of what were utilized and adapted for application in educational programs across the state. Green also pushed from within, vigorously and effectively, seemingly at odds with the ladylike southern persona she projected.

In addition to her school accomplishments, the support organizations in which she was heavily vested were of equal significance to her. For one, she worked toward establishment of the Congress of Parents and Teachers (as the PTA was then known) in Davidson County, beginning in 1911, the year she became primary supervisor.[75] The concept was new then, and many in the schools and even the general public questioned a natural alliance between teachers and parents. A Nashville woman was president of the statewide PTA from 1913 to 1923, during which time the PTA financially supported free lunches for needy children, toward which Green was likely instrumental.[76] For another, she was one of the three founding members who brought the National Education Association to Davidson County in 1933–34, working to transfer the Tennessee Teachers Association to the national union to strengthen her teachers' contracts and salaries.[77] She is credited as a founder of the Nashville chapter of Delta Kappa Gamma, the national honor society for notable women educators, which she used to promote the visibility of local teachers and to professionalize and bring prestige to grade-school teaching.[78] Another of her involvements was the Nashville chapter of the Altrusa Society, a service organization for professional women largely outside of education with whom Green networked to garner women's solidarity for pay increases for teachers. In Altrusa she chaired the committee on vocational education information, reflecting her interest in technical skills development for young people, which paralleled the "career days" she started in county schools to provide students information about future working-world opportunities.[79]

Then there was the Primary Council, later the Association for Childhood Education (ACE), in which Green was heavily involved, as was Lucy Gage. In addition to the domains of primary education, professional leadership in Nashville, and educational advancement connected to Peabody College, the work and worlds of Julia Green and Lucy Gage very much overlapped within the Primary Council and the later ACE. The National Council of Primary Education (NCPE), or Primary Council when it was founded in 1915, immediately grabbed the hearts of Tennessee elementary teachers. This national organization brought schoolteachers together to learn and discuss new ideas in their field and gave them a national platform. Green is credited as having participated in the formation of the NCPE chapter in Tennessee.[80] Tennessee teachers' memberships in the national council and its successor, the ACE, typically were among the very highest participation rates in the entire country, Green herself recruiting phalanxes of members from among her teachers.[81] It was in Memphis in 1930 that the International Kindergarten Union met for its annual convention and voted to disband as a separate entity entirely and join the NCPE in a synergistic organizational fusion of the two groups' modern integrated-early-learning construct.[82] Toward this unification, people like Lucy Gage had been working for years. Both the IKU and the Primary

Council surrendered their prior names, both closed down corporately, and together they cooperatively restructured as the brand-new Association for Childhood Education (currently, the Association for Childhood Education International, or ACEI). The national ACE came to Tennessee just four years later, in 1934, to hold its annual meeting in Nashville.[83] In this mix of primary education associations, Green and Gage were leaders, Green at the state level, Gage nationally.

Gage joined the NCPE at its beginning, when she was still at Western State Normal College and, as she had in IKU, held national positions.[84] Soon after coming to Peabody, she became the Primary Council's vice chair, 1923–25, then headed the overall organization, 1925–27. She continued as a decision maker within NCPE until its closing in 1931, serving on its national board of directors and as the presiding officer over joint sessions of NCPE and IKU as the groups were stepping toward unification. With two other NCPE officers she wrote the sixteen-year history of the Primary Council.[85] Her visibility in these organizations brought status to Gage and to her home university. Right after her years as the national head of the council, she was promoted by Peabody to full professor in 1930.

Green was equally committed to the NCPE-turned-ACE, which she served over the years variously as local chapter president and state president, and when Nashville hosted the ACE national convention in Nashville in 1934, Green co-chaired it. Patty Smith Hill, preeminent scholar, professor, and close personal friend of Gage, and likely of Green as well, was brought to Nashville from Columbia University to give the keynote address for the plenary dinner session, which Green held at Tennessee Agricultural and Industrial State Normal School for Negroes, the African American public university in highly segregated Nashville, a little act of subversion that speaks well of Green.[86] The national ACE referred to Julia Green as "an almost legendary figure."[87] She in turn referred to the ACE as her "beloved" and held a lifetime membership.[88]

The two women vested a great deal professionally in these groups, which were sources of esteem-building and genuine appreciation for them. Moreover, the relationships they formed within IKU-NCPE-ACE were emotional, heartfelt, and affectionate. The level of commitment and involvement of Green and Gage in the primary associations went beyond membership duties for job advancement. The groups were national and provided professional prestige, but they were made up of primary educators, almost all of whom were women. It was these women, the teachers, whom Green and Gage nurtured in the thousands through their careers, who loved them and whom they loved, to whom they opened their homes, hearts, and lives. The relationships in the organizations were personal and transcended work.

These professional yet warm, personal relationships among the women are in contrast to the respectful but formal, negotiated professional relationships between the two primary educators and their male colleagues. The authority the men held in the women's work institutions established tensions that Gage and Green each navigated in her own way. Both Green and Gage moved successfully within their male realms and achieved "new levels of attainment" by carving out acceptable zones of professional advancement, despite impediments. In Green's later years, with so much societal change around her, she reflected back on her years in the world of work and with characteristic grace commented that the difficulties she had faced were overridden by the positive memories. Similarly, Gage's rough edges softened to appreciation and generosity of spirit, but she maintained that women were the ones truly poised to make society's notable advancements.[89]

The difficulties they faced were surely tempered by the exciting times for women in the early twentieth century, when Green and Gage engaged in their professional work. In Tennessee, the legislature permitted women to practice law, hold minor political positions, serve on boards, and be superintendents by 1909; married women could manage their own money in 1911 and their own property in 1913; women got the vote in 1920; and the shared guardianship of children was legalized in 1921.[90] Among the areas of advancement in education were integrated early learning, primary education as a research field, the professionalization of teaching, development of improved state systems for public instruction, the geographic spread of public schools, and the evolving quality of education itself. Green and Gage furthered all of these areas, in great measure, within male-dominated institutions. They both explicitly saw their professional work as "pioneering"—in education as well as in the larger society.[91] Both women were deeply involved with the advancements of their time in children's learning, and they promoted the ideas to the widest possible audiences by disseminating their philosophies through structured systems they themselves participated in establishing. They developed primary education in Tennessee and simultaneously advanced the roles of women.

Both Julia Green and Lucy Gage were apostle-like in their evangelism for primary education.[92] They worked to improve local cultural environments that would generate public demand for the ideals of primary education. They identified areas of need, crafted policies to address those needs, and worked individually and with others to secure the necessary reforms to see their ideas adopted, and the professional organizations in which Green and Gage participated provided them supplementary platforms to facilitate their success and the personal emotional support to achieve in the public world of men.

NOTES

The opening epigraph refers to Lucy Gage, "Women's Part in Reconstruction of World Values" (1933), manuscript collection 162, Box 1, File 22.

1. Julia McClung Green, handwritten autobiographical notes (in the possession of her niece, Florence Weiland, Aug. 8, 1998), n.d. Lucy Gage Papers, Special Collections and University Archives, Jean and Alexander Heard Library, Vanderbilt University (hereafter cited as Lucy Gage Papers).

2. *Annual Report of the State Superintendent of Public Instruction for Tennessee for the Scholastic Year Ending June 30, 1896, Submitted to the Governor* (Nashville: Franc. M. Paul, 1897), 174, 176.

3. Lawrence H. Summers in Derrick Z. Jackson, "Summers's Tortured Logic," *Boston Globe,* Jan. 19, 2005; Daniel J. Hemel, "Summers' Comments on Women and Science Draw Ire," *Harvard Crimson,* Jan. 14, 2005; Marcella Bombardieri, "Harvard Women's Group Rips Summers," *Boston Globe,* Jan. 19, 2005.

4. *Report of the Superintendent of Public Instruction to the General Assembly of Tennessee* (Nashville: J. Geo. Harris, 1839); Solon J. Buck, *The Agrarian Crusade: A Chronicle of the Farmer in Politics* (New Haven: Yale Univ. Press, 1920), 19; John Trotwood Moore and Austin P. Foster, *Tennessee: The Volunteer State, 1769–1923,* vol. 1 (Chicago: S. I. Clarke, 1923), 542ff.; Robert H. White, *Development of the Tennessee State Educational Organization, 1796–1929* (Kingsport, Tenn.: Southern Publishers, 1929); Edwin P. Conklin, "Agriculture," in *Tennessee: A History, 1673–1891,* vol. 2, ed. Philip M. Hamer (New York: American Historical Society, 1933), 681–82, 833; Andrew David Holt, "Forces Retarding Educational Growth," *Struggle for a State System of Public Schools*

in Tennessee, 1903–1936, Contributions to Education 753, Teachers College, Columbia University (New York: Teachers College, Columbia Univ., 1938), 5–30; Austin P. Foster and Albert H. Roberts, *Tennessee Democracy* (Nashville: Democratic Historical Association, 1944); Clement Eaton, "Molding the Southern Mind," in *A History of the Old South: The Emergence of a Reluctant Nation*, 3rd ed., ed. Clement Eaton (New York: Macmillan, 1975), 436–46.

5. *Report of J. B. Killebrew, Assistant Superintendent of Public Instruction for the State of Tennessee to the Thirty-Eighth General Assembly* (Nashville: Jones, Purvis, 1973), 6–7.

6. Ibid., 6–7, 28, 32, 24, 41–40.

7. J. B. Killebrew, "Report of the Assistant Superintendent of Public Instruction, Nashville, March 14, 1872," in *Report of the Hon. W. M. Morrow, Superintendent of Public Instruction, ex officio, to the Called Session of the Thirty-Seventh General Assembly of the State of Tennessee,* 5–28 (Nashville: Jones, Purvis, 1872), 20–21; *Acts of the State of Tennessee Passed by the Thirty-Eighth General Assembly 1873*(Nashville: Jones, Purvis, 1973), chap. 25, 39–51 (hereafter cited as *Acts of Tennessee,* with appropriate dates and citations).

8. *Annual Report of the State Superintendent of Public Instruction for the School Year Ending June 30, 1887, Submitted to the Governor* (Nashville: Marshall & Bruce, 1888), 103–5.

9. As late as 1896, log cabin schools remained 24 percent of Tennessee's school buildings, particularly in rural parts of the state; by 1912, with the mandate for improvement of facilities, log cabins had been reduced to just 4 percent of the official count of schools. *Annual Report* (1896), 132–35; *Biennial Report of the State Superintendent of Public Instruction of Tennessee for the Scholastic Years Ending June 30, 1911–1912, Submitted to the Governor* (Nashville: Brandon Printing, 1912), 138–41. *Acts of Tennessee 1887* called for "planting of trees about the public school builidings, that the grounds may be beautiful and made more attractive, and the minds of the yourng impressed with the importance of the subject" (chap. 172, 297).

10. Dan M. Robison, *Bob Taylor and the Agrarian Revolt in Tennessee* (Chapel Hill: Univ. of North Carolina Press, 1935); Philip M. Hamer, "The Farmer in Politics," in *Tennessee: A History, 1673–1891,* vol. 2, ed. Philip M. Hamer (New York: American Historical Society, 1933), 693–701; Conklin, "Agriculture," 833–34: Between 1860 and 1900, the farms in Tennessee had almost tripled in number and had been reduced in size by nearly two-thirds. In 1860 there were 82,368 farms of an average size of 250.9 acres; by 1900, Tennessee farms were more numerous and were smaller, totaling 224,623 farms of an average size of 90.6 acres.

11. Andrew Holt, "Agencies Promoting Educational Growth," *The Struggle for a State System of Public Schools in Tennessee, 1903–1936,* Contributions to Education 753, Teachers College, Columbia University (New York: Teachers College, Columbia Univ., 1938), 31–74; Mary S. Hoffschwelle, *Rebuilding the Rural Southern Community: Reformers, Schools, and Homes in Tennessee, 1900–1930* (Knoxville: Univ. of Tennessee Press, 1998), 19–20; *Acts of Tennessee 1903,* chap. 254, House Bill 582, 592–96.

12. *Annual Report of the State Superintendent of Public Instruction for the School Year Ending June 30, 1887,* 40.

13. Dick B. Clough, "A History of Teachers' Institutes in Tennessee, 1875–1915," (EdD diss., Memphis State Univ., 1972).

14. Carrie Bailey, "Life and Work of Lucy Gage, Pioneer Teacher and Leader" (master's thesis, George Peabody College for Teachers, 1960); Agnes Snyder, "Lucy Gage (1876–1945), Pioneering Through Life," in *Dauntless Women in Childhood Education 1856–1931,* by Agnes Snyder (Washington, D.C.: Association for Childhood Education International, 1972), 323–54; Darwin L. Henderson, "Elizabeth Peabody and Lucy Gage: A Comparative Study of Their Contributions to the American Kindergarten" (master's thesis, George Peabody College for Teachers, 1976); Nancy Alderman Ransom, "A Comparative History of Faculty Women at George Peabody College for Teachers and Vanderbilt University, 1875 to 1970" (EdD diss., George Peabody College for Teachers of Vanderbilt Univ., 1988).

15. Ella Dobbs, Lucy Green, and Julia Hahn, "History of the National Council of Primary Education," *NCPE Bulletin,* Feb. 1932, on file in the archive of the Association of Childhood Education International, University of Maryland Library Archives, College Park; Lucy Gage, "The Slow Growth of Professionalism in the Field of Education of Young Children," Box 1, File 22, Lucy Gage Papers.

16. Snyder, "Lucy Gage," 339; Bailey, "Life and Work of Lucy Gage"; Henderson, "Elizabeth Peabody and Lucy Gage."

17. Snyder, "Lucy Gage," 340. Examples of thesis topics for which Lucy Gage was the major professor: Frances Lacy, "Teaching of Industry and Art in the Early Elementary Grades" (master's thesis, Department of Elementary Education, Peabody College, 1926); Lillian Sessoms, "A Study of the Rhythmic Element in the Language of Young Children" (master's thesis, Department of Elementary Education, Peabody College, 1929); Pauline Leeman, "A Study Evaluating Children's Drawings in Kindergarten and Early Grades" (master's thesis, Department of Elementary Education, Peabody College, 1930); Ruth Orgain, "Health Education in the Kindergarten" (master's thesis, Department of Elementary Education, Peabody College, 1930); Gardie Kirkman, "The Place of the Kindergarten in the Child's Adjustment" (master's thesis, Department of Elementary Education, Peabody College, 1932); Martha Alexander, "Seventy-three Years of Kindergarten in Kentucky" (master's thesis, Department of Elementary Education, Peabody College, 1938).

18. Gage, "Slow Growth of Professionalism," 4.

19. Lucy Gage, "Pioneering in Education," Box 1, File 1, Lucy Gage Papers; Snyder, "Lucy Gage," 332–34.

20. Ibid.

21. Lucy Gage, "The Kindergarten Training Course as a Department of a University" (paper presented at the Thirteenth Annual Meeting of the International Kindergarten Union, Milwaukee, Apr. 1905), *Kindergarten-Primary Magazine* 18, no. 10 (June 1906): 619–21; Bailey, "Life and Work of Lucy Gage"; Snyder, "Lucy Gage."

22. L. David Norris, "Colleges and Universities, Normal," *Encyclopedia of Oklahoma History and Culture,* Oklahoma Historical Society, http://digital.library.okstate.edu/encyclopedia/entries/C/CO027.html/.

23. Gage, "Kindergarten Training Course," 619.

24. Ray Asplin, "Epworth University," *Chronicles of Oklahoma* 32, no. 4 (Oklahoma City: Oklahoma Historical Society, 1954), 378.

25. Ibid., 375. Note that the two Methodisms did not successfully maintain unity for long; in 1911 the two conferences dissolved their shared venture and terminated Epworth University, which had lasted less than a decade. Other institutions absorbed Epworth's students, properties, programs, and faculty, and Gage's departure in 1907 was timely. Epworth is considered the precursor institution of present-day Oklahoma City University (Asplin, "Epworth University"; John D. Heisch, "Oklahoma City University," *Encyclopedia of Oklahoma History and Culture,* Oklahoma Historical Society, http://digital.library.okstate.edu/encyclopedia/entries/C/CO027.html/).

26. Bailey, "Life and Work of Lucy Gage"; Snyder, "Lucy Gage."

27. Snyder, "Lucy Gage," 334–38.

28. Ibid., 346; Gage, "Kindergarten Training Course"; "International Kindergarten Union Officers," *Proceedings of the Twenty-fifth Annual Meeting of the International Kindergarten Union,* June 24–29, 1918, Chicago; "Maryland," *Journal of Education* 86 (1919): 619.

29. Dobbs, Green, and Hahn, "History of the National Council," 9; Agnes Snyder, *Dauntless Women in Childhood Education 1856–1931* (Washington, D.C.: Association for Childhood Education International, 1972), 372. Gage was also a member of a number of other national educational organizations, including the Progressive Education Association, founded in 1919.

30. Dobbs, Green, and Hahn, "History of the National Council," 2.

31. Bess McCann, "The Faculty of George Peabody College for Teachers 1914–1936" (master's thesis, Department of Higher Education, Peabody College, 1936), 16.

32. George A. Dillingham, *The Foundation of the Peabody Tradition* (Lanham, Md.: Univ. Press of America, 1989), 3.

33. Ibid., 6; Sherman Dorn, *A Brief History of Peabody College* (Nashville: Peabody College of Vanderbilt Univ., 1996); Paul K. Conkin, *Peabody College: From Frontier Academy to the Frontiers of Teaching and Learning* (Nashville: Vanderbilt Univ. Press, 2002).

34. *Acts of Tennessee 1903,* House Joint Resolution 25, p. 1597, urging Peabody trustees to locate in Nashville, and Senate Joint Resolution 20, pp. 1632–33, authorizing some state financial support to develop the college if it be permanently established in Nashville.

35. Hoffschwelle, *Rebuilding the Rural Southern Community,* 21; Dorn, *Brief History,* 1, 12; Dillingham, *Foundation of the Peabody Tradition,* 7; Conkin, *Peabody College,* 129, 211.

36. Dillingham, *Foundation of the Peabody Tradition,* 7.

37. Alfred Leland Crabb, *The Historical Background of Peabody College* (Nashville: George Peabody College for Teachers, 1941); Conkin, *Peabody College.*

38. Dorn, *Brief History,* 10.

39. Paul K. Conkin, "The Academic Side, 1914–1930," in Conkin, *Peabody College,* 205–36; Ransom, "Comparative History."

40. Catharine Beecher, *Suggestions Respecting Improvements in Education: Presented to the Trustees of the Hartford Female Seminary, and Published at Their Request* (Hartford, Conn.: Packer & Butler, 1829).

41. Here are the percentages of Tennessee employed teachers by gender in sample years from 1887 to 1912, based on compiled totals of teachers in all counties and reported in annual reports to the state. In 1887, 68 percent were men, 32 percent were women. In 1888, 67 percent were men; 33 percent were women. In 1889, 64 percent were men; 36 percent were women. In 1896, 56 percent were men; 44 percent were women. In 1900, 54 percent were men; 46 percent were women. In 1903, 48 percent were men; 52 percent were women. By 1903, the gender balance had shifted. In 1910, 37 percent were men; 63 percent were women. In 1912, 34 percent were men; 66 percent were women. *Annual Report* (1887), 108–10; *Annual Report of the State Superintendent of Public Instruction for Tennessee for the Scholastic Year Ending June 30, 1888, Submitted to the Governor* (Nashville: Marshall & Bruce, 1889), 76–78; *Annual Report of the State Superintendent of Public Instruction for Tennessee for the Scholastic Year Ending June 30, 1889, Submitted to the Governor* (Nashville: Marshall & Bruce, 1890), 94–96; *Annual Report* (1896), 125–28; *Annual Report of the State Superintendent of Public Instruction for Tennessee for the Scholastic Year Ending June 30, 1900, Submitted to the Governor* (Nashville: Gospel Advocate Publishing, 1901), 56–58; *Annual Report of the State Superintendent of Public Instruction for Tennessee for the Scholastic Year Ending June 30, 1903, Submitted to the Governor* (Nashville: Foster & Webb, 1904), 55–58; *Biennial Report of the State Superintendent of Public Instruction for Tennessee for the Scholastic Years Ending June 30, 1909–1910, Submitted to the Governor* (Nashville: Ambrose Printing, 1911), 61; *Biennial Report* (1911–12), 130–37. I have not located detailed Tennessee teacher-gender tables prior to 1887 for the full state, but individual counties occasionally provided male-female breakdowns. For example, Washington County in East Tennessee reported for 1872 that fifty-five of its employed teachers were men, fifteen women, or 79 percent men to 21 percent women. *Report of J. B. Killebrew,* 45.

42. *Biennial Report* (1911–12), 481.

43. Alice N. Parker, "The Kindergarten in the South," in *The South in the Building of the Nation,* vol. 10, *History of the Social Life in the South,* ed. Samuel Chiles Mitchell (Richmond: Southern Historical Publication Society, 1909), 380–86.

44. Kathryn Warren, "A History of Public School Kindergartens in Tennessee," unpublished ms., c. 1970, James Walker Library, Middle Tennessee State University. In 1945, the year of Gage's death, the Tennessee legislature acknowledged that city and county school systems "may provide for" programs for children under age six and if so, the Tennessee Board of Education would oversee those programs. In 1973 the legislature set minimum standards for existing public kindergartens but made clear that

kindergarten education was not required in Tennessee; in fact, not until 1992 did the legislature mandate statewide kindergarten education in every public elementary school in Tennessee. *Acts of the State of Tennessee, 1945,* chap. 101, Senate Bill 456, pp. 293–95; *Acts of the State of Tennessee, 1973,* vol. 1, chap. 193, House Bill 566, Minimum Kindergarten Program Law, pp. 604–6, in which Section 3 clarifies that kindergartens are not compulsory; *Acts of the State of Tennessee, 1992,* chap. 535, House Bill 752, pp. 19–49, in which sections 29–30, p. 31, mandate public kindergarten education.

45. Lucy Gage, "Interpreting the Kindergarten to the Community," Box 1, File 19, Lucy Gage Papers.

46. Snyder, "Lucy Gage," 341.

47. For example, Lucy Gage, "The Kindergarten Training Course as a Department of the University," *Proceedings of the Thirteenth Annual Meeting of International Kindergarten Union, Milwaukee, Wisconsin* (1906); Lucy Gage, "New Ideas in Elementary Education at Peabody College," *Peabody Reflector* 4, no. 7 (1921); Lucy Gage, "Freedom, Authority, and Control in Education," *Peabody Reflector* 5, no. 10 (1922); Lucy Gage, "Kindergarten Progress in the Past Twenty-five Years," *Childhood Education* 2, no. 2 (Oct. 1925): 92–95; Lucy Gage, "Teacher Training in the South," *Childhood Education* 4, no. 8 (Apr. 1928): 359–61; Bailey, "Life and Work of Lucy Gage"; Henderson, "Elizabeth Peabody and Lucy Gage"; Snyder, "Lucy Gage."

48. John E. Windrow, as cited in Henderson, "Elizabeth Peabody and Lucy Gage," 44.

49. For example, Gage, "Kindergarten Training Course," "Interpreting the Kindergarten," and "Slow Growth of Professionalism."

50. Letters and notes by friends, students, and colleagues, Lucy Gage Papers.

51. Alfred Leland Crabb and Clara Gibson Haddox, Box 1, Files 3–6, personal communications, in Snyder, "Lucy Gage," 329, 325.

52. Gage, "Slow Growth of Professionalism"; Lucy Gage, *Bulletin of the National Council of Primary Education* 11, no. 4, supplement (Apr. 1928); Snyder, "Lucy Gage," 325–29, 350–51; cf. Amy Chua, *Battle Hymn of the Tiger Mother* (New York: Penguin Group, 2011).

53. Ransom, "Comparative History," 77, 83.

54. Ibid., 88.

55. Ibid., 93.

56. Henderson, "Elizabeth Peabody and Lucy Gage," 44–49.

57. Charles S. Pendleton, "Peabody College Greets Professor Lucy Gage," comments on Gage's retirement, Founder's Day, Feb. 2, 1942, 4, Box 1, File 2, Lucy Gage Papers.

58. In June 1941, a year from Gage's retirement, in a snapshot of Peabody's releases to the city press, the *Nashville Banner* and the *Tennessean* showcase that Dr. Dennis Cooke and Dr. Ray Hamon, professors of school administration at Peabody, were to represent Peabody at a national convention of school administrators that month, and of the more than twenty printed names of leaders attending the conference, none was a woman. A simultaneous press release tells that Miss Janey Hanelin, assistant professor of home

economics, and Miss Mary Wilson, associate professor of foods and nutrition, would represent Peabody at a national home economics education convention. The significance of one group over the other is clear. "38 States to be Represented at Peabody Meeting this Week," *Tennessean,* June 14, 1941; "School Heads Will Convene Here Thursday"; "2 Peabody Teachers to Attend Conference"; all in Nashville Peabody College 1941 clipping file, Nashville Room, Nashville Public Library.

59. Lucy Gage, "Women's Part in Reconstruction of World Values" (1933), 6, Lucy Gage Papers.

60. "Miss Green, Educator, Dies: Teacher Here for 57 Years; Funeral Services Set Tomorrow," *Tennessean,* Oct. 22, 1961, A4; "Julia Green Fund Proposed," *Tennessean,* Oct. 23, 1961; "Miss Julia Green," *Peabody Reflector,* Jan. 1945, 33–34; Carol Farrar Kaplan and Livy I. Simpson, "Julia McClung Green (1873–1961)," in *Remember the Ladies: Women of Mount Olivet Cemetery,* by Carol Farrar Kaplan and Livy I. Simpson (Nashville: Carol Kaplan and Livy Simpson, 1995), 22–23.

61. Julia Green in Ann Caroline Mann, "Miss Julia Ends 40 Years of Service as Teacher," *Nashville Banner,* Sept. 11, 1944, 9; Green, handwritten autobiographical notes; Florence Weiland (niece of Julia Green), handwritten biographical notes about her Aunt Julia (in possession of Florence Weiland, Aug. 8, 1998).

62. Green, handwritten autobiographical notes.

63. Cf. David Moss Hilliard, "The Development of Public Education in Memphis, Tennessee, 1848–1945" (PhD diss., Univ. of Chicago, 1946).

64. Mann, "Miss Julia Ends 40 Years," 9.

65. Lucille Rogers, *Light from Many Candles: A History of Pioneer Women in Education in Tennessee* (Nashville: Xi State, Delta Kappa Gamma, 1960), 243–46.

66. "Miss Julia Green," 33; Green, handwritten autobiographical notes.

67. The Davidson County Superintendent, writing in *Biennial Report* (1911–12), informed the state about the new position he created and Green's promotion: "As a means of securing greater efficiency in primary work, our board has appointed one of our skilled primary teachers, under the direction of the County Superintendent, to supervise the work of teachers of first, second, and third grades. She is to visit schools where special instruction is needed, and at each monthly meeting to give suggestive outlines for the next month's work. The indications are that this plan will be very satisfactory."

The plan must have been quite satisfactory, as other counties soon thereafter also began appointing supervisors to offer direct oversight for the many elementary teachers; other than through training institutes, school boards up to then must not have provided teachers with much personal guidance by their principals or superintendents. In 1925 the Tennessee legislature legitimized and defined Green's supervisory position in a new act of the general assembly that modified and restructured the existing "uniform system of Public Education" in Tennessee: "County Boards of Education may employ one or more supervisors for the supervision of teaching the elementary schools of the county." W. C. Anderson, "Davidson County," *Biennial Report* (1911–12), 480–81; *Acts of Tennessee 1925,* chap. 115, House Bill 780, Section 7, Supervisors, 333.

68. White, *Educational Organization,* 235; *Annual Report of the Public Schools of Nashville, Tennessee, Scholastic Year 1903–1904,* Metropolitan Government of Nashville and Davidson County Archives (Metro Archives); *Annual Report of the Davidson County Public Schools, 1944–1945,* Metro Archives; "Board of Education," Box 19, File 19-1, Metro Archives; *Annual Report of the Public Schools of Nashville, Tennessee, Scholastic Year 1945–1946,* Metro Archives.

69. Kaplan and Simpson, "Julia McClung Green," 22.

70. Mann, "Miss Julia Ends 40 Years," 9; "Miss Green, Educator, Dies," A4; Patricia Mann, narrator, transcript from *Your Neighbor* radio program on Julia Green, WLAC, Nashville, Nov. 12, 1949, 4:45 P.M..

71. William M. Green, *Life and Papers: A. L. P. Green, D.D.,* ed. Thomas O. Summers (Nashville: Southern Methodist Publishing House, 1877); Carter T. Cullen, "Dr. Alexander Little Page Green," *History of the Tennessee Conference and a Brief Summary of the General Conferences of the Methodist Church: From the Frontier in Middle Tennessee to the Present Time* (Nashville: Cullen T. Carter, 1948), 73–75; James Penn Pilkington, *The Methodist Publishing House: A History,* vol. 1, *Beginning to 1879* (Nashville: Abingdon Press, 1968). Alexander Little Page Green's role in the founding of Vanderbilt University is not recorded in most histories of Vanderbilt. Dr. A. L. P. Green came to rural middle Tennessee and to Nashville in the 1820s and established and served Methodist churches, circuits, stations, and districts throughout the central area of the state over the course of his lifetime, in a rural, hardscrabble frontier when he first arrived. In Nashville, living monuments to his ministry are everywhere. He founded McKendree Methodist Church in downtown Nashville and was its first minister. He founded, operated, published, and wrote for the Methodist Publishing House in Nashville, which with the Civil War and the split in the church would become the Southern Methodist Publishing House for many years. In his capacity as church leader, he was one of the early prime movers, well before the Civil War, for the idea of a central university in the South for the training of young men to prepare for the ministry. He served on the executive board of this Central University and helped develop its charter even as the money for it was secured and construction of its buildings was begun.

He was its unflagging champion and for decades worked, along with other church leaders, to generate support for the concept both inside the church and outside of it, to continue to push for the university, and to never let the concept die, even during the Civil War, when it was put on the back burner for a time. Commodore Cornelius Vanderbilt eventually provided the funds to realize Dr. Green's long-nurtured dream—even though by the time the charter came to fruition, the final negotiations had been passed into other hands. Green himself, who died in 1874, did not live to see the school dedicated in 1875. But A. L. P. Green was without question one of the primary heroes in the story of the creation of Vanderbilt, and he was cited at the university's dedication, October 4, 1875, by Chancellor Landon Garland as the man whose portrait deserves most to hang on the walls of Vanderbilt University along side that of Commodore Vanderbilt. (A. L. P. Green's portrait does not hang at Vanderbilt, nor is Green referred to much, if at all, in the many histories of Vanderbilt, other than by Edwin Mims in his 1946 history.) A. L. P. Green lived to see the birth of his granddaughter Julia McClung Green in 1873.

Landon C. Garland in Edwin Mims, *History of Vanderbilt University* (Nashville: Vanderbilt Univ. Press, 1946), 34: "There was in our midst one spirit which did not quail, one breast which hope did not forsake; and if there be any man whose portrait deserves to hang on these walls by the side of that [of the Commodore] which has just been unveiled, it is that of the wise, the prudent, the brave, the gentle and now sainted, A. L. P. Green. Without him, we should have postponed, probably to an indefinite period, the matter in hand." Cf. Harvie Branscomb, *Vanderbilt University: The Commodore's Best Investment* (New York: Newcomen Society in North America, 1950); Robert A. McGaw and Reba Wilcoxon, *A Brief History of Vanderbilt University, 1872–1982* (Nashville: Vanderbilt Univ., 1983); Paul K. Conkin, *Gone with the Ivy: A Biography of Vanderbilt University* (Knoxville: Univ. of Tennessee Press, 1985); Bill Carey, *Chancellors, Commodores, and Coeds: A History of Vanderbilt University* (Nashville: Clearbrook Press, 2003).

72. "Woman of the Week," *Nashville Good News Weekly*, Aug. 6, 1947, 3; Julia M. Green, handwritten autobiographical notes; Florence Green Weiland (niece of Julia McClung Green), personal interview, Aug. 8, 1998.

73. "Well Done," editorial clipping commenting on the professional contributions of Julia Green, *Nashville Banner*, 1944.

74. Ibid.

75. "Miss Julia Green," 34; cf. Perry Leah Roberts, *Tennessee Congress of Parents and Teachers: History, Forty-six Years in Retrospect, 1911–1957* (1942; reprint, Nashville: Tennessee Congress of Parents and Teachers, 1957).

76. Council of Community Agencies, *Free School Lunches: A Study of the Free Lunch Program in the Nashville Schools* (Nashville: Council of Community Agencies, 1962), vi.

77. "Miss Julia Green," 34; Cavit C. Cheshier, *An Environmental Scan of the Tennessee Education Association: Its Beginnings, Development, Present Status, and Future* (Nashville: Tennessee Education Association, 1993), 28.

78. Mann, *Your Neighbor* transcript; Mann, "Miss Julia Ends 40 Years," 9; Rogers, *Light from Many Candles*, 243–46.

79. "Woman of the Week," 3; Altrusa International, Inc., "The History of Altrusa," Altrusa International, http://www.altrusa.com/General/History.asp/ (accessed Aug. 28, 2004); Altrusa International, Inc., District Four, "Altrusa International, Inc. of Nashville, TN," http://www.districtfouraltrusa.org/nashville.htm/ (accessed Aug. 28, 2004); "Altrusa" clipping collection, *Nashville Banner*, Jan. 14, 1944, and Oct. 29, 1945, Nashville Room, Nashville Public Library; "Woman of the Week," 3. In addition to memberships in professional and service organizations, both Julia Green and Lucy Gage belonged to the exclusive Centennial Club of Nashville, the city's premier women's social and civic club that accrued personal stature, connections, and influence to its elite

members. Charlotte A. Williams, The Centennial Club of Nashville: A History from 1905–77 (Nashville: Centennial Club, 1978), 449, 451.

80. Rogers, *Light from Many Candles,* 245–46.

81. Annual yearbooks of the National Council of Primary Education and the Association of Childhood Education, archive of the Association of Childhood Education International, University of Maryland Library Archives, College Park (hereafter cited as ACEI archive); Mann, *Your Neighbor* transcript.

82. "Program, Thirty-Seventh Annual Meeting of the International Kindergarten Union, April 22–26, 1930, Memphis, Tennessee," Box 2, Series 5, Record Group III, ACEI archive.

83. "Program, Forty-First Annual Convention of the Association of Childhood Education, May 1–5, 1934, Nashville, Tennessee," Box 2, Series 5, Record Group III, ACEI archive.

84. Dobbs, Green, and Hahn, "History of the National Council," 9.

85. Ibid.; Snyder, "Lucy Gage," 345–52.

86. Ibid.; "Program, Thirty-Seventh Annual Convention of the International Kindergarten Union"; "Program, Forty-First Annual Convention of the Association of Childhood Education."

87. Alberta L. Meyer, "Julia Green Dies," *Childhood Education* 38, no. 5 (Jan. 1962).

88. Mann, "Miss Julia Ends 40 Years," 9.

89. Dobbs, Green, and Hahn, "History of the National Council," 9; Mann, *Your Neighbor* transcript; Gage, "Women's Part in Reconstruction"; Lucy Gage, letter of farewell, Aug. 1942, in Snyder, "Lucy Gage," 354.

90. A. Elizabeth Taylor, *The Woman Suffrage Movement in Tennessee* (New York: Bookman Associates, 1957), 138; *Acts of Tennessee 1909,* chap. 508, House Bill 517, "An Act . . . to define the qualifications of the County Superintendent of Schools . . . [for] which he or she [might be] an applicant . . . [verifying] his or her moral character," 1830–31. There had already been women superintendents in Tennessee prior to the 1909 legislation (*Annual Report 1896,* 174, 176) in rural counties, where perhaps no men had been qualified to fill the post: Miss Rutha Davis had been superintendent in remote Campbell County since 1893. State legislation to authorize women superintendents followed the reality sixteen years later. The same situation was true in the case of Julia Green's appointment to supervisor in 1911; legislation to legitimize her professional designation was passed by the Tennessee General Assembly in 1925, fourteen years later.

91. Gage, "Pioneering in Education"; Green in Mann, "Miss Julia Ends 40 Years"; "Honor Well Earned," newspaper clipping in possession of Florence Weiland, Aug. 8, 1998 (references the building of Julia Green Elementary School).

92. Pendleton, "Peabody College Greets Professor Lucy Gage."

Chapter 8

Sport and the Outward Life: Young Women Athletes as Progressive Players

Mary Ellen Pethel

Hippity-hus Hippity-hus!
What in the thunder's the matter with us?
Nothing at all! Nothing at all!
We are the girls who play basketball.

—University of Tennessee women's basketball team, 1906

In the annual yearbook for Knoxville, Tennessee's Central High School in 1912, basketball team member Carolyn Sowers wrote of her team, "As practice makes perfect, surely our zenith lies not far in the future, for we have practiced at every possible chance with untiring interest and energy."[1] This description characterizes not only the girls' basketball team at Central High but also the growing interest of many southern young women to participate in competitive sports. Strangely foreshadowing the development of women's athletics to come later in the century, Sowers gives symbolic insight to the movement of women in sport: "We see just a little way in the future an air castle, and in that castle the reward of perseverance and hope—the success of a championship. We shall practice with the same untiring interest and energy to behold our goal, and press forward crying in unison, Excelsior."[2]

Her words are laden with imagery and meaning that epitomize the struggle of female athletes in the public sphere from 1895 to the end of World War I. These young women simply wanted to experience the thrill of sport, but in the process they helped to redefine acceptable notions of gender in Tennessee during this pivotal period of change and progress. Female athletes during this time may not have gained the public's approbation, but their efforts and competitive spirit certainly laid the groundwork that would ultimately lead to a women's movement within sport. The success achieved by female athletes today is surely a "reward of perseverance and hope" manifested by Tennessee's vanguards of women's sport.

During the 1890s and early 1900s, sport and leisure provided a springboard that served to propel Tennessee's young women who were actively involved in school sports into the public sphere of competitive athletics. Young women who played sports did not carry banners, hold rallies, or intentionally advance a political movement, but their competitive athleticism publicly contested the Old South order of class and gender.[3] Sport allowed female students to unknowingly champion a cause that directly challenged definitions of southern propriety on the physical plane; therefore these young, upper-class women represented progressivism at its most basic level. Additionally, the development of women's sports accompanied other developments during the period that had an impact on young women's physicality and shifted society toward new norms of modernity benefiting the emerging new woman.[4] Such changes included women's clothing, growing health awareness, and increased democratization and commercialization of leisure/recreation.

Women's sports developed almost entirely under the umbrella of education.[5] Beginning in the 1890s, increasing numbers of upper-class Tennessee females attended institutions of secondary and higher education. A significant number of these women also represented a new generation of girls who believed that playing sports should be just as acceptable as playing the violin or learning to sew. Traditional principles of femininity, which supported the education of women in "domestic science" or training in the modern ideas of housekeeping, came also to recognize the value of "Physical [C]ulture" for the health and well-being of young women.[6] As such, Victorian ideologies transitioned, allowing women to participate increasingly in physical activities.

The Progressive Era developed differently in the South compared to other regions of the United States. Because southern society remained entrenched in patriarchy and traditional social structures, Knoxville and Nashville offer an excellent lens through which to view women's athletics in New South progressivism. Knoxville served as the home of the state's leading public university as well as several new secondary schools. Known as the "Athens of the South," Nashville legitimized its title with the emergence of coeducational universities and a leading women's high school and college in the 1870s and 1880s. Education and sport played a large role in the new cityscapes of both Middle and East Tennessee.

The young women athletes of Knoxville and Nashville indelibly shaped new cultural norms, just as they were shaped by them. Sport transformed women from passive members of private spheres to active participants in public spaces. As unlikely agents of change, female athletes were not purposeful firebrands who sought to identify and address problems in society, as did other Progressive women in Tennessee. These girls did not participate in sport for the purposes of posterity or social change. They just played. They unknowingly scrimmaged for the cause of women's public visibility and personal strength each time they battled one another in the gym or on the field. Each game may have produced a winner and a loser, but in the larger historical narrative women athletes were collectively victorious in expanding perceptions and acceptance of women's roles in southern society.

Knoxville and Nashville: Cities in Context

The "Lost Cause" narrative in southern rhetoric following Reconstruction functioned to maintain on her high pedestal of femininity and domesticity the "Lady of the South," who "receives recognition at any convention she attends, . . . stands out in any company, and shows by every word and deed, her superiority."[7] Such gendered images conjured pride and a regional unity that recreated a southern and northern hybrid between progress and tradition, filled with change and contradictions, good intentions, and variegated outcomes, from 1895 to 1918. Emerging from the Civil War, the New South vision to transform largely agrarian areas into industrial centers animated certain southern cities. Due to the benefits of federal occupation during the war, Nashville was poised to progress into the postbellum vision of modernization, and Knoxville during the postwar years transformed from a modest town to one of the major urban centers of East Tennessee.[8]

By the turn of the twentieth century Knoxville was a sizable city of approximately 15,700 inhabitants, largely because of location and the establishment of new industries in the area.[9] Drawn to new opportunities for employment, East Tennesseans who moved into the city from surrounding rural areas caused a rapid population increase in Knoxville during the early 1900s.[10] From 1900 to 1910, the number of inhabitants in the county more than doubled; new businesses, churches, and schools were established and flourished throughout these years.[11] Connected to Nashville by rail and road, Knoxville served as the eastern platform of commerce into North Carolina and Virginia. As home to the state's public university and situated in the foothills of the Appalachian Mountains, the city maintained a distinctive flavor of mountain culture, intermingled with an intellectual ethos.

Nashville's population nearly tripled from the late nineteenth into the twentieth century, growing from 43,350 in 1880 to 80,865 in 1900 and 118,342 in 1920.[12] Nashville retained Old South values but combined them with a New South economic drive.[13] The shift of southern commerce from the seaboard to the Piedmont took place in urban centers such as Nashville and Atlanta because of their geographic positions as railroad centers with easier access to markets in the North, Midwest, and West Coast. The Nashville, Chattanooga, and St. Louis Railway became a major artery connecting Nashville to the rest of the nation.[14] As early as 1885, Nashville was gaining recognition for its importance as a city and cultural arts center, having "grown to be a commercial emporium, the *entrepot* of a rich, wealthy, tax-paying division of the State, and the educational center of the South."[15]

There existed a special symbiotic relationship between urban development and education in both Knoxville and Nashville, cities that had gained head starts in educational opportunities in their respective regions, with growth that increased steadily after the Civil War. Educational policy changes at the state level had developmental effects across Tennessee through the late 1800s, which increased in scope and implementation after 1903 to energize "the most intensive and extensive educational crusade in the history of the state."[16] Education advocates traveled the state during the century's first decade, preaching the cause of public education in hopes of ensuring the passage of important legislation. Women's clubs and labor unions grew vocal in support of educational improvement and attended rallies with featured speakers on education.

New private city schools and public county schools were built to respond to the need for education in Knoxville and its surrounding areas. Central High School, a county high school located in the Knoxville suburb of Fountain City, opened in 1907 as a result of the crusade for expansion of education. Also, well-established public schools such as Knoxville High School broadened and improved facilities, faculty, and curricula in the twentieth century. On the college level, the University of Tennessee had been established as a state institution of higher education in Tennessee since 1794. The university did not accept female students until 1892, when four women received admission to the normal school by special action of the faculty, and in 1893 the trustees approved a general admission policy.[17]

In greater Nashville, while new high schools were chartered, certain private secondary schools and colleges emerged as leading educational institutions of the region. In 1913, Ward Seminary, founded in 1865, merged with Belmont College, founded in 1890, to form one of the South's most prestigious women's high school/junior colleges. Fisk University, which opened in 1865, was the premier southern center of higher education for African Americans.[18] Nashville's Peabody College and David Lipscomb College served specific educational niches: Peabody trained teachers and Lipscomb, then Nashville Bible College, trained preachers. The state's second largest collegiate institution, Vanderbilt University, established in 1873 on an original endowment by Cornelius Vanderbilt, quickly gained the reputation as an elite southern university. One or two women per class attended Vanderbilt from its inception, arranged under special circumstances, but women did not fully matriculate there until 1895.[19]

Aside from urban growth and educational reform, the period from 1895 to 1918 produced major social and political reform. In the South, reform followed many processes that trickled down from the northern cities; however, the South laid claim to its own peculiar type of southern progressivism. Some historians have judged southern progressivism "to be too little, too late,"[20] but to say that the South did not experience progress is clearly a falsehood. The South resisted certain changes that would disrupt the traditional social order and system of patriarchy and white superiority, but slowly but surely, the cultural heritage of the South would be transformed by urbanization, industrialization, and higher education. New South modernization provided the conditions within which women would challenge societal stereotypes and women in education would leave an ineffaceable mark on sports in Tennessee.

Formation of the Female Athlete

In 1903 *The Iris,* the annual of Ward Seminary for Young Ladies, revealed an intriguing dichotomy in an editorial titled "Two College Preparatory Girls: The Ideal and the Other." Agnes Amis, treasurer of the senior class, stated, "My ideal is, like the other, preparing for college; but—O, the difference between them!"[21] Her submission documents the shifting self-perception and self-projection of many women attending institutions of higher education in the Progressive Era. Interestingly, Amis describes two very different models of femininity: the lovely southern lady focused on fashion and marriage versus the serious-minded student-athlete. In truth, most educated southern women emerged as a hybrid of the two—a "Modern Belle" of sorts. Amis views herself as the ideal student, exhibiting pride as an autonomous and independent woman. Yet she also upholds the merits of the more traditional "other":

> "Miss Ideal" is quite a studious girl, who is very fond of her books; stands high in her classes; and scorns with a "pooh!" any mention of or allusion to a boy as a beau. . . . She takes any caller she happens to have out and plays tennis or ball or runs races with him. She is very proud of her prowess in athletic sports; and, in fact, is fond of telling how she distanced one of her "beaux" in a foot race. She spends much time on her books, and likes nothing better than to dream of Wellesley, . . . herself, in cap and gown, as part of

> the landscape. In personal appearance, she almost approaches the masculine; she wears her hair parted and pulled (or slicked) back; she has an entire disregard for "style" . . . yet she has a distinct style of her own. In school, her manner is entirely polite, though cold and forbidding; while out of school, she is a jolly, good fellow all around.[22]

Conversely, "Lady Other" is quite different, though equally acceptable in the South:

> [She] is entirely different, for she is a graceful feminine creature; cares much for style—not "Miss Ideal's" sort, however. . . . Her desires and also herself are entirely opposite from "Miss Ideal's." The delights of her heart are [dancing] balls, beaux (really true ones), and to be real young lady. . . . She is the same in school as she is out. . . . She is seemingly very frivolous and light, but beneath that runs a strong current of the good. . . . Taken all in all, they are very different, yet each quite attractive in her way; still, they form a striking contrast.[23]

The same dichotomy was articulated as early as 1898 at Vanderbilt when collegiate sportswomen were presented as atypical of other females, such as Rowena Reed, "the pride of all the college girls . . . who broke the woman's record for the broad jump . . . won the 120-yard hurdle race and the running high jump."[24] Although Miss Reed's athletic prowess is positively noted, the article certainly paints her in a masculine light: At "160 pounds . . . 5 feet 8 1/2 inches tall . . . she can ride, swim, fence, row, run, handle Indian clubs, play football and basketball with the best."[25] The account curiously describes Reed as the "pride of all college girls" but makes clear she was exceptionally robust and masculine in contrast to the average size of the beauty-queen, boy-crazy "typical Vandy co-ed" of the time.

Agnes Amis's account of her "Miss Ideal" and "Lady Other" reflects the struggle of the South to come to terms with a more Progressive image. Even as Amis portrays herself as the more Progressive "Miss Ideal" she seems to acknowledge that many in Nashville and other southern urban areas see her epitome of a strong modern woman both as unattractive and incompatible with the southern belle ideology, describing "Miss Ideal" as "approach[ing] the masculine" with slicked back hair, dreaming of autonomy gained through higher education instead of men and marriage. "Miss Other," on the other hand, is a stylish, "graceful feminine creature" who desires dancing and dating. The women who viewed education and sport as a means to gain autonomy were seen as modern but more masculine as they challenged the previously limited roles for women as married ladies and dutiful mothers. Yet it is also clear that young females increasingly viewed education, and the social and professional mobility it provided, as both congenial and in vogue.[26] Amis presents the paradox of what many young women at the turn of the century regarded as ideally modern versus the more traditional prototype perpetuated by older generations. Although a shift was occurring regarding the value of women's education and attitudes toward female autonomy in social and professional settings, the South remained profoundly traditional. Sports added further complexity to the competing images.

Education served as a primary springboard for upper-class women in the South into more active outward lives, but debates raged regarding appropriate curriculum for women, their intellectual capacity, education's effects on them, and the consequences of educated women in male-run society.[27] A pattern of progress, backlash, and accommodation developed when a traditional limitation was challenged, encountered reactions of varying degrees, then became some form of socially acceptable modification. Such cycles pulsed the shift from antebellum and Victorian values to a more modern, Progressive vision of acceptable behavior for southern women. High schools and colleges in Knoxville and Nashville reflected the momentum-inertia pattern of change experienced by females struggling with their roles as students, young women, and affluent constituents of the New South, as the South itself wrestled with identity and redefinition. The generation of educated young women who emerged by the end of World War I, not exactly as traditional southern belles or as autonomous women, helped to create and shape a new model—from a trajectory abounding with contradictions and combining southern realities with reform, innovation, and industry. These young women presented as a hybrid of old and new—part gentry and part jock.

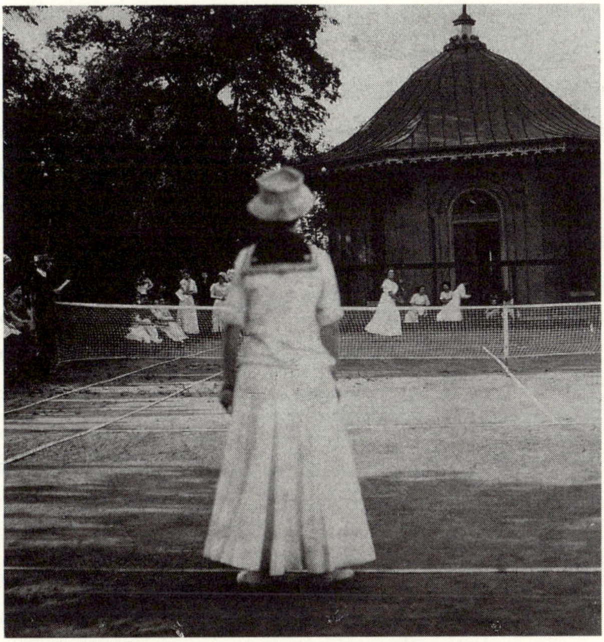

Women from all of Nashville's colleges wore uniforms, but dress became less confining by 1915. Pictured here are students from Ward-Belmont playing tennis in sailor-style physical education uniforms that reflect changes in women's dress in the early twentieth century. Courtesy of the Harpeth Hall School Archives, Nashville, Tennessee.

Under the umbrella of education, women also advanced their engagement in physical activity. The generation of young women who participated in molding new definitions of suitable behavior and occupations for women also altered perceptions of women's sport and leisure and the acceptability of those activities in public spaces. Victorian era trends had already begun to emphasize the development of good health. Yet from 1895 to 1918, young women made significant progress toward a new image that included physical education and sport,[28] and the structures for and organization of women's sports advanced as well.[29] Physical education activities in colleges, high schools, and women's seminaries, which included walking, tennis, gymnastics, and basketball, allowed girls to exercise and begin to compete for the very first time.[30] Athletics and physical education reflect the "strategies New Women in the New South adopted and some of the tensions and anxieties they faced as they negotiated the contested ground of gender redefinition at the turn of the century."[31] Higher education was a powerful, although acceptable, wedge between appropriate female behavior and evolving notions of gender in the New South, and women's athletics drove the wedge further.

In part, changes in clothing and style at the turn of the twentieth century facilitated the transformation of southern belles into women with greater autonomy and athleticism. Nineteenth-century women's clothing—long dresses, skirts, petticoats, bustles, corsets, and other layers of underclothing—had restricted women's physical movements. Instead of changing the style of dress for ease and mobility, social propriety had rather altered the sport to accommodate women's prescribed attire: The sidesaddle, for instance, was developed before the Civil War to allow respectable women to ride horses.[32] Unsuitability of women's wear helps explain the approval of certain activities for females but discouragement of others that were traditionally masculine. In short, women were simply not dressed to play, yet American culture did not view any other style of dress as acceptable.[33]

With the 1890s arrived the new trend of bicycling, which became immensely popular and found wide participation among women. As early as 1897, Vanderbilt called for the creation of a bicycle club that "would add much to the pleasure . . . in this university to have certain times appointed for spins to different points of interest."[34] Many saw riding bikes more as entertainment than exercise, but middle-class women in particular realized that bicycling gave them a socially approved form of physical activity. With long skirts and several layers of underclothing, the dress of women encumbered them while bicycling. The emphasis placed on health began to aid the transition of clothing because medical findings officially discovered that the daily wearing of tight corsets by women directly led to headaches, back troubles, and fainting spells.[35] The invention of elastic in the 1880s also contributed to fewer layers of underclothing for women and promoted the popularity of bloomers, the new style of pants that soon became the preferred alternative for active women. By the turn of the century, the style of acceptable athletic clothing for women transformed into a new look consisting of a middy blouse, bloomers, and dark woolen stockings.[36] In addition, skirts became shorter and underclothing minimized, with many women eliminating corsets altogether. In 1901, George J. Englemann, a physician and pioneer in the fields of gynecology and obstetrics, reported that "while 47 percent of the girls enter schools wearing corsets, these are given up, in consequence of advice and teachings of the instructors in physical training."[37]

The changes that occurred in the United States from 1895 to the end of World War I reflect a social scene that correlated clothing appropriate for enjoying physical activity to increasing opportunities for participation in sport, paralleling changes in dress with social acceptance of strenuous exercise for women. New physical freedom helped women "throw off . . . nineteenth century attitudes and fashions."[38] Accompanying the emerging concept of the new women, in 1903 *Colliers* magazine predicted that "the time is not far distant when the clothes of women will help to keep them vigorous and active, and not waste their energy; will encourage instead of hindering natural action and development."[39] In Nashville, the girls of Ward Seminary reflected such patterns of new fashion and physical activity at the turn of the century. Known as the "Ward Ducks," students hiked in lines of two every afternoon behind the principal, J. D. Blanton, and his wife. They wore navy blue, bloomer-like pants, with white sailor hats and tops in the summer. One of the favorite downtown promenades included a hike up to Capitol Hill, while other days the students were granted greater privilege as they rode "bicycles or horses in divided skirts" as far as Mount Olivet, a cemetery in East Nashville.[40]

Although new ideas in women's education brought with them new ideas about clothing, physical health, and exercise, and introduced competition, sport, and sweat to middle- and upper-class southern women, the conservative South was slow to change. Still thought to prefer "Ladies' Amusements," southern women enjoyed social pleasures in which ambition and vanity remained the focus; before 1900 the typical southern female "was not interested in playing games for her own sake, nor did she participate in sports where she had no male companion."[41] Even as basketball, gymnastics, and tennis gained popularity in the early 1900s,

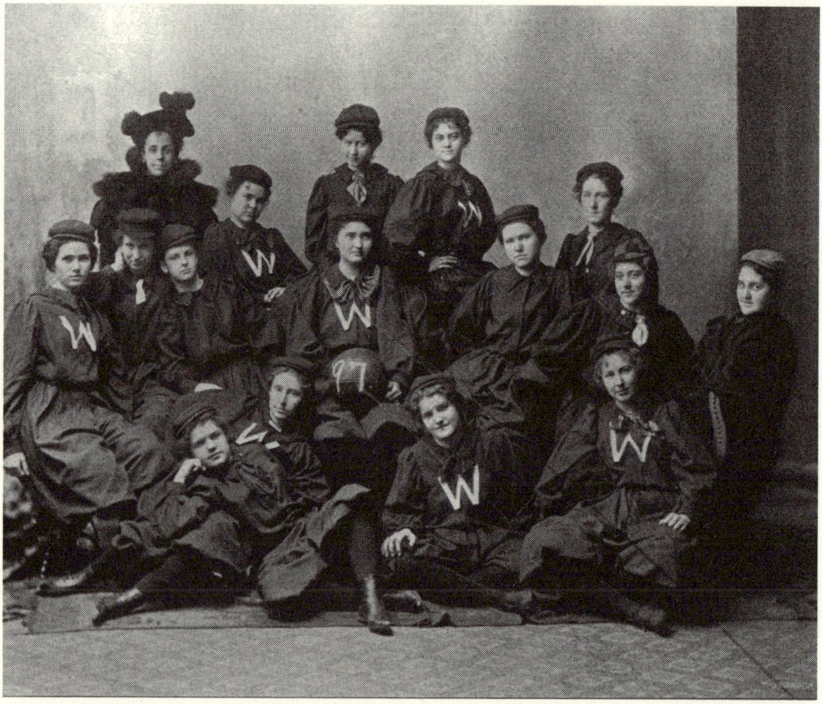

The 1897 Ward Seminary basketball team, pictured above, played the Vanderbilt women's team in the first recorded women's basketball game in Tennessee. The Vanderbilt team, led by alumnae and coach Stella Vaughn, won the contest with a score of 5-0 and played in front of an all-female crowd as male students were not allowed to watch. Courtesy of the Harpeth Hall School Archives, Nashville, Tennessee.

many advocates sought societal approval for women's sports by emphasizing the assets sports could provide to a new and improved form of femininity in modern society: Physical exercise resulted in better health and reproductivity; shooting "a basket was not the point . . . [but rather] form, poise, and grace while doing so were."[42] Indeed, many of the first women participants in college sports were not viewed as, or even called, athletes.[43] Despite all the justifications, women's competitive athletics signaled a new arena within which women were entering the public sphere and public consciousness. Throughout the first two decades of the twentieth century, women playing sports gained increasing acceptability and a sense of normalcy.

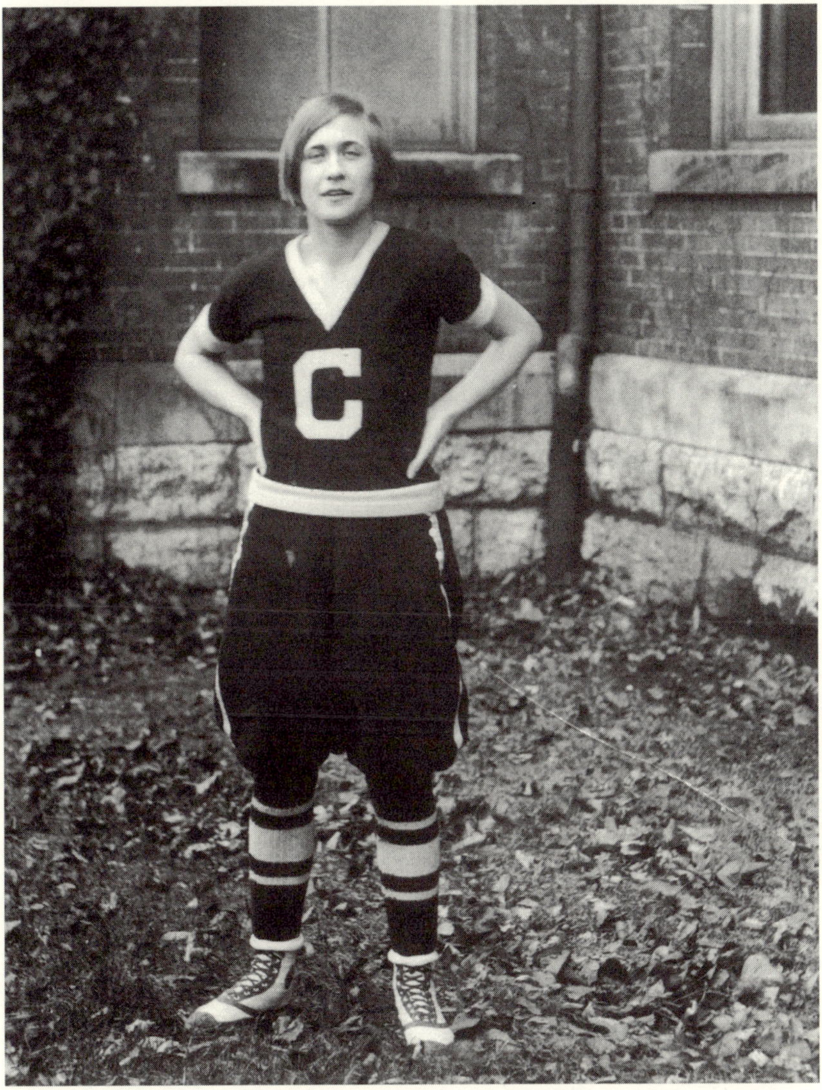

By the 1920s, after thirty years of increasing athleticism and competition, women's sports clothing had become more practical, as shown in the women's basketball team uniform of Cumberland College, Lebanon, Tennessee, worn here by team member Cornelia Adelaide Smartt (Hendley Hodges), c. 1926. Progress in women's sports would be redirected with the formation of Women's Division of the National Amateur Athletic Federation (WDNAAF) in the mid-1920s, which mostly reduced competitive play between women's teams to the intramural level by the 1930s. Courtesy of the Evins-Smartt family collection.

Tennessee's Progressive Players

In 1899, Knoxville High School sophomore Hattie Harrell established a "Fencing Club, secured the foils and equipment, arranged times and locations for regular practice, and assumed the duties of director."[44] With nine charter members, these young ladies grew "so skilled in the art of fencing as to consent to give a drill on the evening of Commencement."[45] Another report states, "As the close of school drew near the members found it expedient to practice oftener. The practicing in it has been a source of pleasure to the participants, and they enjoy the exercise it provides."[46] It remains doubtful that the young women in the fencing club were even considered athletes. However, these Knoxville students organized a physically competitive club, exerted self-discipline to learn the sport, publicly engaged in the masculine art of combat, and did so amid cheers from the community. Hattie Harrell and her fencing club teammates served a greater Progressive good, even if they remained unaware of their cause or, retrospectively, their success.

In the first two decades of the twentieth century, several other women's and coed athletic clubs were formed. In 1904, the women of the University of Tennessee established the Barbara Blount Tennis Club with eight members, and in 1905 six women joined together to form the Girls' Boat Club.[78] On the secondary level, by 1914 both Knoxville High and Central High organized tennis clubs that maintained an open admission policy to both men and women.[48] These high school clubs remained interclass and intramural and did not compete with other schools; the focus was on wholesome physical exercise, inclusiveness, camaraderie, and school spirit over competition. Members simply played for the fun and refrained from recording individual scores. As a faculty sponsor claimed in the 1915 annual, "Our philosophy relies not on producing a winner and a loser but on the improvement of all."[49] Through analysis of reports and articles dealing with girls involved in athletic clubs, girls generally enjoyed participating in these physical activities, which were not limited to the athletically inclined or sport-oriented woman but drew from a wide range of girls.

Ward Seminary also maintained an early interest in athletics, although largely noncompetitive and under the title of "Physical Culture." At Ward

Seminary the 1902 basketball team maintained eight members and provided a commencement exhibition that included exercises such as the "hoop drill, German Bell exercise, Swedish gymnastics, fancy march, and combination bell and wand drill."[50] The team appeared to be more like an acrobatic dance team than a modern basketball squad, yet their visibility and participation still signaled a shift to more serious exercise and sport for women. In the same year, Ward Seminary announced that "regardless of criticism, [the Ward woman] adopts the divided skirt" in order to vigorously ride horses just as the men, rather than be relegated to side saddle.[51] In 1911, Ward Seminary offered a description of "physical culture" that solidified the systemic shift of sport from unfeminine to an essential part of development: "Physical culture is made a special feature of Seminary life. The gymnasium and bowling alleys afford abundant indoor exercise. Lessons in swimming are offered throughout the session. In addition, . . . the extensive campus at Ward Place furnishes abundant facilities for tennis, basketball, croquet, field hockey, and other outdoor sports."[52]

Although very much in the minority in the student body, Nashville's Vanderbilt coeds also actively participated in student culture, "from a woman editor on the *Observer* to a reporter on the *Hustler,* from a basketball team that never lost a game for several years to a girls' club, which they formed in 1909."[53] Such participation mirrored national trends reflecting greater interest in women's clubs and sports already by 1895: "The colleges for women are beginning to take a very active interest in athletics. Fencing is greatly in vogue at Smith College. At Vassar . . . basketball has become the popular pastime."[54]

Females became more aware of issues in health and more active in opportunities for physical exercise through school athletics, but what of competition and adrenaline pumping rivalry between schools during this time period? Competitive women's sports of the early twentieth century do not compare to today's standards and schedules of team competition. In the Knoxville area, 1903 marks the first year of organized basketball for women at the University of Tennessee, and in that year UT women played no other teams.[55] In 1904, with the addition of Grace Hood, who transferred from Maryville College's basketball team, interest increased, and several female students joined Hood to push for university sanction to practice their sport on campus in university facilities. Eventually, the university's board allowed women to use the main campus gymnasium one afternoon a week from 4:00 to 6:00 P.M.[56] In that inaugural season, the University of Tennessee female students played nearby Maryville College, Fountain City High School, and Concord Academy. The women played in uniforms quite different from their male counterparts, donning knee-length dresses and high stockings.[57] Although the game scores were omitted from the yearbook records, strong recognition should be accorded their accomplishment of organizing and playing the first girls' competitive basketball season in the area.

In 1907 the University of Tennessee women's team gained noticeable respect when T. S. (Thomas Snoddy) Myers, an active junior and president of the UT Student Association, became coach.[58] More attention followed when Alice Perkins joined the team, the daughter of Charles Perkins and Angie Warren Perkins, he the chair of the Physics and Electrical Engineering Department and she the first dean of the Women's Department of the university in 1899.[59] However, despite the early good fortunes of the team, after the 1910 season, women's basketball was dissolved at UT until the 1920s. Whatever the explanation for its disappearance after only six years, the first era of women athletes at the University of Tennessee laid a foundation upon which future female athletes would build.

Although Knoxville area high schools started girls' basketball teams later than did the University of Tennessee, their programs achieved more success overall in the early years. Not only did the high school teams survive from 1910 to 1920, the decade when the UT team lapsed, but they attracted wider community interest, participation, and school support. The girls who played on these teams were well-rounded, intelligent students with a broad range of accomplishments. For example, in 1908 Juanita McFarland, member of Knoxville High School's basketball team, participated also in the "Kodak Klub," Art Club, and Literary Club. Another teammate, Elizabeth Ferrell, served as an officer of the Literary Club.[60] After graduation in 1908, Elizabeth Ferrell was accepted to the University of Tennessee, where she played with the newly formed "Lady Volunteers" until the team disbanded in 1910.[61] She then went on to become a member and officer of the Barbara Blount Literary Club at the university and graduated with a literary degree in 1912.[62]

In 1912 basketball team member Marguerite Kehr was elected secretary of the Central High School Athletic Association, an organization that helped to govern all student related extracurricular activities, while teammate Audrey Capps captured the superlative for "Cutest Girl." One of Central's star players, Anna French, was the president of the "Noise Brigade," comparable to today's pep club or cheerleading squad.[63] During the early 1900s, when no separate cheerleaders existed for either boys' or girls' high school athletics, some of the female athletes themselves doubled as "sponsors" or members of "Rooters Clubs and Noise Brigades." Basketball players Mary Dooley, Dorothy Cox, and Ella Hodges all participated as "sponsors" for both basketball and football at Knoxville High from 1913 to 1914.[64] These well-rounded student-athletes served to normalize the perception of girls who played sports.

The girls who participated in the team sport of basketball did so with enthusiasm and enjoyment. They practiced daily with intensity and fought for victory in each game. The 1916 *Centralite* reported that the Central High School "girls' basketball team began practice shortly after the opening of school and kept it up almost daily until the close of the season . . . [and] turned out the strongest team in the history of the school with a record of 8 wins and 2 losses."[65] After playing together for three years, the team members grew "deeply committed to one another and to sport."[66] In most yearbook entries recapping both high school and collegiate girls' basketball teams, practice was emphasized and success noted, showcasing the dedication of the girls who were the first generation of young women to compete athletically in organized school sports.

Basketball was introduced to female students in Northampton, Massachusetts, in 1892 at Smith College, where the first women's game was played in that year.[67] Race relations, unstable economies, and a hot climate may all partially explain sports lag in the South.[68] The first publicly viewed women's basketball game in the South did not occur until three years later, in 1895, when students of Sophie Newcomb College in New Orleans, Louisiana, played a demonstration game.[69] Once basketball reached the South, however, it became instantly popular among high school and college girls. Tennessee schools began organizing competitions in 1896, forming club teams and holding demonstration games between schools beginning in 1898 in cities such as Knoxville, Nashville, Johnson City, and Memphis. A hundred years later, sports programs for women at Tennessee colleges and high schools are premier programs and Tennessee women athletes among the very finest in the nation.

Gendered Competition and the Public Sphere

In 1897, the Vanderbilt women's basketball team, still a club sport, began receiving coverage in the student newspaper. The reports, however, remained less than attractive and essentially dismissive of the women athletes. As a covert male reporter published, "In spite of the precautions and vigilance of don't-let-a-man-come-in girls . . . I gained admission to the gymnasium and hid myself in a corner. Soon the crowd began to gather, consisting of the girls' schools and old and young ladies. On the faces of the sweet schoolgirls were not seen the usual 'bewitching' smiles. Something was lacking. What was it? . . . It must have been the absence of the college boys, whom, alas, the teachers had excluded from the rare sight of seeing girls play basketball."[70] From a college man's perspective, lack of "bewitching" smiles indicated male attention was missing; that the women were intently focused on their game seems not to have occurred to him. Before the Vanderbilt–Ward Seminary match, the doors had been locked and the windows covered to safely sequester the women's sport. The spy reporter did, however, acknowledge that the "agility of some of [the women] was really surprising, as they got around after the ball in a manner that would put some of our gym graduates to shame."[71] The game, publicized as the first organized women's contest in Tennessee, ended in a loss for Ward Seminary, 0–5.[72]

In 1898, interest in basketball was reflected by regular competitions between Ward Seminary and Vanderbilt, whose "school girls are almost as enthusiastic over the game as the men."[73] Although by 1910 Vanderbilt women had solidified teams in not only basketball, but also in rowing and tennis, even if only on a club or intramural level. Ada Raines, captain of the Vandy 1909–10 women's basketball team, proudly admitted that her team "always had a way of winning their games under the excellent coaching of Miss Stella Vaughn," but the season's wins and losses were not officially recorded; the men, however, achieved a 10–3 season record.[74] Stella Vaughn, one of the first females to matriculate, graduated from Vanderbilt in 1896 and joined her father on the faculty as the women's physical education director (without pay). As the first female faculty member, she organized, coached, and played on the women's basketball team for over twenty years.[75]

As men's competition grew more intense, women's competition remained understated. While men played before large crowds, women played behind closed doors in Nashville until 1905. All of these limitations to women's sports "den[ied] the emerging reality that southern college women were in fact learning to be strong, self-reliant, and competitive, as well as graceful, loyal, and cooperative."[76] After 1910 Vanderbilt women expanded their season schedule, playing more games and traveling to colleges in Kentucky, Ohio, and other regional cities. In part this development was less about the acceptability of women's sports and more about the growth of scholastic sport in general. From 1895 to 1918 the number of women's teams grew tremendously, particularly with the decrease in male sports during World War I.

The tactic of promoting the boys' sports but minimizing the girls' sports was true in Knoxville as well. At Central High School from 1901 to 1916 only four instances record the numerical scores and opponents of games played by the women's teams.[77] For much of this time period, a brief report summarizing the season, with occasional references to the overall outcomes of the season, remained the only specifics of women's sport. Deemphasis and discouragement of girls' competition were apparent; exercise and recreation, "the improvement of our girls physically and mentally," sufficiently justified athletics for women.[78]

The 1915 report read, "We had one of the best Girls' Basketball teams this year that ever represented C.H.S. They won nearly every game, except two and one of these was against a college team. The second team also played a number of games winning most of them."[79] Despite such a strong, proud athletic year, that small summary was the extent of the record. In contrast, the boys' teams, football, basketball, and track, were reported in great detail.[80] Symbols of school spirit and unity, the men's teams encouraged student support and game attendance; the women's teams served as educational play only, not spectator sport.

Now Lipscomb University, Nashville Bible College also fielded men's teams in basketball and tennis by 1910, but both sports were intramural, rarely competing outside of school. Lipscomb basketball had two women's teams, five girls each on the "Haughty Hits" and the "Dandy Doers," with six girls listed as "Scrubs" to substitute for either team. The tennis club—its motto "First come, first served!"—maintained about twelve to twenty members annually from 1910 to 1917.[81] Similar to Lipscomb, other schools also encouraged women students to play tennis, which was considered a more feminine, thus acceptable, sport, with players exhibiting grace and poise. In the early 1900s, area schools held an annual girls' tennis tournament, which included students from Peabody, Ward Seminary, Belmont, and Vanderbilt who played before a "large and enthusiastic crowd" on the grounds of the Nashville Tennis Club in Centennial Park.[82] Athletic contests that exhibited females as spectacles of sport remained rare, however, until after 1910, when women's teams and programs grew more widespread.

Another example of the stifled nature of coed campus interaction in the late 1890s can be seen in the begrudged acceptance and gendered curriculum of gym class at Vanderbilt University. When a note appeared on a campus bulletin board in 1897 that informed male students to avoid the gym one afternoon, male students responded with considerable complaint.[83] The men did not seem opposed to women's exercise or sport, but they did mind when their time and space were infringed upon. Ironically, the men also took issue with the fact that women and men could not exercise together. One student commented, "We are perfectly willing to share with the co-eds, . . . but our only objection is to the exclusion of either sex at any time. Let us have co-gymnastics or let us have our gym."[84] Yet physical education classes would not be held with both male and female students together until the 1930s, and many schools would not adopt coeducation for gym classes until the 1950s and 1960s. Neither the nation nor the region was ready to place hormonal young adults in circumstances that increased their "physical" education more than already allowed under school policy.

The emphasis placed on sports by most educational institutions, however, remained determined that girls should play purely for gentle exercise, adhering to standards in sports for girls set by the National Education Association in 1915 as worthwhile for personal enjoyment and healthful for physical development.[85] In Knoxville and Nashville, girls' athletics doggedly subscribed to the principle that female sport was solely healthy recreation. In truth, most school girls were not accustomed to intense physical workouts that required coordination, agility, strength, and perspiration. To the general female student population, these physical demands—associated especially with basketball—remained extreme. The desire to reinforce "womanly qualities" continued as a cultural driver: Whether or not women could play sports without a serious challenge to their femininity was a contentious argument.[86]

Female athletes answered this question in Middle and East Tennessee by revealing that they were not girls who would become overly absorbed by the sports, that their interest in sports did not mean they were masculine girls; many of them participated in a good balance of other extracurricular activities and were actively involved in art, literature, other academic subjects, and other clubs. Yet the love of their sports grew among young women. Girls seemed to view athletics as liberating, and their teams inspired their loyalty. As Ward-Belmont student Rosalyn Kirsch wrote in a poem in her memory book, "There's a school in Tennessee, where we all just love to be. / Everyone should want to see, the sports at W-B. / We've tennis in the spring and fall, in winter we play basketball. / We stand together one and all, and loyalty is our call."[87] And as the girls played, their successful participation necessitated practical changes in clothing, which over time reinforced the propriety and greater acceptance of their sporting activities. From the first game in 1897 through World War I, interest in women's health, organized athletics, and competition expanded in Tennessee, alongside increasing student and community support.

Successes and progress in women's athletics are not to say, however, that women's sports received widespread and strong encouragement, nor that the girls who competed from 1895 to 1918 continued to be anything other than a minority of the student populations. Traditional principles of femininity still stood in the way of full acceptance of the legitimacy of women's sports. And certain constricting attitudes powerfully persisted, especially the view that female emotionality and physical weakness made women ultimately too delicate for the intensity and vigor required for serious sports.

Conclusion

Despite negative perceptions and societal restrictions, as the twentieth century progressed, so did the acceptability of an increasing range of activities for young women in Tennessee, providing them with greater choices and redefining their world.[88] Earlier sanctioned public interactions, such as church youth groups, lectures, club meetings, theater, and parks, transitioned to social functions permitting greater independence. With expanded social freedoms, parties, dances, fraternities and sororities, and football games associated with schools, colleges, and universities, increased from 1910 to 1918, when movies and automobiles began replacing theaters, dance halls, and streetcars.[89]

As Nashville and Knoxville both modernized and expanded, so did the roles and public visibility of the cities' women. As the national movement toward ever greater health awareness and women's involvement in sports activities advanced, so too did local Tennessee high schools and colleges' participation in those advancements, adding physical education programs to their academic curricula. Within these programs, basketball quickly claimed its place as the standard competitive sport for Tennessee's girls. However, beyond the game at stake on the basketball court, the girls fought a battle of larger significance: Girls' sports were changing the culture around them and changing their opportunities.

This first generation of women athletes in Tennessee envisioned a figurative castle in the clouds to signify success on the basketball court. They never would have dreamed that a century later women's teams would play in front of over twenty thousand spectators. Tennessee continues to serve as a bastion for women's sports, with stellar high school teams and renowned college programs such as Vanderbilt's Lady Commodores, and of course the Lady Vols of the University of Tennessee. Knoxville and Nashville played, and continue to play, a central role in the formation of women's sport both regionally and nationally.

Although women's sports had not attained mainstream acceptability in the early 1900s, Tennessee's female athletes played with dedication and enthusiasm. By the time the United States approached its entrance into World War I, athletic participation for females was becoming more commonplace and suitable within proper society. Women's basketball drew closer to being a mainstream sport by 1918, although some of the attention given to girls' basketball was not intended to encourage participation. While the number of spectators increased, many who attended the games came more as voyeurs, to see what girls could do with a basketball rather than to watch a display of skilled, competitive talent or ability. Some spectators found themselves pleasantly surprised "when one of the gals made a good play."[90] Still, women athletes did not receive adequate credit or affirmation for mastering the skills of coordination and agility, nor were they recognized for any natural athletic aptitude.

To many female students, the physical demands of hard-driven sports, especially basketball, still seemed inappropriate. Reinforcement of girls' femininity continued to serve as a societal mandate; whether playing sports would seriously challenge a young woman's feminine qualities remained in question.[91] Female athletes in Tennessee, however, showed by their actions and interests that they had not been damaged by the assumed masculinity of sports. On the contrary, most of the girls who played sports were active in many other areas—in their social lives, their churches, their academics, and a broad range of extracurricular activities. Although the girls who competed in sports, from the first game in 1897 to the 1918 season, continued to be a minority of the female student population in Tennessee schools with athletic programs for women, competitive sports and health-related physical activities grew, as did increasing support and acceptance for them within schools' student bodies and within their communities.

Once these young sportswomen stepped foot in the door of athletic sport, their success in outward physical activities necessitated a practical change in their clothing, which over time gained acceptability and further reinforced the propriety of the sporting life. Women's athletics would develop into the 1920s, but certain prejudices and stereotypes concerning presumed female mental and physiological weakness would persist, as would the opinion that women's sporting activities should not be competitive. Nonetheless, without the strong foundation first built by this early Progressive Era cohort of productive, versatile girl athletes, women's sports could not have survived the anticompetition philosophy put in place in 1923 by the Women's Division of the National Amateur Athletic Federation (WDNAAF), which minimized competition in women's athletics through the late 1960s.[92]

Not until second-wave feminism and pressure on the federal government for the 1972 Title IX legislation did women's high school and intercollegiate sports push more aggressively into serious women's athletic competition. Since then, women have made overwhelming gains in amateur and professional sport.

The early efforts made by the girls of the Progressive Era in Tennessee opened doors for serious women's sports and helped set the stage for the present-day female athlete. Beginning in the 1890s, reformed views on health, education, femininity, and clothing began shifts for women into an outward life that included competitive sports. Without girls such as Knoxville High's Hattie Harrell, who singlehandedly established the school's fencing club; Grace Hood, who brought basketball to the University of Tennessee; and Stella Vaughn, who brought sport and physical education to Vanderbilt, women might never have reached their "air castle."

They pursued their interests on the court and on the field with determination, keen to be involved in something new and fun, but likely not conscious of the wider feminist ramifications of their sportswomanship. As a result of the aggressive interests of these girls, the previously separate spheres of femininity and sport were brought together to form the unified identity of the female athlete in Tennessee. These were the early heroines who first competed, whose failures and successes were vanguards of women's athletics, and who blazed a Progressive trail. Perhaps Pat Head Summit, renowned Lady Volunteers' basketball coach emerita, best summarized the purpose of women's sports: "It's more than basketball. It's about life skills, and life stories, . . . trading in old, narrow definitions of femininity for a more complete one . . . [and] exploring all of the possibilities in yourself."[93]

NOTES

Portions of this chapter have been taken from my PhD dissertation, "Athens of the South: College Life in Nashville, a New South City, 1897–1914" (Atlanta: Georgia State Univ., 2008), http://digitalarchive.gsu.edu/history_diss/20. The opening epigraph refers to *The Volunteer,* 1906, 127. Available at the University of Tennessee Scholarly Collection; also available on line at http://www.lib.utk.edu/digitalcollections/ut.html.

1. *Sequoyah: Yearly Annual of Central High School,* 1912. Knox County purchased the building and grounds previously occupied by the Holbrook Tennessee Normal School (1893–1904). Central High School, founded in 1906, was one of the first public high schools in the county and remains on the same thirteen-acre campus.

2. Ibid.

3. Education and urbanization created a dialectic that produced a new generation of moneyed young adults who thought and acted differently from their parents. See Rebecca Edwards, *New Spirits: Americans in the Gilded Age, 1865–1905* (Oxford: Oxford Univ. Press), 2006.

4. Margaret A. Lowe, *Looking Good: College Women and Body Image,1875–1930* (Baltimore: Johns Hopkins Univ. Press, 2003). For more on the New Woman and sports, see Pamela Grundy, "From Amazons to Glamazons: The Rise and Fall of North Carolina Women's Basketball, 1920–1960," *Journal of American History* 86 (2000): 112–46.

5. In contrast, men's sports developed professionally and recreationally beyond the high school and college campus. Sport certainly played an increasingly large role in the male college experience. However, education was not the sole medium for the evolution of modern male sport, nor was sport seen as a challenge to the order of southern gender. In fact, many in the South saw male sport as a safety valve of sorts, a way to express regionalism and achieve success after the Civil War.

6. *Ward Seminary Bulletin,* 1911, 63. The *Ward Seminary Bulletin* was published annually, beginning in the 1880s, to promote its curriculum, faculty/staff, student body, and facilities.

7. Mike Ramirez, "The Lost Cause in a New South City; Nashville, 1890–1910," in "Nashville as a Historical Laboratory for Teaching Undergraduates," ed. Don H. Doyle, presented in "The City as Historical Laboratory" session, Organaization of American Historians' annual meeting, April 1979. This paper is archived in Special Collections, Jean and Alexander Heard Library, Vanderbilt University, Nashville, Tenn. Even as the South selectively followed the models of northern cities such as Boston, Philadelphia, Chicago, and New York in industrialization and urbanization, southerners continued to maintain their notions of "superiority."

8. The first southern city to be occupied by Union forces, in 1862, Nashville escaped the devastation experienced by many southern cities. Robert Wiebe, in *The Search for Order, 1877–1920* (New York: Hill and Wang, 1967), argues that during the Gilded

Age/Progressive Era, urban areas grew increasingly connected to smaller "island" communities. From downtown Nashville the city grew to link outlying communities such as Belle Meade and connect by railroad to formerly distant towns such as Murfreesboro and Lebanon.

9. *Knoxville City Directory,* 1900, 5.

10. *Knoxville City Directory,* 1901, 640–49. Factories such as Brookside Mills, Paper Box Factory, Riverside Cotton Mills, and the Knoxville Cotton Mills provided jobs for both men and women in Knoxville by the year 1901.

11. *Knoxville City Directory,* 1915, 20–26.

12. Census Bureau, U.S. censuses, 1880–1920.

13. Ramirez, "Lost Cause in a New South City," 3.

14. Don Doyle, *New Men, New Cities, New South: Atlanta, Nashville, Charleston, Mobile, 1860–1910* (Chapel Hill: Univ. of North Carolina Press, 1990); Lawrence Larson, *The Urban South: A History* (Lexington: Univ. of Kentucky Press, 1990); Arthur M. Schlesinger, *A History of American Life,* vol. 12, *The Rise of the City 1878–1898* (New York: Macmillan, 1931); Edwin Mims, *The Advancing South: Stories of Progress and Reaction* (Garden City, N.Y.: Doubleday, Page, 1926); Raymond Mohl, *The New City: Urban America in the Industrial Age, 1860–1920* (Arlington Heights, Ill.: Harlan Davidson, 1985).

15. *Memphis Ledger,* 1885, taken from *W. E. Ward's Seminary Annual Announcement,* 1885–86, 19. The rest of the quote states, "We are all proud of Nashville, not only on account of its historic associations, its commanding position, and political relations with the rest of the State, but for the intelligence, culture, and hospitality of the people."

16. J. H. Warf (Tennessee commissioner of education, 1968–71), *Tennessee State Department of Education, 1900 to 1968* (Nashville: Department of Education, 1968), 11.

17. *University of Tennessee Record,* 1898, 38. Five women had attended Blount College, including Barbara Blount, in 1804. Blount College was the predecessor to the University of Tennessee.

18. Fisk University, Lipscomb University, and Peabody College are not heavily considered in this study as they did not maintain substantial women's sport teams or programs. The women's teams that did exist for each school were mostly engaged in intramural sports until the 1930s.

19. Paul K. Conkin, *Gone with the Ivy: A Biography of Vanderbilt University* (Knoxville: Univ. of Tennessee Press, 1985), 81–82.

20. Glenda Elizabeth Gilmore, *Gender and Jim Crow* (Chapel Hill: Univ. of North Carolina Press, 1996), 148; Allen Davis, *Spearheads for Reform: The Social Settlements and the Progressive Movement, 1890–1914* (Camden, N.J.: Rutgers Univ. Press, 1984).

21. *Iris,* 1903, 70.

22. Ibid.

23. Ibid., 70–71.

24. *Hustler* 9, no. 19 (Mar. 3, 1898): 4.

25. Ibid. According to "From Menarche to Menopause: Trends among US Women Born from 1912 to 1969," in the *American Journal of Epidemiology,* the average women in the United States in 1910 measured approximately five feet three inches in height and weighed 115 pounds.

26. This new image is similar to the national trend that emerged in the 1890s of the Gibson Girl, who was an All-American girl, a female who was rational and placed an emphasis on education, and who played sports but was still aristocratic. The Gibson Girl "was taller than the other women currently seen in the pages of magazines, infinitely more spirited and independent, yet altogether feminine. She appeared in a stiff shirt-waist, her soft hair piled into a chignon, topped by a big plumed hat. Her flowing skirt was hiked up in back with just a hint of a bustle. She was poised and patrician. Though always well bred, there often lurked a flash of mischief in her eyes" (Susan E. Meyer, "Charles Dana Gibson and the Gibson Girls," in *America's Great Illustrators,* http://www.livelyroots.com/things/gibsongirl.htm/).

27. With the creation of the Department of Education in 1867, the National Teachers Association (NTA) in 1867, the Southern Association of Colleges and Schools (SACS) in 1895, the Association of Collegiate Alumnae (ACA), and the Southern Association of College Women (SACW), educational reform began to take place in the South. The NTA is today the National Education Association (NEA). However, the NTA absorbed three smaller organizations: the American Normal School Association, the National Association of School Superintendents, and the Central College Association. The NTA is credited with lobbying Congress for a federal department of education, a goal that was achieved in 1867, the same year the NTA officially established itself as a national organization. The NTA initially formed in 1857 with meetings in New York. For more, see Christopher J. Lucas, *American Higher Education* (New York: Palgrave Macmillan, 2006); and Arthur M. Cohen, *The Shaping of American Higher Education* (San Francisco: Jossey-Bass, 1998).

28. Lowe, *Looking Good.* Lowe argues that body image had shifted to women actually working to gain weight, as opposed to present standards, which encourage women to be thinner.

29. Ellen W. Gerber, *Innovators and Institutions in Physical Education* (Philadelphia: Lea and Febiger, 1971).

30. Bruce Bennett, ed., *The History of Physical Education and Sport* (Chicago: Athletic Institute, 1972); Mabel Lee, *A History of Physical Education and Sports in the U.S.A.* (New York: John Wiley and Sons, 1983); June A. Kennard, "History of Physical Education," *Signs* 2, no. 4 (1977): 835–42.

31. Pamela Dean, "'Dear Sister' and 'Hated Rivals': Athletics and Gender at Two New South Women's Colleges, 1893–1920," *Journal of Sports History* 24 (Fall 1997): 341.

32. Reet Howell, "Generalizations on Women and Sport Games and Play in the U.S. from Settlement to 1860," in *Her Story in Sport: A Historical Anthology of Women in Sports,* ed. Reet Howell (New York: Leisure Press, 1982), 91.

Mary Ellen Pethel

33. Nancy G. Rosoff, "'Every muscle is absolutely free': Advertising and Advice about Clothing for Athletic American Women," *Journal of American Culture* 25 (Spring 2002): 25–31.

34. *Hustler* 8, no. 25 (Apr. 14, 1897): 1.

35. Barbara N. Noonkester, "The American Sportsman from 1900–1920," in *Her Story in Sport: A Historical Anthology of Women in Sports,* ed. Reet Howell (New York: Leisure Press, 1982), 178–79.

36. A middy blouse was a loose-fitting top with a large, navy-style collar, and bloomers were knee-length, baggy pants similar to knickerbockers worn by young men.

37. George J. Engelmann, "The American Girl of Today," *American Physical Education Review* (Mar. 1901): 35–66.

38. Maxwell Howell and Reet Howell, "Women in Sport and Physical Education in the United States, 1900–1914," in *Her Story in Sport: A Historical Anthology of Women in Sports,* ed. Reet Howell (New York: Leisure Press, 1982), 157.

39. "Editorial," *Colliers,* Nov. 7, 1903, 5.

40. Louise Davis, "A Quiet, Even Growth," *Tennessean Magazine,* Nov. 28, 1948, 7–8.

41. Karen Kenney, "American Women in Sport and Physical Activity, 1850 to 1900," in *Her Story in Sport: A Historical Anthology of Women in Sports,* ed. Reet Howell (New York: Leisure Press, 1982), 108.

42. Dean, "'Dear Sisters' and 'Hated Rivals,'" 351.

43. Carl E. Klafs, *The Female Athlete* (St. Louis: C. V. Mosby, 1973), 7.

44. *The Voice: Yearly Annual of Knoxville High School,* 1899, 27.

45. Ibid.

46. Ibid.

47. *The Volunteer,* 1905.

48. *Sequoyah,* 1914.

49. *Sequoyah,* 1915, 59. In fact, over half of the tennis club was comprised of females.

50. *The Iris,* 1902, 83.

51. Ibid., n.p.

52. *Ward Seminary Bulletin,* 1911, 63.

53. *Observer,* 213. The *Observer* served as a published periodical of Vanderbilt while the *Hustler* was the school's weekly newspaper. Also, the girls' basketball team first formed during the 1896–97 school year.

54. *Hustler* 7, no. 12 (Dec. 12, 1895): 3.

55. *The Volunteer,* 1903, 159.

56. Dan Ray, "History of Women's Basketball at U.T." (master's thesis, Univ. of Tennessee, 1978), 2.

57. Ibid., 8.

58. *The Volunteer,* 1907, 177; *The University of Tennessee Record,* 1908, 128.

59. *University of Tennessee Record,* 1908, 39; 1899, 8.

60. *The Voice,* 1908.

61. *The Volunteer,* 1910, 88.

62. *University of Tennessee Record,* 1912, 131.

63. *Sequoyah,* 1908.

64. *The Voice,* 1914.

65. *Centralite,* Feb. 1916, 18.

66. Ibid.

67. Women's Basketball Hall of Fame, Historical Timeline, http://www.wbhof.com/timeline.html/.

68. John Betts, *American Sporting Heritage:1850–1950* (Reading, Mass.: Addison-Wesley 1974), 190.

69. Joan Paul, "Clara Gregory Baer: Catalyst for Women's Basketball," in *A Century of Women's Basketball: From Frailty to Final Four,* ed. Joan Hult and Marianna Trekell (Reston, Va.: NAGWS, 1991), 37.

70. *Hustler* 8, no. 22 (Mar. 17, 1897): 1.

71. Ibid.

72. Ibid. Publishing game scores would not be a regular trend, as statistics for the women's teams were typically not reported.

73. *Hustler* 9, no. 15 (Feb. 3, 1898): 1.

74. Bill Traughber, "Vandy's Men's and Women's 1909–1910 Seasons," *Commodore History Corner,* Feb. 6, 2007, 3–4.

75. Ibid. Stella Vaughn was the daughter of mathematics chair William J. Vaughn. Stella Vaughn was officially named dean of women in 1925. Upon her death in 1960, Vaughn was called the "Grand Old Lady of Vanderbilt." The Vaughn home, once a boardinghouse for female students and one of the original faculty houses, remains on campus.

76. Dean, "'Dear Sisters' and 'Hated Rivals,'" 353.

77. *Sequoyah,* 1901–16; *Centralite,* 1901–16.

78. *Sequoyah,* 1910.

79. *Sequoyah,* 1915, 52.

80. *Centralite,* 1915, 17.

81. Nashville Bible College, *The Ark,* 1910, 11–68.

82. *Hustler* 17 (May 17, 1906): 1.

83. *Hustler* 8, no. 22 (Mar. 17, 1897): 1.

84. Ibid.

85. *Standards in Sports for Girls and Women* (Washington D.C.: AAHPER, 1915), 16.

86. Shelia Scraton, *Shaping Up to Womanhood: Gender and Girls' Physical Education* (Buckingham, UK: Open Univ. Press, 1992), 29.

87. Rosalyn Kirsch Scrapbook, 1920, Belmont University Special Collections, Nashville, Tenn.

88. M. Deborah Bialeschki, "'You have to have some fun to go along with your work': The Interplay of Race, Class, Gender, and Leisure in the Industrial New South," *Journal of Leisure Research* (Jan. 1998): 2–3; note that chaperonage was still common and expected through 1918, particularly for official dating within the upper class.

89. Sarah Mercer Judson, "Leisure Is a Foe to Any Man: The Pleasures and Dangers of Leisure in Atlanta during World War I," *Journal of Women's History* 15, no. 1 (2003): 94.

90. Dave Babelay, "First Central Class Makes 70th Year," *Halls/Fountain City Shopper,* June 1978.

91. Scraton, *Shaping Up to Womanhood,* 1992, 29.

92. Adam Hornbuckle, "Women's Sports and Physical Education at the University of Tennessee: 1899–1939" (master's thesis, Univ. of Tennessee, 1983), 101–3.

93. Pat Summit, *Raise the Roof: The Inspiring Inside Story of the Tennessee Lady Vols' Undefeated 1997–1998 Season* (New York: Broadway Books, 1998), 280. For more on Pat Summit and the University of Tennessee Women's Athletic Program since 1974, see Debby Schriver, *In the Footsteps of Champions: The University of Tennessee Lady Volunteers, the First Three Decades* (Knoxville: Univ. of Tennessee Press, 2008).

Contributors

Carole Stanford Bucy is professor of history at Volunteer State Community College in Gallatin, Tennessee. She earned her PhD in 2002 from Vanderbilt University. Her dissertation, "Exercising the Franchise, Building the Body Politics: The League of Women Voters of the United States," is under revision for publication. Her published works include *Women Helping Women: The YWCA of Nashville, History Carved in Stone: The Nashville City Cemetery*, two elementary textbooks based on the Tennessee state social studies curriculum standards for fourth and fifth grades, and numerous published articles about Tennessee women.

Mary A. Evins is associate professor of U.S. history at Middle Tennessee State University and coordinates the university's American Democracy Project, which promotes civic learning and democratic engagement across the disciplines. She earned her PhD from the University of Chicago in culture history and political economy developed from fieldwork in a Kurdish region of southeastern Turkey. Her current research concentrates on gender, women's work, and women's history in Tennessee and the U.S, including Tennessee women progressives in social reform as well as the changing gender roles and family politics in Tennessee immigrant communities. Her most recent essay is on twentieth century political history in rural Middle Tennessee for an anthology on the Tennessee Upper Cumberland.

Jean Shepherd Hamm, who recently retired from teaching, received her doctorate from Virginia Tech in curriculum and instruction and has taught at both East Tennessee State University and Radford University. Her undergraduate and master's degrees are in English, which she taught at the secondary and community college levels. She has a life-long interest in history that led her to pursue the oral history and archival research for her chapter in this volume. She has also published the *Term Paper Resource Guide to Medieval History* (2010) as well as pedagogical and critical articles. Dr. Hamm serves as the chair of a non-profit organization seeking to restore and adaptively reuse Konnarock Training School.

PAULA K. HINTON is associate professor of history at Tennessee Technological University where she specializes in women's history and the history of crime. Her publications include "The Unspeakable Mrs. Gunness: The Deviant Woman in Early-Twentieth-Century America," in *Lethal Imagination: Violence and Brutality in American History*, 1999; "'Just Like One of the Family': An Immigrant Murderess in Turn-of-the-Century America," *Ohio Valley Historical Journal,* 2006; and "The Belle Gunness Serial Murder Case: The Fiendish Widow," in *Famous American Crimes and Trials*, 2004. She received her PhD from Miami University of Ohio.

JANICE M. LEONE is interim associate dean of the College of Liberal Arts and professor of history at Middle Tennessee State University. She earned her PhD at The Ohio State University and teaches courses in U.S. women's history, the history of higher education, and twentieth-century U.S. history. Her research interests are focused on the social reform work of the Woman's Missionary Council of the Methodist Episcopal Church, South, especially at the turn of the last century. Her most recent publication is an edited collection of essays in honor of MTSU's centennial celebration in 2011. In the past few years, Dr. Leone has worked closely with middle and high school teachers in Teaching American History grants and the NEH Landmarks of American History program. She continues to collaborate with the MTSU College of Education and local school systems on grants and projects focused on improving the teaching of history.

ELISABETH ISRAELS PERRY is emeritus professor of women's studies and history at Saint Louis University, where from 1999–2008 she co-held the John Francis Bannon, S.J., chair in history. After earning her PhD in French history from UCLA, she turned to research and writing in U.S.

women's history. In that field she first published *Belle Moskowitz: Feminine Politics and the Exercise of Power in the Age of Alfred E. Smith*, 1987, and then co-authored or co-edited *The Challenge of Feminist Biography: Writing the Lives of Modern American Women*, 1992; *America: Pathways to the Present*, 1994; *We Have Come to Stay: American Women and Political Parties, 1880–1960*, 1999; and *The Gilded Age and Progressive Era: A Student Companion*, 2006. She has also published articles on the early political career of Eleanor Roosevelt, the history of girl scouting in Tennessee, issues in Progressive Era historiography, and New York City women and politics after suffrage. Her most recent publication is an essay on race and gender in the 2008 election. Her current project is a book entitled *La Guardia's Women: Feminism and Politics in Twentieth-Century New York City.*

Mary Ellen Pethel received her PhD from Georgia State University in 2008 and currently teaches at the Harpeth Hall School, Nashville, Tennessee, and Belmont University, and serves as the archivist at Harpeth Hall. Her dissertation, "Athens of the South: College Life in a New South City, 1897–1917" explored issues of southern urbanization, education, and leisure during the Gilded Age/Progressive Era. Her most recent publication is *Berry College: A Century of Music*, 2010, and she is currently working on an essay that analyzes the roles of African American women in Nashville during the late nineteenth and early twentieth centuries, as well as a project that documents the history of women's higher education in Tennessee.

Sonya Ramsey is an associate professor of African American history and women's and gender studies at the University of North Carolina at Charlotte. She has also taught at the University of Texas at Arlington. She received her PhD in United States history at the University of North Carolina at Chapel Hill. She is the author of several articles, books, and chapters, including "We Are Ready [to Desegregate] Whenever They Are: African American Teachers and the Desegregation of the Public Schools in Nashville, Tennessee, 1954–1966," *Journal of African American History,* 2005; *Reading, Writing, and Segregation: A Century of Black Women Teachers in Nashville* (University of Illinois Press, 2008); and "Of Culture and Conviction: African American Women Non-Fiction Writers and the

Gendered Definition of Class," *The Southern Middle Class in the Long Nineteenth Century*, edited by Jonathan Daniel Wells and Jennifer R. Green (Louisiana State University Press, 2011).

MINOA D. UFFELMAN is associate professor of history at Austin Peay State University in Clarksville, Tennessee. She received her MA from APSU and PhD from the University of Mississippi. She has published numerous encyclopedia entries and book reviews, as well as an article on *Plessy v. Ferguson*, "Homer Plessy, Civil Rights Activist," in *The Human Tradition in the Civil Rights Movement* series, 2006. Her primary areas of interest are southern history and women's history of the late nineteenth and early twentieth centuries, and she is currently researching the Civil War and post-war diaries and correspondence of Nannie Haskins Williams, who at age 16 began recording the unsettling events in her life and community during the Union occupation of Clarksville and Reconstruction (University of Tennessee Press, forthcoming).

Index

Tennessee Women in the Progressive Era was designed and typeset on a Mac OS 10.6.8 using InDesign CS5 software. The body text is set in 11/14 Adobe Garamond Pro Regular and display type is set in Adobe Garamond Pro Semibold. This book was designed and typeset by Barbara Karwhite and manufactured by Thomson-Shore, Inc.